IMAGES
of America

ITALIAN AMERICANS OF THE GREATER MAHONING VALLEY

ON THE COVER: SONS OF ITALY CONVENTION. In 1923, the Ohio Chapter of the Order of the Sons of Italy in America held its annual convention in Youngstown, Ohio. Italian Americans from around the Mahoning Valley stood on the steps of the US Post Office in downtown Youngstown, displaying pride in their heritage and love for their adopted country. (Courtesy of Youngstown Lodge No. 858 Order of the Sons of Italy in America.)

IMAGES
of America

ITALIAN AMERICANS OF THE GREATER MAHONING VALLEY

Dr. Donna M. DeBlasio
and Dr. Martha I. Pallante

ARCADIA
PUBLISHING

ISBN 978-1-4671-1479-0

Published by Arcadia Publishing
Charleston, South Carolina

Printed in the United States of America

Library of Congress Control Number: 2015942092

For all general information, please contact Arcadia Publishing:
Telephone 843-853-2070
Fax 843-853-0044
E-mail sales@arcadiapublishing.com
For customer service and orders:
Toll-Free 1-888-313-2665

Visit us on the Internet at www.arcadiapublishing.com

Contents

ACKNOWLEDGMENTS

Italian Americans of the Greater Mahoning Valley was truly a labor of love. We could not have done this book without the help of many people who shared their photographs and their stories with us. They are as follows: Anthony Cafaro Sr., the Cassese family, Carl and Edith D'Altorio Ritch, Garrett Guerrieri, Joe Merlo, Nicole Marino, the Marino and Massullo families, Noreen Modarelli and family, Niles Historical Society (NHS), Oblate Sisters of the Sacred Heart, Our Lady of Mount Carmel Basilica (Msgr. Michael J. Cariglio), Frank Pape, Rosanne Pasquinelli Dando and family, Adelia Marsch Moritz, Audrea Marsch Neri and Robert Bartolli, Napoleone Colaianne Lodge No. 858 (Order of the Sons of Italy in America, Youngstown), Rosyln Torella, Warren Italian American Heritage Festival Committee, Anthony Worrellia, and Toni and Dom D'Urso.

We would be remiss in not thanking Ben Lariccia. Not only did he loan us family photographs, he connected us with other Italian Americans he knew had collections of images we might use. It was Ben who linked us with Carl and Edith Ritch and their amazing storehouse of family history. We also used several of Ben's translations.

No work like this is done without the help of the keepers of our history, the archivists. Our thanks to the Catholic University of America's American Catholic History Research Center and University Archives (CUA), the Francis Loeb Library of Harvard University, Brian Brennan and the Youngstown State University Archives (YSU), and, most especially, Martha Bishop of the Ohio History Connection's Youngstown Historical Center of Industry and Labor Archives Library (OHC-YHCIL).

We would also like to thank the YSU graduate students who helped with the scanning: Valerie Waksmunski and Carmella Cadusale. Without the scanning, we would not have a book. We also thank our administrative assistant, Grimilda Ocasio, for editing.

Finally, our most sincere thanks to all of the Italians who made the brave decision to leave their homeland in search of a better life and found it here in the Mahoning Valley. Your presence has enriched our community in countless ways, large and small, contributing to the quality of life and bringing a distinctive ethnic flavor to the Valley.

Unless otherwise noted, all images are from the collections of the authors. All author royalties go to the Youngstown Historical Center of Industry and Labor.

INTRODUCTION

Between 1890 and 1924, there was a large influx of Italian immigrants to the Mahoning Valley, in particular to Youngstown and Niles. The majority of the Italians who came here were from southern Italy, a region that lacked opportunities for its native population. Thanks to industrialization, northern Italy prospered, while *il mezzogiorno* ("the land of the noon sun"), or southern Italy, lagged behind in education, wealth, and literacy. High taxes and tariffs contributed to poverty in the south, forcing many to consider emigration.

In Ohio's Mahoning Valley, new jobs in the burgeoning iron and steel industries, as well as in allied industries, beckoned. While the work was hard, the opportunities and relatively high wages proved irresistible. The mills and factories rimmed the Mahoning River as it wound its way from Warren toward Lowellville on the border of Pennsylvania. While a number of these immigrants were single men—the "birds of passage" that planned to make money and return to their native Italy—many more remained in the Mahoning Valley. These people often called for their families to join them in the New World, resulting in chain migration.

Arriving in the Mahoning Valley beginning in the late 1880s, the earliest arrivals frequently settled in the shadows of the factories and furnaces where they labored. Those who followed often settled in the same neighborhoods as had other people from their homeland. In the city of Youngstown, two areas, Smoky Hollow, just east and north of downtown, and Brier Hill, on the north side, had significant populations of Italian Americans. In Trumbull County, the city of Niles, with its Niles Fire Brick Company and Trumbull Blast Furnace, also attracted many Italians, who became the city's dominant immigrant and ethnic group. Warren, Trumbull County's seat, hosted a fully integrated steel mill—originally Trumbull Steel and later part of Republic Steel—that also became a mecca for Italian men seeking opportunities. Smaller communities, such as Campbell, Struthers, and Lowellville in Mahoning County and Girard, Hubbard, and McDonald in Trumbull, also beckoned.

While many living in these ethnic enclaves found jobs in steel or related industries, other forms of work provided much-needed income for their families. Italian Americans opened grocery stores in their neighborhoods, providing staples like olives and Italian cheeses that were not available in "American" stores. Many families took in boarders: single men who could not yet afford their own house got a bed and meals in family homes. Small two-bedroom houses sheltered as many as 10 borders, plus the family members themselves. These men were usually from the same hometown as the host family. This was not an unusual practice in growing industrial communities like those in the Mahoning Valley.

Once settled in the area, Italian immigrants found ways to become "American" and yet retain their Italian identity and culture. Organizations such as the Bagnoli Irpino Club and the Golden Eagles Club provided a social outlet for Italian American men and their families. The Roman Catholic Church was also a safe haven; soon, Trumbull and Mahoning Counties boasted Italian Catholic parishes. At the region's amusement park, Idora Park, Italian Americans had their own "day" to enjoy its attractions. Summer festivals celebrating the immigrant past and the Italian American present enlivened the Valley. Evidence of assimilation and integration into the larger community is seen in less institutional fashion, as well. Every resident of the Mahoning Valley knows about Brier Hill pizza, wedding soup, and the cookie table.

Life, however, was not always easy. The native-born white Anglo-Saxon Protestants did not always welcome them. While the owners of large businesses were happy to have their labor, Italians (and other Eastern and Southern European immigrants, as well as African Americans) often faced hostility and outright intimidation. In the Mahoning Valley, the resurgence of the Ku Klux Klan at the end of World War I put fear in the hearts of the immigrant community. Throughout the early and middle 1920s, numerous communities elected candidates running on Klan platforms. The resulting tensions occasionally erupted into violence. For example, in 1924, the Italians and Irish of Niles, anticipating a KKK parade in their community, retaliated and put an end to the Klan's show of power. Discrimination often took subtler forms. Italians often were not given promotions in the workplace. There were neighborhoods in which they were not allowed to live, organizations they could not join, and places where they were not welcome.

In spite of this, the Italian Americans of the Mahoning Valley prospered. Unlike the national stereotype forged in large metropolises, they knew the value of an education and how it could make their lives, and those of their children, better. Over time, they became accepted, and many became leading citizens in the Mahoning Valley. For example, two of the largest shopping-mall developers in the United States, Edward J. DeBartolo and William M. Cafaro, were Italian Americans, both hailing from Youngstown—the former from Smoky Hollow, and the latter from Haselton on the east side. DeBartolo's interests are centered in Mahoning County, while Cafaro is based in Trumbull County. The region has Italian American mayors, legislators, educators, doctors, lawyers, skilled tradespeople, clerical workers, shopkeepers, and, yes, steelworkers.

This book focuses on the Italian American experience in the Mahoning Valley from the 1890s until 1960. The images cover topics ranging from the immigration experience to the formation of neighborhoods, the building of communities, the contributions to workplaces, the achievement of prosperity, and commemorations. The lives of these immigrants have rarely been explained accurately and in this manner. Previously, many Italian Americans focused on the present and the creation of a better future. Most of our forebearers claimed that they did not have an important story. They were wrong. Understanding the real stories of these immigrants and how they impacted the area is of tremendous importance, not just to Italian Americans, but to the entire community. This group is just one of many who gave the Mahoning Valley its rich ethnic diversity.

One

Coming to America

In the late 19th and early 20th centuries, immigrants flooded the shores of the United States, seeking better lives in the New World. Historians refer to this as "second-wave" immigration. These "new" immigrants came largely from Southern and Eastern Europe, unlike earlier immigrants, who were from Northern and Western Europe. In the first three decades of the 20th century, over 14 million newcomers arrived in the United States. Of that 14 million, there were over 3 million Italians. While the United States was not the only destination of choice, this nation's lure was distinctive, because Americans looked to the future, not the past. The term "immigrant" appeared in 1789 to describe foreign settlers in New York City, rather than the more traditional "emigrant"—the implication being that newcomers were entering a new land rather than leaving an old one. Making the decision to leave familiar surroundings and loved ones was not easy; the impetus for such a move varied. Old and new immigrants left because of political, economic, and/or religious discontent. The industrial and agricultural revolutions in this period transformed society. The result was a rapid growth in population, which, in places like Italy, threatened the standard of living. Food shortages became common, and agricultural jobs disappeared thanks to increasing mechanization. Political upheavals, such as the lengthy process of Italian unification, were another factor pushing people to immigrate. Yet, the United States was not the welcoming presence promised in the poem at the Statue of Liberty. Discrimination and the distrust of native-born Americans made life difficult, and many immigrants were disillusioned about the fabled *La Merica*. As one Italian immigrant said: "I heard that the streets were paved with gold. When I got here, I found out they weren't paved with gold, they weren't paved at all, and I was expected to pave them."

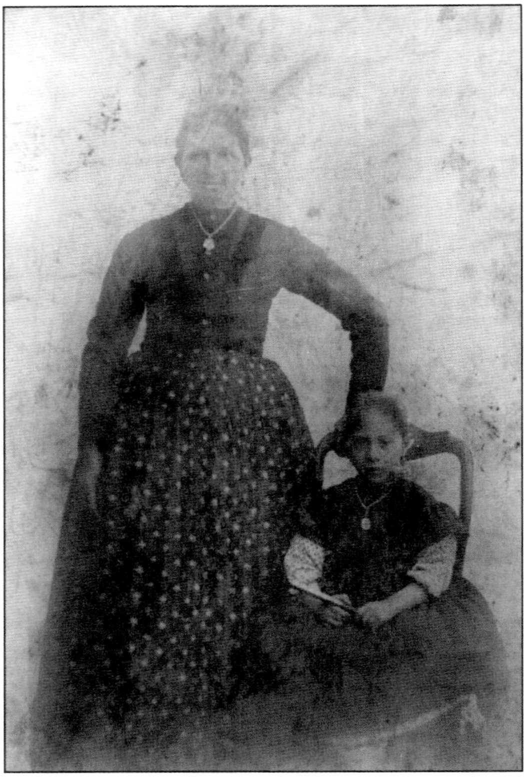

Lucia and Rafaela Clemente. The photograph at left, taken in Bagnoli Irpino about 1885, depicts Rafaela Calatrella and her five-year-old daughter, Lucia Clemente. Lucia's attachment to this photograph was so deep that she kept it throughout her life, which included two transcontinental moves. While many Italian immigrants traveled "without papers" or legal documents, many sought the security that documentation provided. In the late 19th century, travel papers were just that—official permissions to travel, signed and stamped by local officials. The below photograph comprised part of the documentation carried by Guiseppi Clemente when he, his wife, Rafaela Calatrella, and their daughter Lucia ventured from Bagnoli Irpino, Campania, to Brazil in 1886–1887. Note the "fingers" pointing toward each emigrant and the "M" stamped on Lucia's dress, indicating her status as a minor.

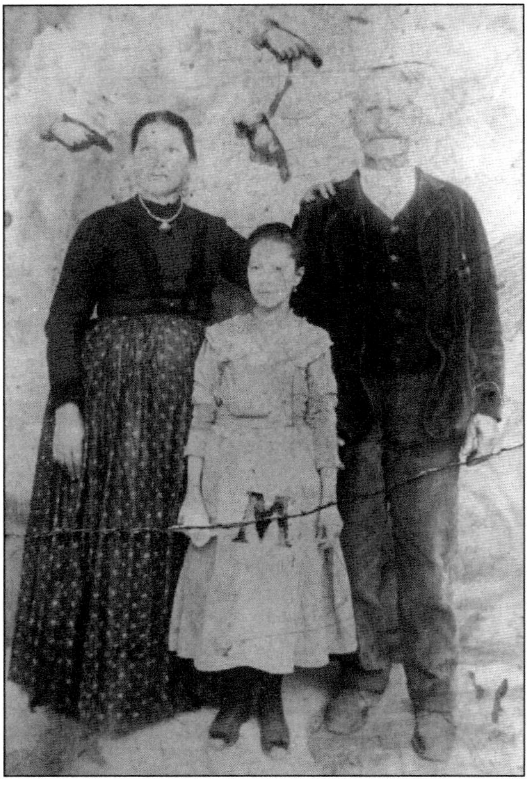

Baptismal and Marriage Certificates. For Roman Catholics, verification of Baptism was important, especially for those seeking marriage in the church or for a man wishing to enter the priesthood. Baptismal certificates could be used in lieu of birth certificates. Paolo Guerrieri, who was born and baptized in 1898, proved his age in 1961 in order to collect retirement benefits (right). If a couple was married in Italy, they also needed proof that they were husband and wife. The marriage certificate shown below verifies that Nicolo Bernardo Piccoli wed Maria Caterina DeRochis in December 1909. (Right, courtesy of Garrett Guerrieri; below, courtesy of Noreen Modarelli.)

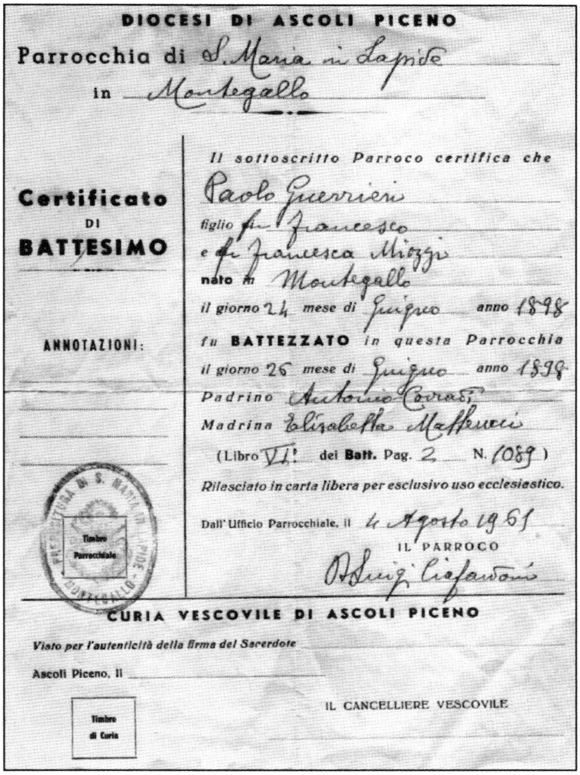

DIOCESI DI ASCOLI PICENO

Parrocchia di S. Maria in Lapide

in Montegallo

Certificato di BATTESIMO

ANNOTAZIONI:

Il sottoscritto Parroco certifica che

Paolo Guerrieri

figlio fu Francesco

e fu Francesca Miozzi

nato in Montegallo

il giorno 24 mese di Giugno anno 1898

fu BATTEZZATO in questa Parrocchia

il giorno 26 mese di Giugno anno 1898

Padrino Antonio Corradi

Madrina Elisabetta Mattucci

(Libro VI dei Batt. Pag. 2 N. 1089)

Rilasciato in carta libera per esclusivo uso ecclesiastico.

Dall'Ufficio Parrocchiale, li 4 Agosto 1961

IL PARROCO

Timbro Parrocchiale

CURIA VESCOVILE DI ASCOLI PICENO

Visto per l'autenticità della firma del Sacerdote

Ascoli Piceno, li

Timbro di Curia

IL CANCELLIERE VESCOVILE

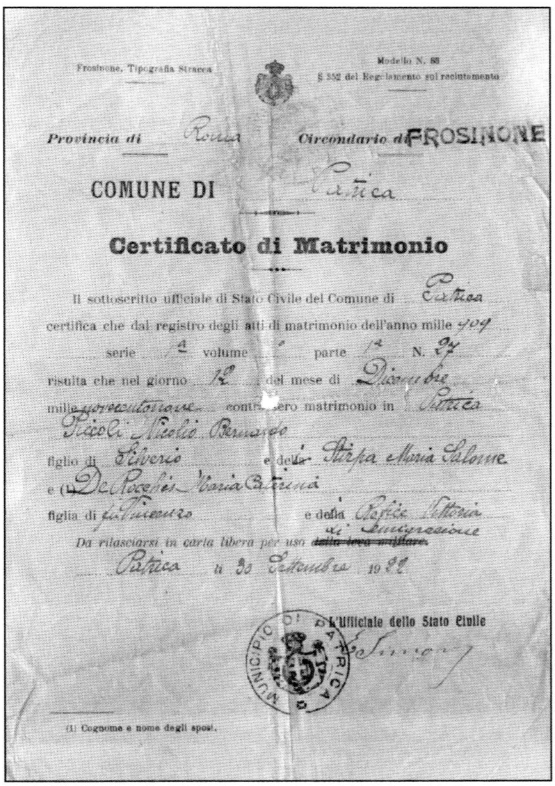

Frosinone, Tipografia Stracca

Modello N. 88
§ 352 del Regolamento sul reclutamento

Provincia di Roma Circondario di FROSINONE

COMUNE DI Patrica

Certificato di Matrimonio

Il sottoscritto ufficiale di Stato Civile del Comune di Patrica certifica che dal registro degli atti di matrimonio dell'anno mille 909 serie 1a volume parte 1a N. 27 risulta che nel giorno 12 del mese di Dicembre mille novecentonove contrassero matrimonio in Patrica

Piccoli Nicolò Bernardo

figlio di Silverio e della Stirpa Maria Salome

e (1) DeRochis Maria Caterina

figlia di fu Vincenzo e della Poffice Vittoria

Da rilasciarsi in carta libera per uso ~~della leva militare~~ di emigrazione

Patrica li 30 Settembre 1922

L'Ufficiale dello Stato Civile

MUNICIPIO DI PATRICA

(1) Cognome e nome degli sposi.

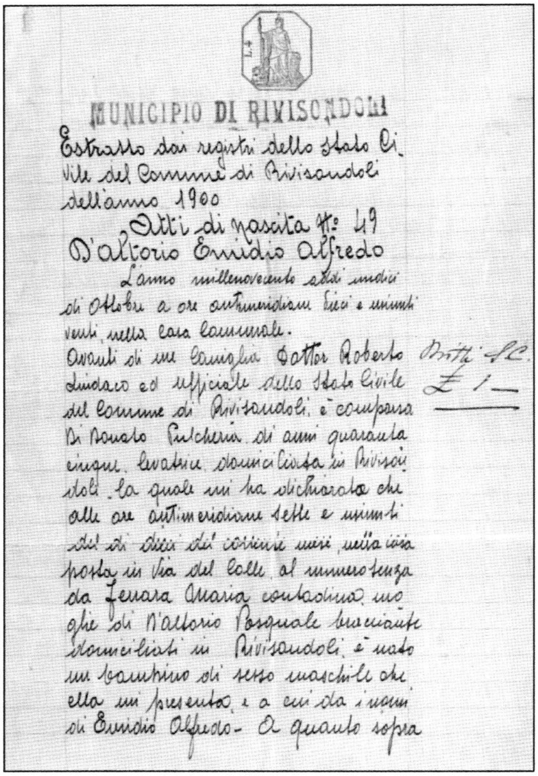

MUNICIPIO DI RIVISONDOLI

Estratto dai registri dello Stato Ci-
vile del Comune di Rivisondoli
dell'anno 1900

Atti di nascita N° 49

D'Altorio Emidio Alfredo

L'anno millenovecento addì undici
di Ottobre a ore antimeridiane dieci e minuti
venti nella casa comunale.
Avanti di me Caniglia Dottor Roberto
Sindaco ed Ufficiale dello Stato Civile
del Comune di Rivisondoli è comparsa
Di Donato Pulcheria di anni quaranta
cinque levatrice domiciliata in Rivison-
doli la quale mi ha dichiarato che
alle ore antimeridiane sette e minuti
venti del dì dieci del corrente mese, nella casa
posta in Via del Colle al numero senza
da Ferrara Maria contadina mo-
glie di D'Altorio Pasquale bracciante
domiciliati in Rivisondoli è nato
un bambino di sesso maschile che
ella mi presenta e a cui da i nomi
di Emidio Alfredo- A quanto sopra

Diritti SC. £ 1 —

D'Altorio Birth Certification. Since many Italians did not bring legal documents on their journey, they often had to contact officials in their native land to verify their birth. This letter confirms the birth of Emidio Alfredo D'Altorio. The first two sentences read: "On October 11, 1900, at 10:20 a.m., in the town hall, Midwife Pulcheria Di Donato, age 45, resident of Rivisondoli, appeared before me, Doctor Roberto Caniglia, Mayor and Officila of the Vital Records Office of the town. She declared at 6:20 a.m. on the 10th of the current month, at the house on Hill Street, that Maria Ferrara gave birth to a baby of the masculine sex." The document is an extract from the Rivisondoli Vital Records of 1900, issued in 1926. In D'Altorio's case, he needed this document "for the purposes of contracting marriage." (Both, courtesy of Edith and Carl Ritch; translation by Ben Lariccia.)

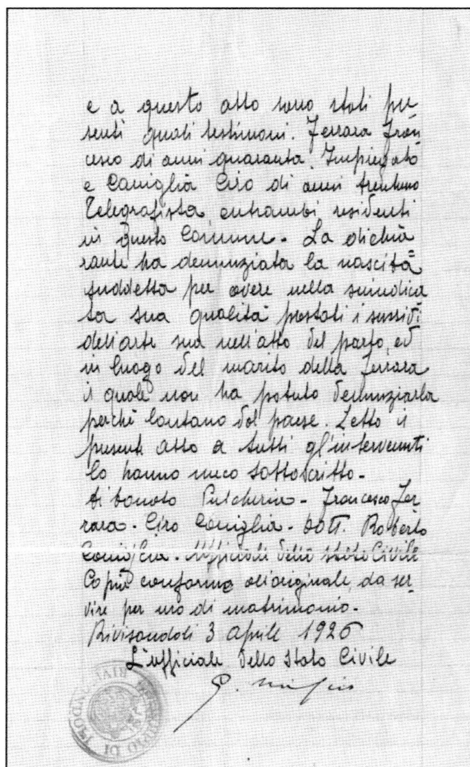

e a questo atto sono stati pre-
senti quali testimoni Ferrara Fran-
cesco di anni quaranta Impiegato
e Caniglia Ciro di anni trentuno
Telegrafista entrambi residenti
in questo Comune. La dichia-
rante ha denunziata la nascita
suddetta per avere nella suindica-
ta sua qualità prestati i suoi
ufficii dell'arte sua nell'atto del parto ed
in luogo del marito della puerpera
il quale non ha potuto denunziarla
perchè lontano dal paese. Letto il
presente atto a tutti gl'intervenuti
lo hanno meco sottoscritto.
Di Donato Pulcheria - Francesco Fer-
rara - Ciro Caniglia - Dott. Roberto
Caniglia - Ufficiale dello Stato Civile
Copia conforme all'originale da ser-
vire per uso di matrimonio.
Rivisondoli 3 aprile 1926
L'Ufficiale dello Stato Civile

Bevilaqua Family and Steamship Ticket. Prior to coming to the United States in 1911, several members of the Bevilaqua family posed for the camera. Shown at right are, from left to right, Antonia Mascio Bevilaqua, Elisabetta Bevilaqua (Caniglia), and Antonio Bevilaqua. Antonio died at the age of six from diphtheria, but the rest of the family, including the patriarch, Francisco, settled in Ravenna, Ohio. The family's steamship ticket (below) indicates that Antonia sailed from Naples with her daughters Elisabetta and Filomena, ages eight and one, respectively. The family arrived in Philadelphia before joining Francisco in Ravenna. One of the Bevaliqua daughters, Corinne, married Emidio Alfredo D'Altorio in 1926. D'Altorio's pending nuptials precipitated the need for the official verification of his birth. The newlyweds settled in Warren, Ohio. (Both, courtesy of Edith and Carl Ritch.)

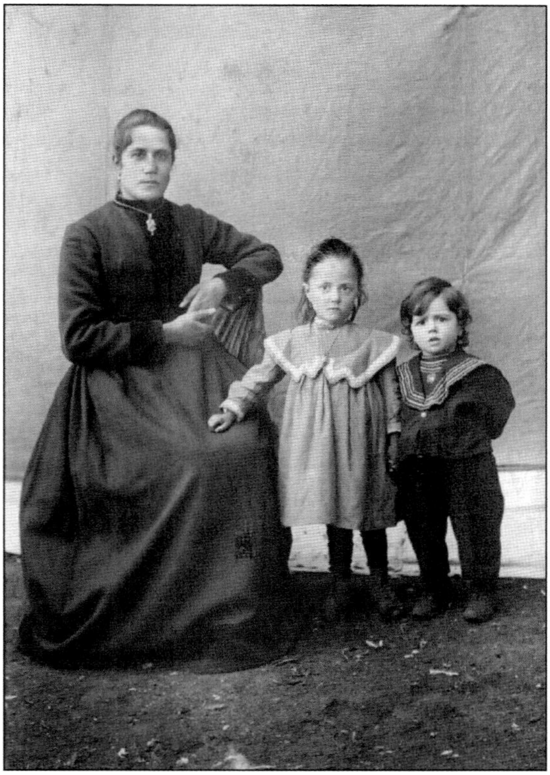

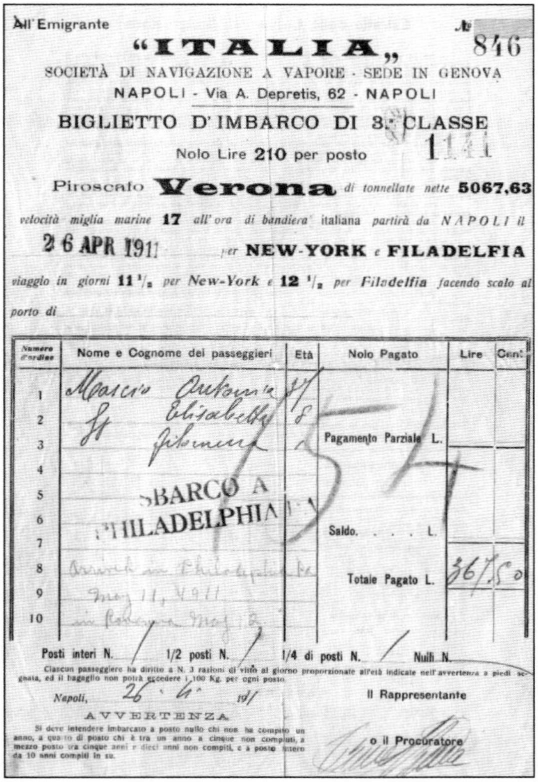

All'Emigrante № 846

"ITALIA,,

SOCIETÀ DI NAVIGAZIONE A VAPORE - SEDE IN GENOVA

NAPOLI - Via A. Depretis, 62 - NAPOLI

BIGLIETTO D'IMBARCO DI 3.ª CLASSE 1141

Nolo Lire 210 per posto

Piroscafo **Verona** di tonnellate nette 5067,63

velocità miglia marine 17 all'ora di bandiera italiana partirà da NAPOLI il

26 APR 1911 per NEW-YORK e FILADELFIA

viaggio in giorni 11 ½ per New-York e 12 ½ per Filadelfia facendo scalo al porto di

Numero d'ordine	Nome e Cognome dei passeggieri	Età	Nolo Pagato	Lire	Cent.
1	Mascio Antonia	37			
2	" Elisabetta	8			
3	" Filomena	1	Pagamento Parziale L.		
4					
5	SBARCO A				
6	PHILADELPHIA		Saldo. . . . . L.		
7					
8	Arrived in Philadelphia		Totale Pagato L.	367.50	
9	May 11, 1911				
10	in Ravenna May 12				

Posti interi N. 1 1/2 posti N. 1 1/4 di posti N. 1 Nulli N.

Ciascun passeggiere ha diritto a N. 3 razioni di vitto al giorno proporzionate all'età indicate nell'avvertenza a piedi segnata, ed il bagaglio non potrà eccedere i 100 Kg. per ogni posto.

Napoli, 26 · 4 · 911

Il Rappresentante

AVVERTENZA

Si deve intendere imbarcato a posto nullo chi non ha compito un anno, a quarto di posto chi è tra un anno a cinque non compiuti, a mezzo posto tra cinque anni e dieci anni non compiti, e a posto intero da 10 anni compiti in su.

o il Procuratore

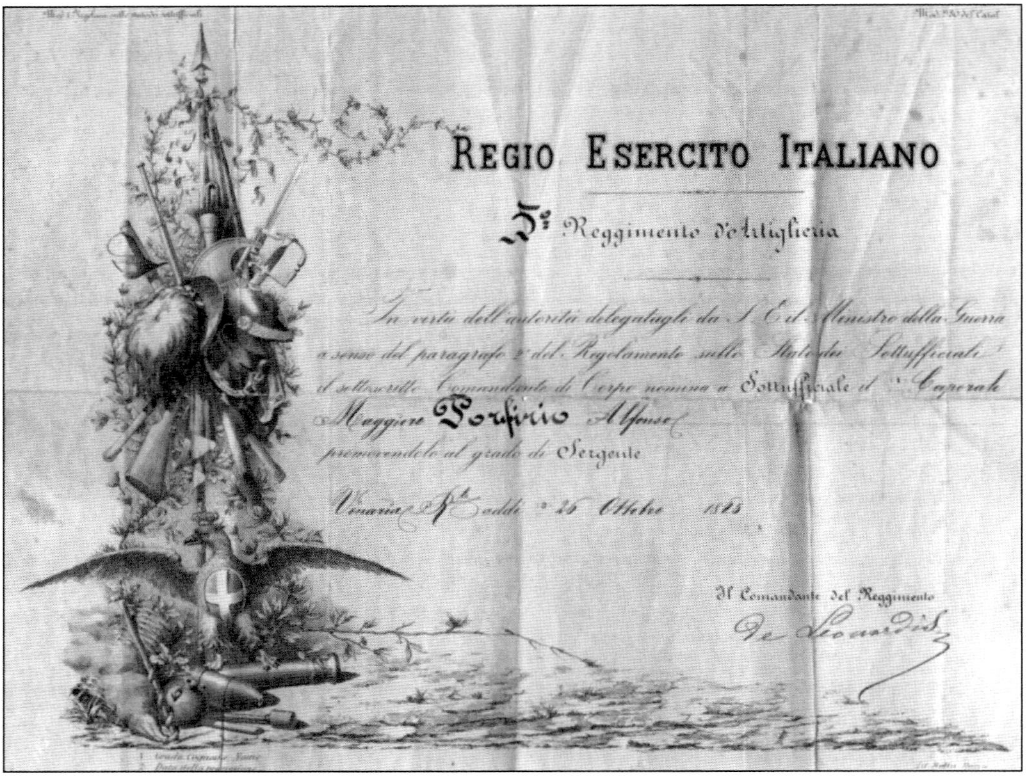

REGIO ESERCITO ITALIANO

5° Reggimento d'Artiglieria

In virtù dell'autorità delegatagli da S. E. il Ministro della Guerra a senso del paragrafo 2 del Regolamento sullo Stato dei Sottufficiali il sottoscritto Comandante di Corpo nomina a Sottufficiale il Caporale Maggiore Porfirio Alfonso promovendolo al grado di Sergente

Venaria R.le addì 26 Ottobre 188[illegible]

Il Comandante del Reggimento

De Leonardis

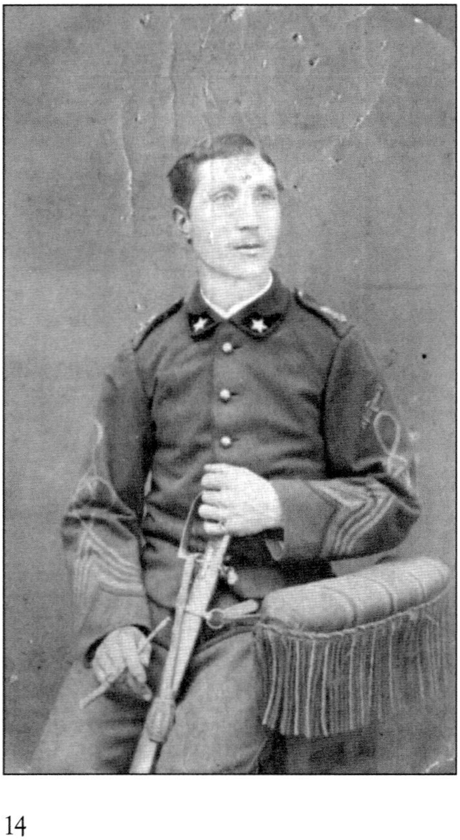

ALFONSO PORFIRIO. Cost and space often limited what Italian emigrants could carry with them to their new homes in the Americas. Photographs were one of the relatively few mementoes that they could easily transport. Alfonso Porfirio chose to preserve the memory of his military service during the 1880s. He carried the certificate marking his promotion to the rank of sergeant in the Cinque d'Reggimento Artiglieria (5th Artillery Regiment) (above) and a photograph of himself in regimental uniform (left). In 1903, Porfirio left his hometown of Trivento in what is now Molise to sail to the United States. His wife and daughter followed in 1904.

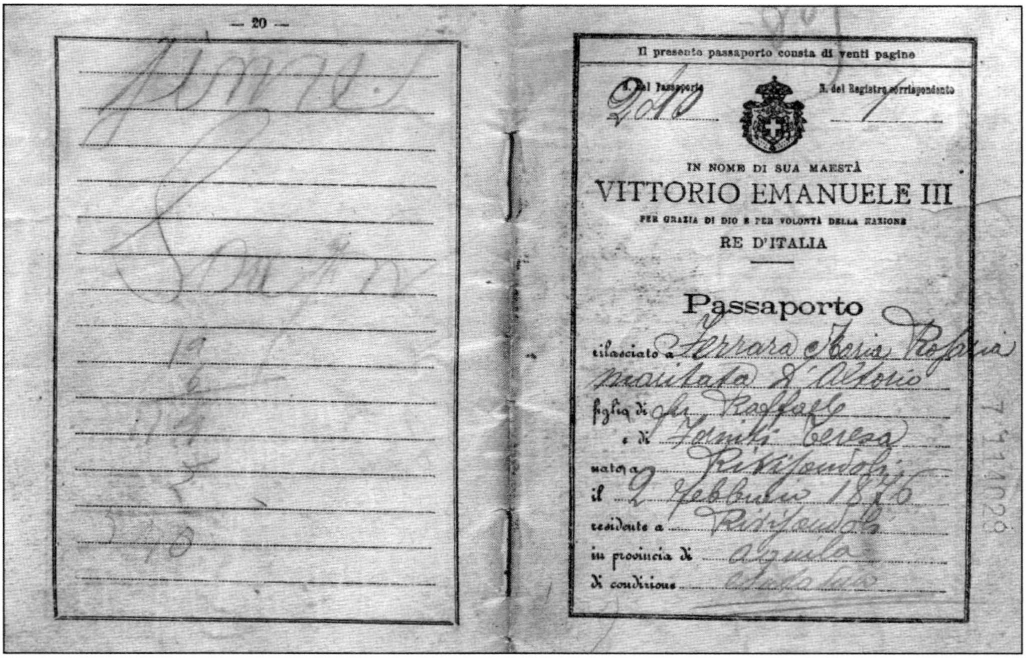
— 20 —

Il presente passaporto consta di venti pagine

N. del Passaporto 2010 N. del Registro corrispondente 1

IN NOME DI SUA MAESTÀ

VITTORIO EMANUELE III

PER GRAZIA DI DIO E PER VOLONTÀ DELLA NAZIONE

RE D'ITALIA

Passaporto

rilasciato a Ferrara Maria

maritata D'Altorio

figlia di fu Raffaele

e di Teresa

nata a Rivisondoli

il 2 febbraio 1876

residente a Rivisondoli

in provincia di Aquila

di condizione

D'Altorio Passport. In 1916, Maria Ferrara D'Altorio left Rivisondoli in southern Italy and joined her husband, Pasquale, in the United States. On Italian passports, a married woman was legally identified by her birth and married last names (above). With Maria journeyed their three children, Emidio (15), Elodia (11), and Ida (7). The minor children did not have their own passports, but were listed on their mother's papers (below). Pasquale, or Patsy, who emigrated in 1900, quickly found work in the Mahoning Valley's steel industry. By the time the family arrived, Patsy worked at the Trumbull Steel Company, eventually part of Republic Steel. (Both, courtesy of Edith and Carl Ritch.)

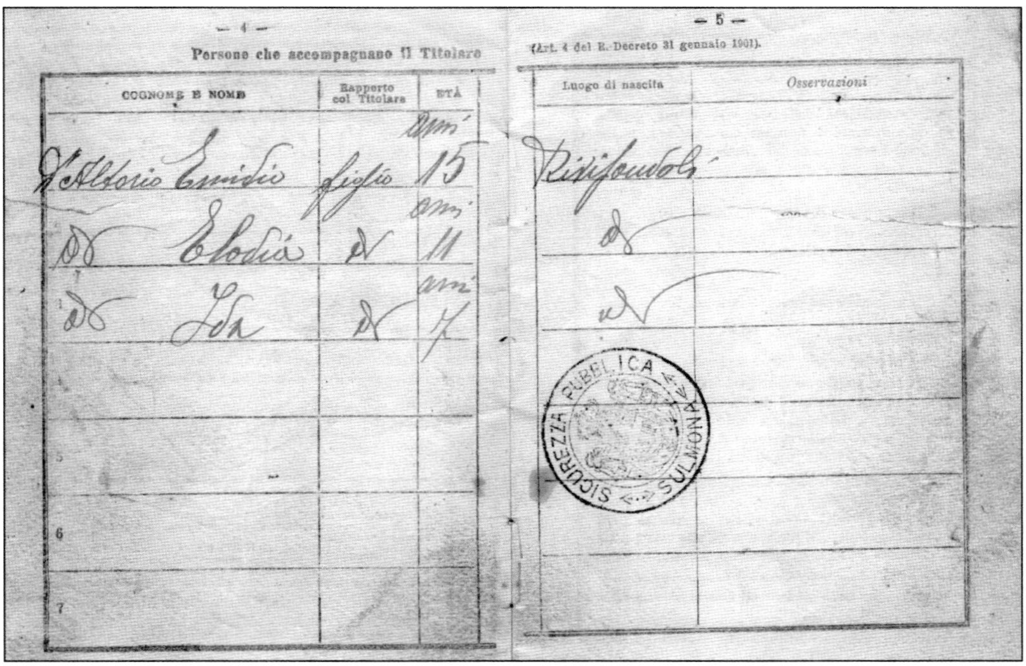
— 4 —

Persone che accompagnano il Titolare

COGNOME E NOME	Rapporto col Titolare	ETÀ
D'Altorio Emidio	figlio	anni 15
do Elodia	do	anni 11
do Ida	do	anni 7

— 5 —

(Art. 4 del R. Decreto 31 gennaio 1901).

Luogo di nascita	Osservazioni
Rivisondoli	
do	
do	

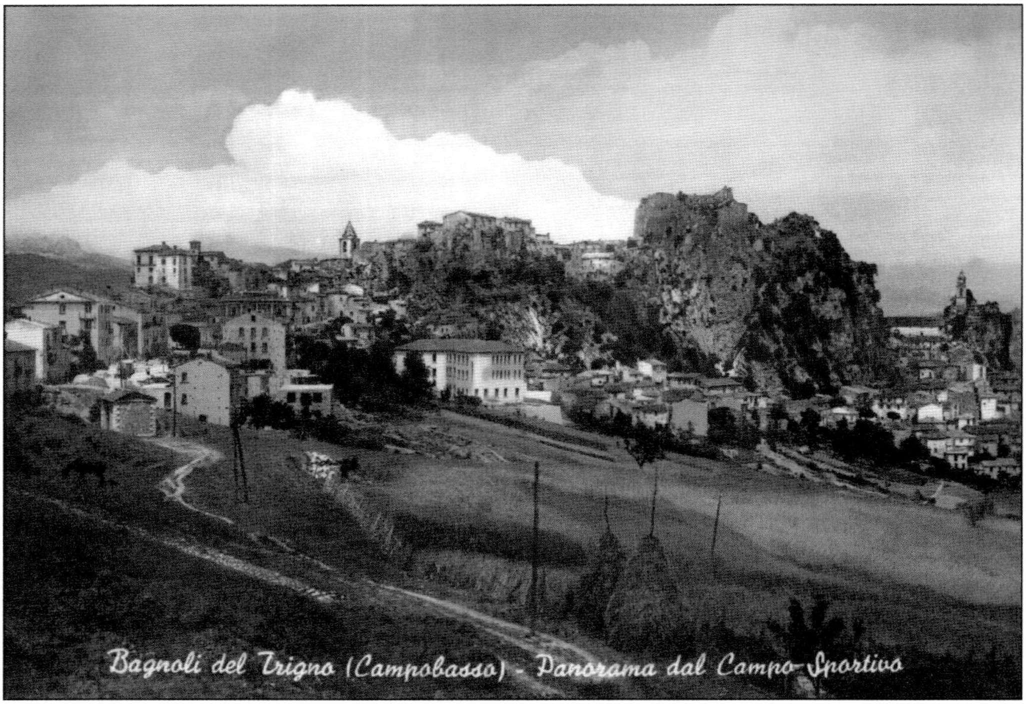

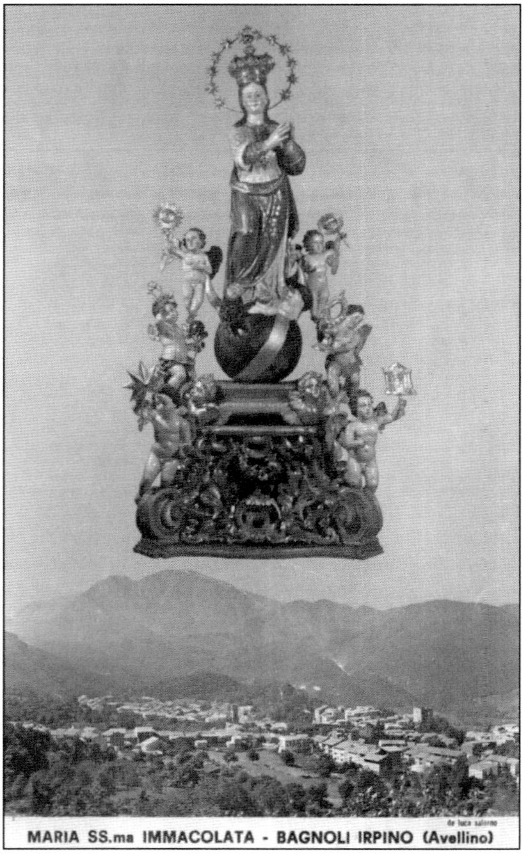

Two Bagnolis. As late as the 1950s, chain migration into the Mahoning Valley continued. In a nation devastated by World War II, few opportunities presented themselves to Italy's young adults. One of the anomalies of immigration to the Valley was that some early immigrants were residents of two villages named Bagnoli. A significant number of Smoky Hollow's residents hailed from Bagnoli del Trignio (above), located in the province of Campobasso in the Abruzzi region. Similarly, Bagnoli Irpino (left), in the Avelino region of Campania, was the home of many of the settlers in Niles. Although these villages are romanticized in postcards as idyllic locations, the postwar recession encouraged many residents to join family and friends in the Mahoning Valley.

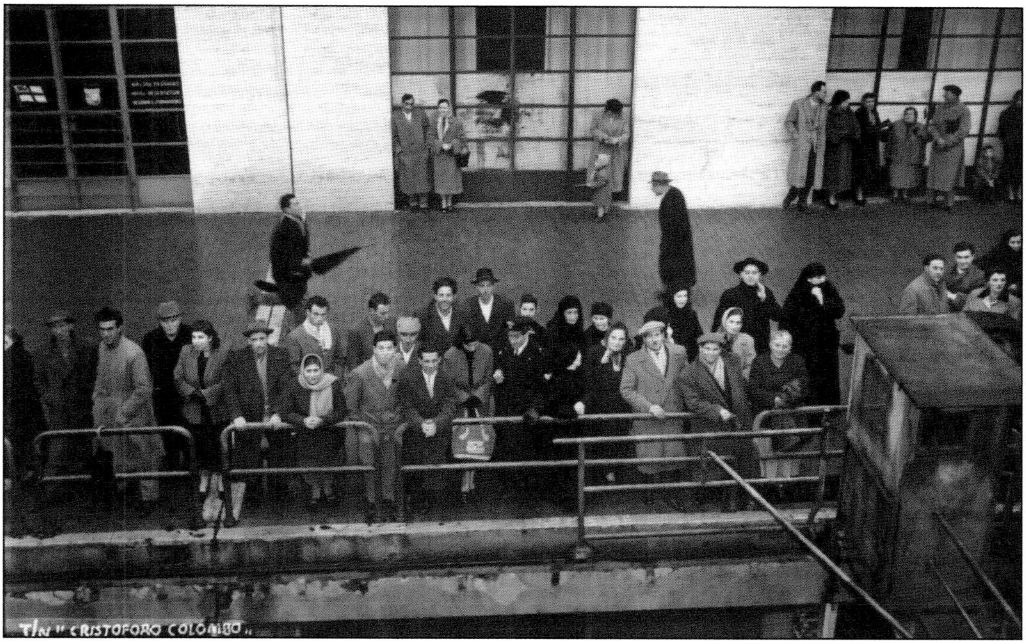

Oblate Sisters. In 1949, the Oblates of the Sacred Heart established a convent in the Mahoning Valley, when 10 of its members flew from Rome, with the permission of Bishop James A. Mc Fadden of the Roman Catholic Diocese of Youngstown. This was the first Oblate convent in the United States. In 1957, a number of their sisters, sailing on the *Cristoforo Colombo,* joined them. The above photograph was taken from the ship as family and friends waved goodbye. Below, several of the sisters may be participating in a mass onboard the ship. Note the orchestra in the background. The women wear head covers—hats and mantillas—in accordance with pre–Vatican II doctrine. (Both, courtesy of the Oblates of the Sacred Heart.)

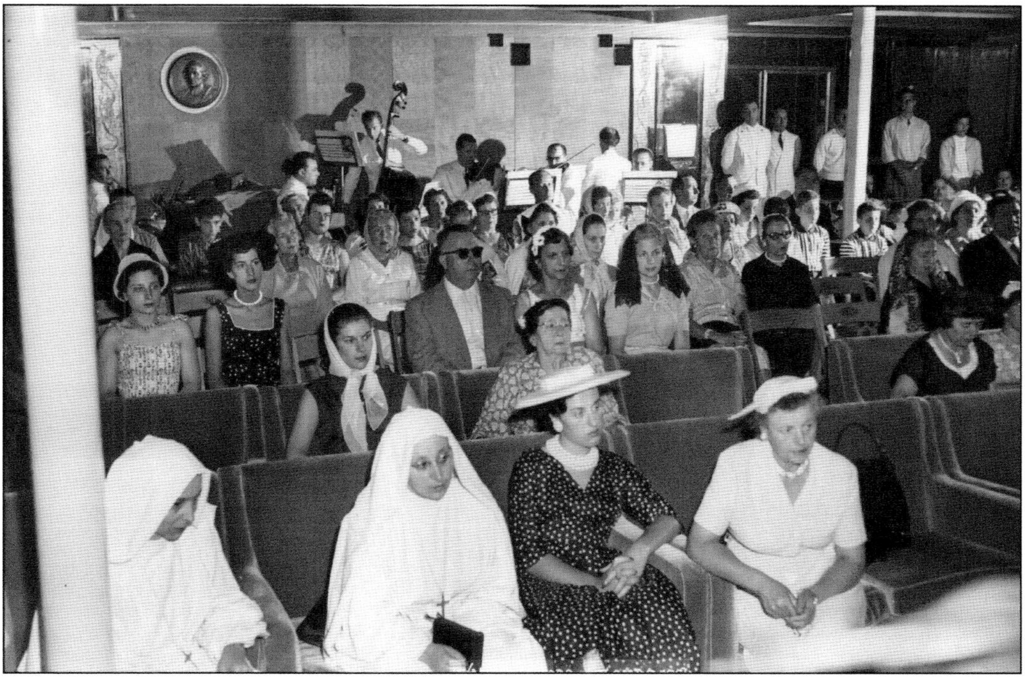

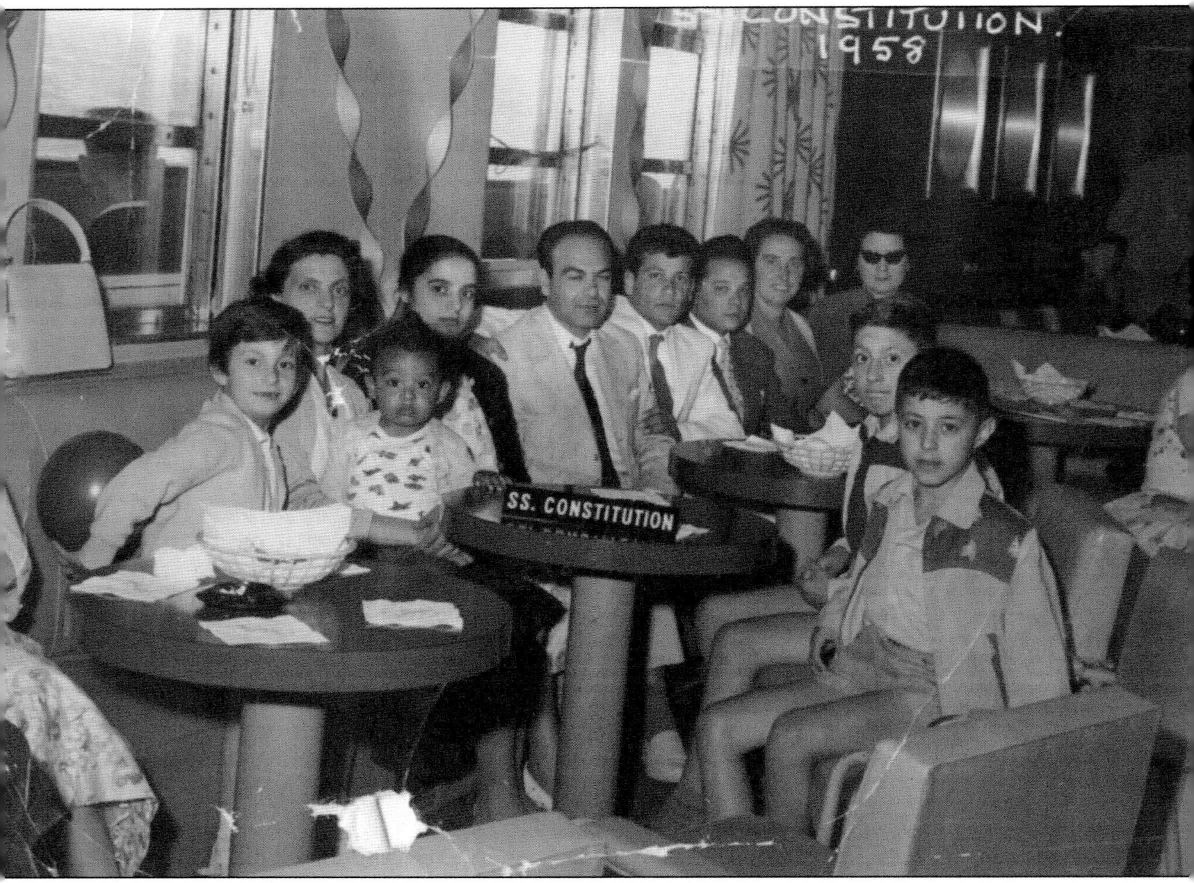

TRANSATLANTIC VOYAGE. The voyage across the Atlantic Ocean was a perilous one, as ships braved storms, icebergs, and other hazards. The early sailing ships often took weeks or months for the crossing. Steamships brought improvements in passenger comfort—not to mention shorter journeys. By the early 20th century, large steamship companies—Great Britain's Cunard and White Star Lines, and Germany's Hamburg-Amerika Line—engaged in cutthroat competition for customers. While travelers in first class and second class journeyed in comfort, the steamship companies made their profit on steerage passengers. Over time, conditions in steerage, or third class, improved, although the quarters were still crowded, noisy, and located near the engine room. Here, members of the Listorti family travel on the SS *Constitution* in 1958. This particular ocean liner became immortalized in American popular culture when it appeared in several episodes of *I Love Lucy* and in the Cary Grant/Deborah Kerr film *An Affair to Remember.* (Courtesy of Frank Pape.)

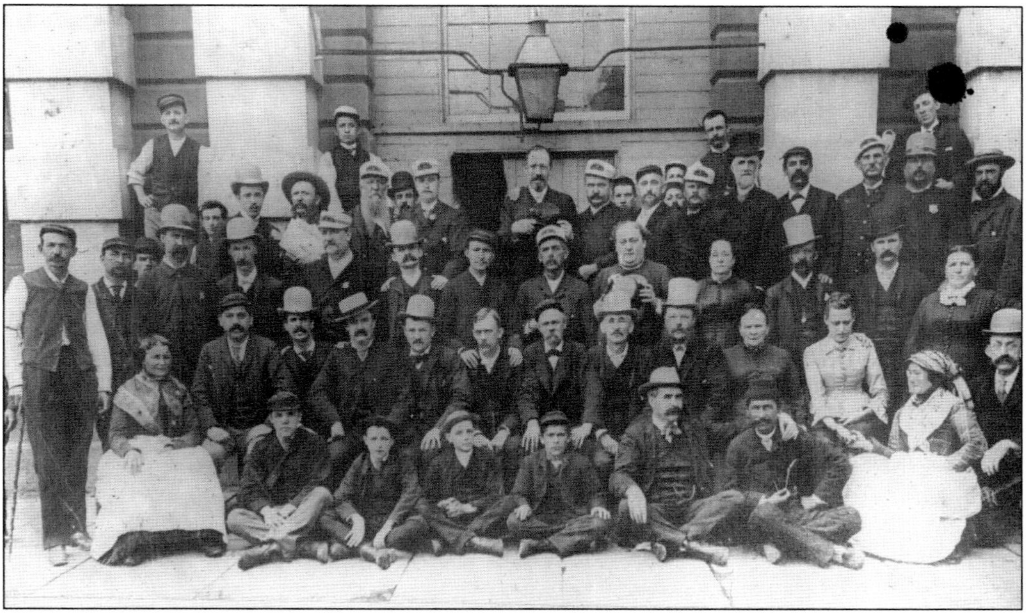

BARGE OFFICE AND ELLIS ISLAND PLAN. While cities up and down the East Coast served as ports of entry for European immigrants, New York was by far the most popular destination. Castle Garden, located at the southern tip of Manhattan, closed in 1890 due to poor conditions, just as Italian immigration accelerated. The Barge Office, seen above with immigration officials, served as the temporary immigration station from April 19, 1890, through December 31, 1891. Ellis Island opened officially on January 1, 1892, and soon became the gateway through which Italian immigrants passed into the United States. The plan of the site (below) illustrates the complexity and scope of the procedures involved in the processing of immigrants. (Both, courtesy of CUA.)

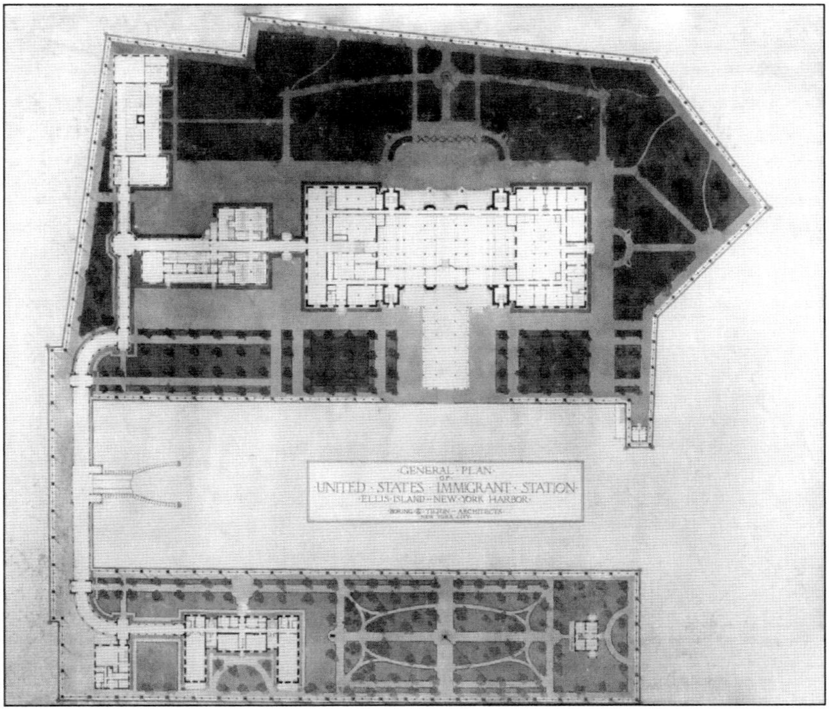

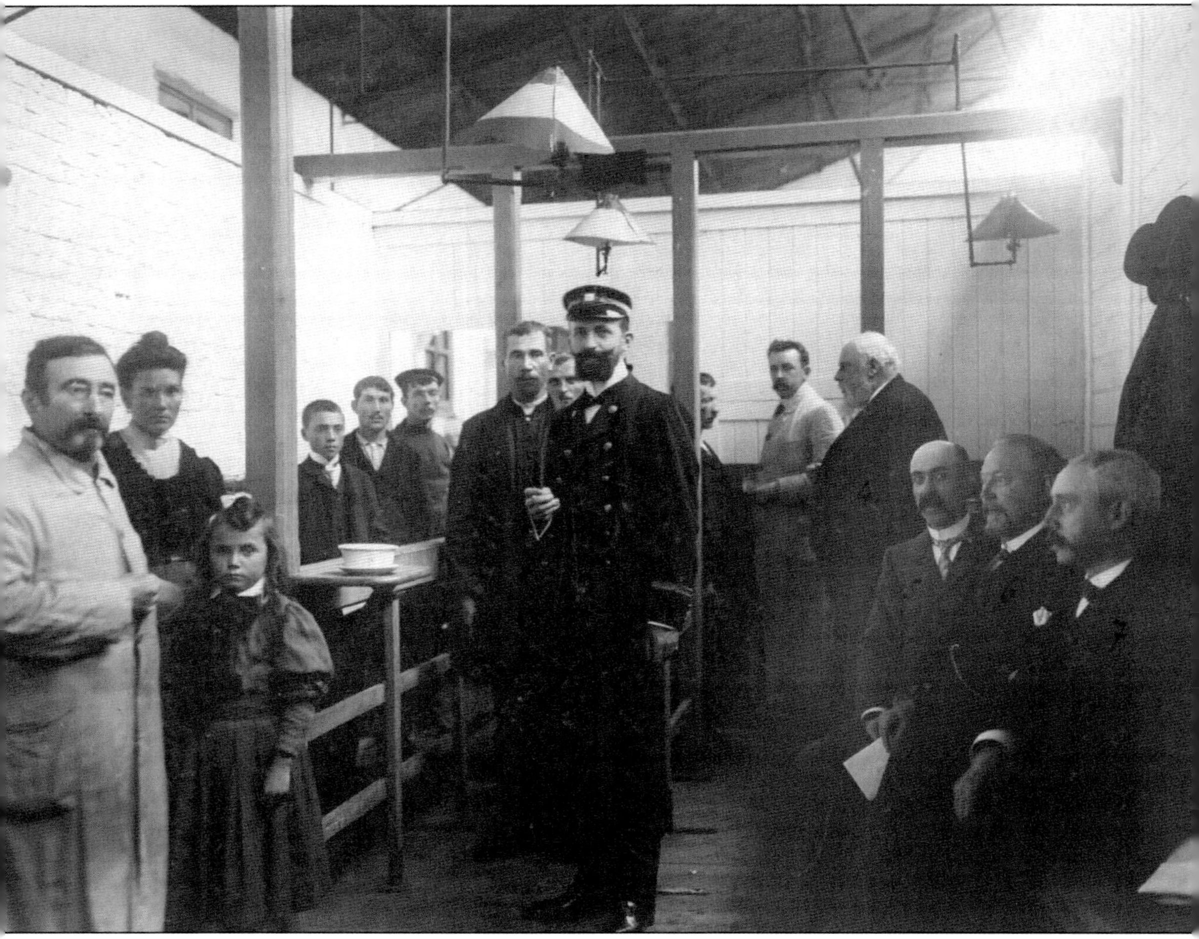

INSPECTION. All immigrants to the United States underwent a process to screen out undesirables, enduring rigorous medical, mental, and political tests of fitness. They also had to prove that they were in no danger of becoming "public charges." In such cases, "class" really mattered. Those traveling to the United States in first or second class had their interviews and medical exams onboard the ship. They proceeded directly to the docks, bypassing the Ellis Island experience. Part of the rationale for this was that, while steerage passengers usually listed their occupation as "laborer" or "farmer," many in first and second class referred to themselves as "gentlemen" or "ladies." This photograph, taken on a ship of the Belgian Red Star Line, the SS *Zealand*, is dated August 26, 1906. (Courtesy of CUA.)

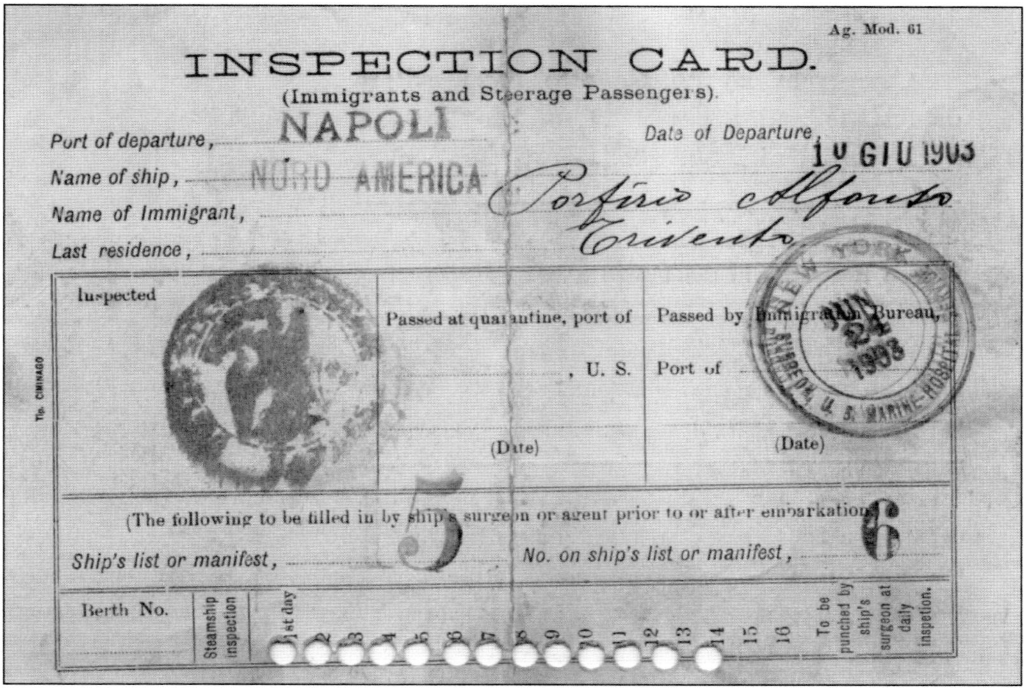
Ag. Mod. 61

INSPECTION CARD.

(Immigrants and Steerage Passengers).

Port of departure, NAPOLI   Date of Departure, 10 GIU 1903

Name of ship, NORD AMERICA

Name of Immigrant, Porfirio Alfonso

Last residence, Trivento

Inspected | Passed at quarantine, port of ……, U. S. (Date) | Passed by Immigration Bureau, Port of …… (Date)

NEW YORK JUN 24 1903 SURGEON, U. S. MARINE-HOSPITAL

(The following to be filled in by ship's surgeon or agent prior to or after embarkation)

Ship's list or manifest, 5   No. on ship's list or manifest, 6

Berth No. | Steamship inspection | 1st day 2 3 4 5 6 7 8 9 10 11 12 13 14 15 16 | To be punched by ship's surgeon at daily inspection.

Inspection Cards. The majority of Italian immigrants endured long queues and exhausting waits as they met with inspectors. Each stamp or punch on an inspection card was another step toward their new home. In the early 20th century, native-born Americans feared that these newcomers would become public charges—hence the exams that went on for hours. Alfonso Porfirio and his daughter Venturina received their "golden tickets" in 1903 (above) and 1904 (below), respectively. Like many Italian immigrants, Alfonso left his native land and sent for his family once he was established in his new home.

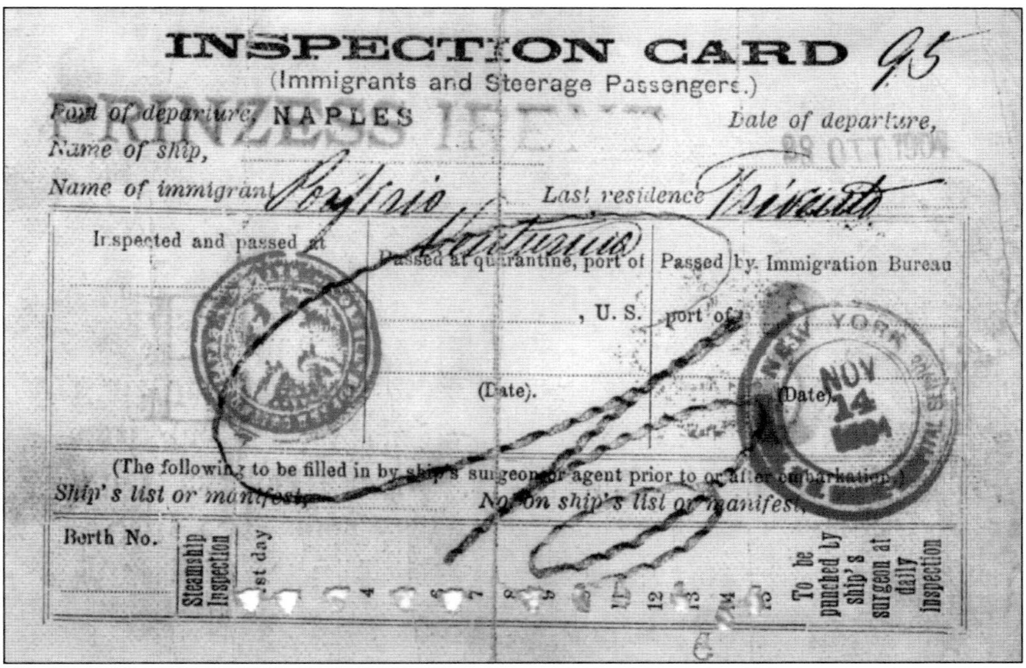
INSPECTION CARD 95

(Immigrants and Steerage Passengers.)

Port of departure, NAPLES   Date of departure, 28 OTT 1904

Name of ship, PRINZESS IRENE

Name of immigrant Porfirio Venturina   Last residence Trivento

Inspected and passed at | Passed at quarantine, port of ……, U. S. (Date). | Passed by Immigration Bureau port of …… (Date).

NEW YORK NOV 14 1904

(The following to be filled in by ship's surgeon or agent prior to or after embarkation.)

Ship's list or manifest,   No. on ship's list or manifest,

Berth No. | Steamship Inspection | 1st day … 12 13 14 15 | To be punched by ship's surgeon at daily inspection

6

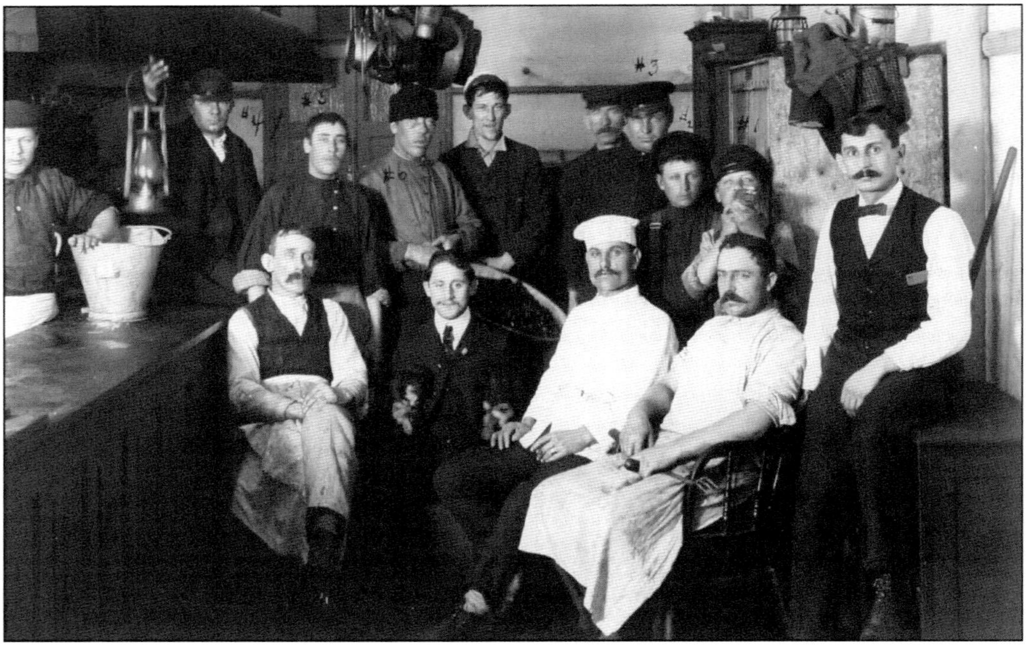

Ellis Island Kitchen and Food Counter. Many immigrants were detained at Ellis Island for various reasons. Above, several detained immigrants are put to work in the facility's kitchen. The men identified with numbers 1, 2, 3, 5, and 6 are immigrants. The below photograph shows the railroad ticket department's food counter. The original caption noted that the person indicated by No. 1 is "Squire Maetin." Wearing a cap with an eagle on it, he is "impersonating a government officer." No. 2 is Emile Schwab, the restaurant's privilege holder, and No. 3 is a pile of bags of prepared lunches. Note the immigrant family on the left and the menu listed in five languages (English, Italian, German, Yiddish, and Polish). (Both, courtesy of CUA.)

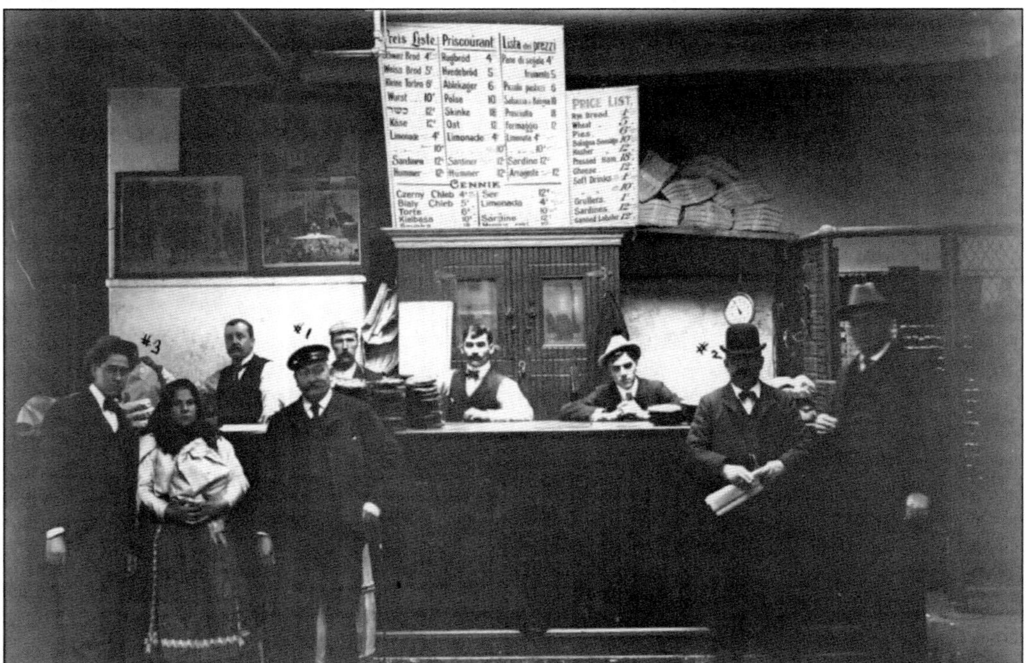

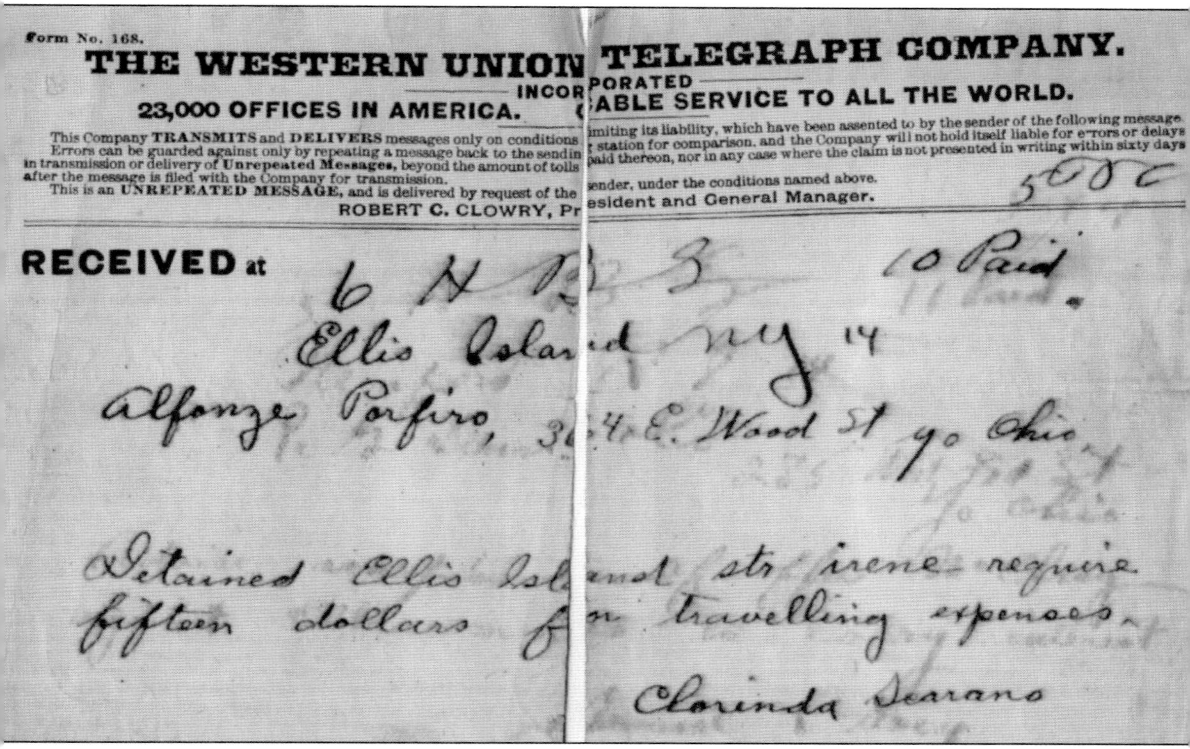

Form No. 168.

THE WESTERN UNION TELEGRAPH COMPANY.

INCORPORATED

23,000 OFFICES IN AMERICA. CABLE SERVICE TO ALL THE WORLD.

This Company TRANSMITS and DELIVERS messages only on conditions limiting its liability, which have been assented to by the sender of the following message. Errors can be guarded against only by repeating a message back to the sendin[g] station for comparison, and the Company will not hold itself liable for errors or delays in transmission or delivery of Unrepeated Messages, beyond the amount of tolls paid thereon, nor in any case where the claim is not presented in writing within sixty days after the message is filed with the Company for transmission.
This is an UNREPEATED MESSAGE, and is delivered by request of the sender, under the conditions named above.

ROBERT C. CLOWRY, President and General Manager.

RECEIVED at 6 H B 3 10 Paid.

Ellis Island NY 14

Alfonze Porfiro, 364 E. Wood St Yo Ohio

Detained Ellis Isl and str irene require fifteen dollars for travelling expenses.

Clorinda Scarano

TELEGRAM. Immigrants who made it successfully through the inspection process still had to reach their destination. New York City and its environs was not always the journey's end. Since many of the immigrants had no prior experience traveling overseas, they underestimated the cost of food and other necessities to be purchased on the ship. Upon arrival in the United States, many did not have enough money for passage to their final destination. In the case of the Porfirio family, mother Clorinda and minor daughter Venturina arrived in the New World one year after Alfonso. At Ellis Island, they discovered that they lacked the necessary funds to continue to Youngstown. With the concern that the two females would become public charges, they were detained until money arrived for their train tickets. Clorinda, signing her maiden name (Scarano), sent this telegram to her husband: "Detained Ellis Isle and str [steamer] Irene. Require fifteen dollars for travelling expenses."

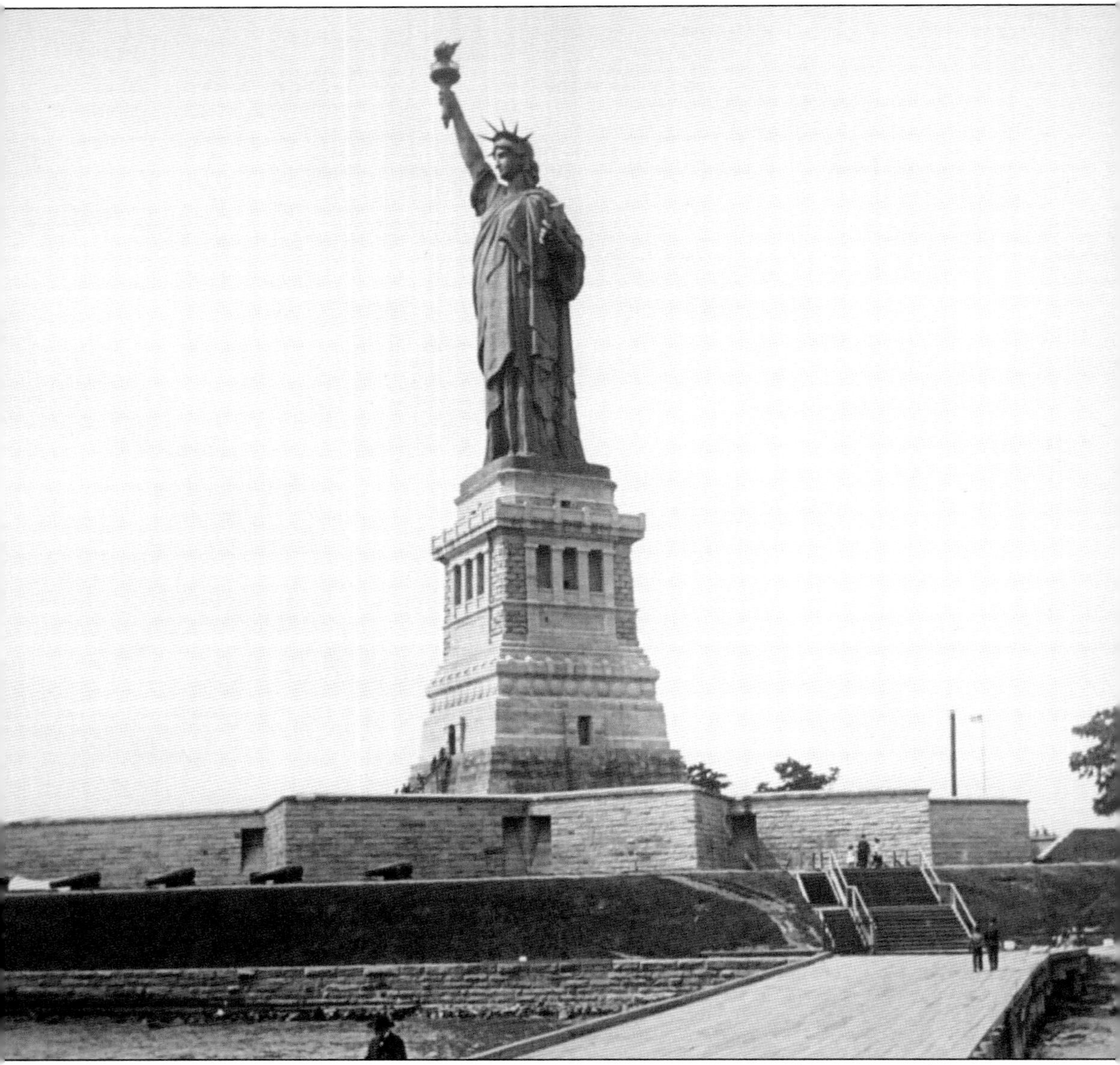

STATUE OF LIBERTY. An American icon, the Statue of Liberty marked the end of the journey to the United States. Designed by Frédéric Auguste Bartholdi, the statue was a gift from the French people. Its full name is "Liberty Enlightening the World." Due to political problems in France, the United States had to raise funds to provide for the site and the pedestal. After a lengthy fundraising campaign, the statue was installed on what was then called Bedloe's Island in New York Harbor, now Liberty Island, and dedicated on October 28, 1886. The famous poem by Emma Lazarus, "The New Colossus," with its celebrated words, "Give me your tired, your poor / Your huddled masses yearning to breathe free," is inscribed on a plaque in the museum at the pedestal's base. Many immigrants took heart upon seeing the Statue of Liberty as they arrived in their new home. They carried with them their hopes and dreams for a better life in America. (Courtesy of the Francis Loeb Library, Harvard Graduate School of Design.)

Two

Becoming American

In many ways, the Mahoning Valley is a microcosm of American society. This is most evident in the history of immigration at the turn of the 20th century. Similar to most of the United States, the "Steel Valley" prior to 1880 was dominated by people who claimed ethnic origins in Northern and Western Europe. By 1930, the picture changed dramatically. Burgeoning steel and iron factories drew Italian immigrants like magnets. At first, they came in ones and twos, but the numbers quickly multiplied. According to the Annuals of Ohio, in 1880, there were seven Italians residing in the Mahoning Valley; by 1890, there were a little over 600. By 1930, Italians and Italian Americans constituted almost 10 percent of the total population (31,151 of 359,205). Most came to the Valley as the result of chain migration: a brother, a cousin, or a friend in America told them there was work to be had, so they eagerly followed. Husbands and fathers sent money for wives and children to join them. Several factors, however, place this community outside the "normal" patterns of immigration to the United States. Women and children represented a much larger percentage of the population than was the norm in early immigrant communities, and the birds of passage were much rarer. The immigrants moved quickly toward home ownership and defied national trends in Italian American communities for education. In other words, most rushed to become Americans. Lorenzo Russo offered a poignant interpretation: "This is the best country in the world. I kiss that flag (the US one) every day. In Italy we respect the flag. I live here now, and I am an American."

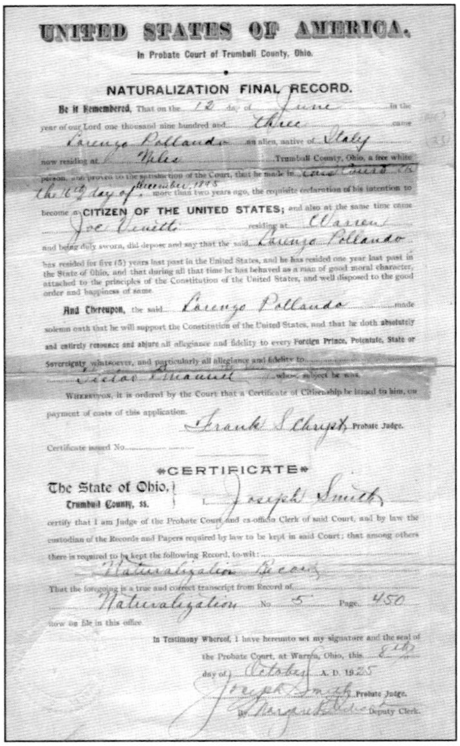

UNITED STATES OF AMERICA.

In Probate Court of Trumbull County, Ohio.

NATURALIZATION FINAL RECORD.

Be it Remembered, That on the 12 day of June in the year of our Lord one thousand nine hundred and three came Lorenzo Pollando an alien, native of Italy now residing at Niles Trumbull County, Ohio, a free white person, and proved to the satisfaction of the Court, that he made in ... the 4th day of December, 1895 more than two years ago, the requisite declaration of his intention to become a CITIZEN OF THE UNITED STATES; and also at the same time came Joe Venetti residing at Warren and being duly sworn, did depose and say that the said Lorenzo Pollando has resided for five (5) years last past in the United States, and he has resided one year last past in the State of Ohio, and that during all that time he has behaved as a man of good moral character, attached to the principles of the Constitution of the United States, and well disposed to the good order and happiness of same.

And Thereupon, the said Lorenzo Pollando made solemn oath that he will support the Constitution of the United States, and that he doth absolutely and entirely renounce and abjure all allegiance and fidelity to every Foreign Prince, Potentate, State or Sovereignty whatsoever, and particularly all allegiance and fidelity to Victor Emanuel whose subject he was.

Whereupon, it is ordered by the Court that a Certificate of Citizenship be issued to him, on payment of costs of this application.

Probate Judge.

Certificate issued No.

CERTIFICATE

The State of Ohio, Trumbull County, ss. I, Joseph Smith certify that I am Judge of the Probate Court and ex-officio Clerk of said Court, and by law the custodian of the Records and Papers required by law to be kept in said Court; that among others there is required to be kept the following Record, to-wit: Naturalization Record

That the foregoing is a true and correct transcript from Record of Naturalization No. 5 Page 450 now on file in this office.

In Testimony Whereof, I have hereunto set my signature and the seal of the Probate Court, at Warren, Ohio, this 8th day of October A.D. 1925

Joseph Smith Probate Judge.

By Deputy Clerk.

Naturalization Papers. US citizenship was the most obvious way to become American. While many Italian immigrants were often reluctant to become citizens—partly due to a distrust of authority—some, like Lorenzo Pallante (misspelled "Pollando" in the document at left), did. He filed his intent to apply for citizenship in 1895 and had met all the requirements established by the US government. In 1903, when Pallante filed his final papers, his friend, Joe Venetti, testified that the former was a man of good character and "well disposed" toward the US Constitution. Cesare Speroni (below) arrived in the United States in 1914. He became a citizen in 1936, most likely because it would be easier for him to claim retirement benefits under the Social Security Act of 1935. Note the differences in the two sets of naturalization papers. Speroni did not need to have another person testify of his intention to stay in the United States or vouch for his character.

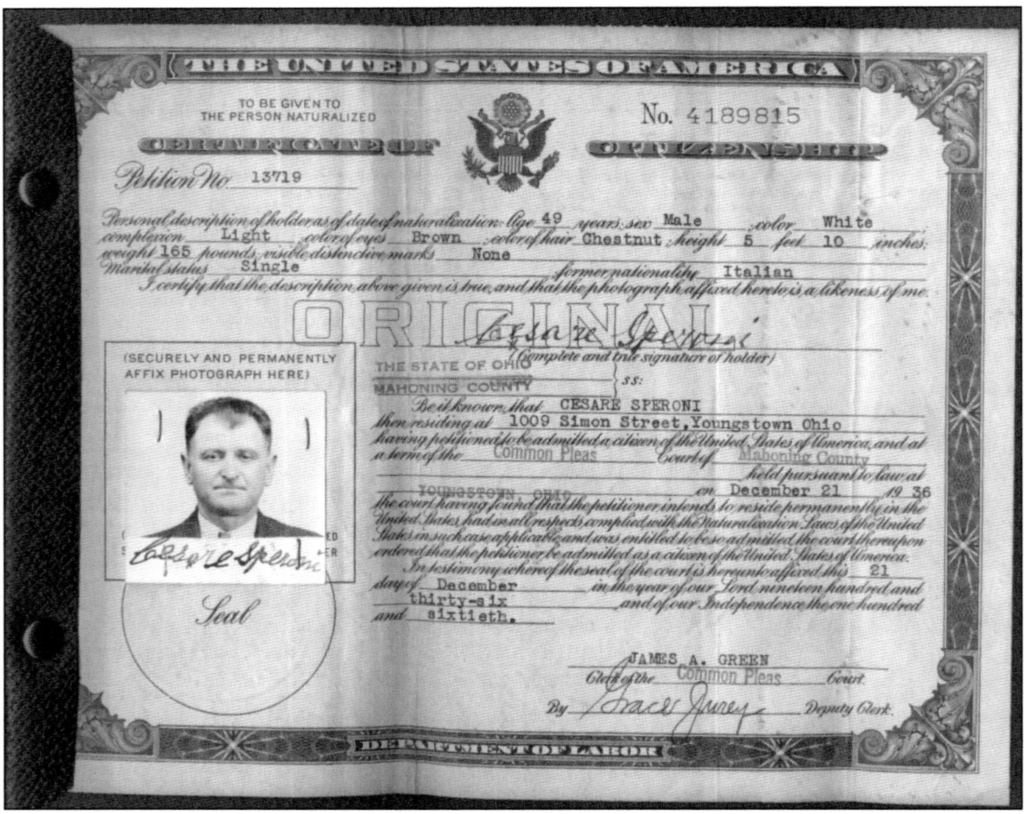

THE UNITED STATES OF AMERICA

TO BE GIVEN TO THE PERSON NATURALIZED

No. 4189815

CERTIFICATE OF CITIZENSHIP

Petition No. 13719

Personal description of holder as of date of naturalization: Age 49 years; sex Male color White complexion Light color of eyes Brown color of hair Chestnut height 5 feet 10 inches; weight 165 pounds; visible distinctive marks None

Marital status Single former nationality Italian

I certify that the description above given is true, and that the photograph affixed hereto is a likeness of me.

ORIGINAL

Cesare Speroni (Complete and true signature of holder)

(SECURELY AND PERMANENTLY AFFIX PHOTOGRAPH HERE)

THE STATE OF OHIO } ss: MAHONING COUNTY

Be it known that CESARE SPERONI then residing at 1009 Simon Street, Youngstown Ohio having petitioned to be admitted a citizen of the United States of America, and at a term of the Common Pleas Court of Mahoning County held pursuant to law at YOUNGSTOWN OHIO on December 21 1936 the court having found that the petitioner intends to reside permanently in the United States, had in all respects complied with the Naturalization Laws of the United States in such case applicable, and was entitled to be so admitted, the court thereupon ordered that the petitioner be admitted as a citizen of the United States of America.

In testimony whereof the seal of the court is hereunto affixed this 21 day of December in the year of our Lord nineteen hundred and thirty-six and of our Independence the one hundred and sixtieth.

Seal

JAMES A. GREEN Clerk of the Common Pleas Court.

By Grace Jurey Deputy Clerk.

DEPARTMENT OF LABOR

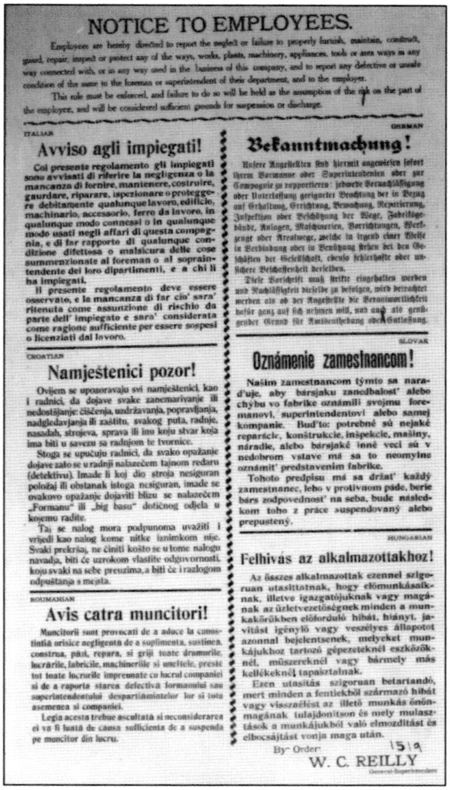

NOTICE TO EMPLOYEES.

Employees are hereby directed to report the neglect or failure to properly furnish, maintain, construct, guard, repair, inspect or protect any of the ways, works, plants, machinery, appliances, tools or area ways in any way connected with, or in any way used in the business of this company, and to report any defective or unsafe condition of the same to the foreman or superintendent of their department, and to the employer.

This rule must be enforced, and failure to do so will be held as the assumption of the risk on the part of the employee, and will be considered sufficient grounds for suspension or discharge.

ITALIAN

Avviso agli impiegati!

GERMAN

Bekanntmachung!

CROATIAN

Namještenici pozor!

SLOVAK

Oznámenie zamestnancom!

ROUMANIAN

Avis catra muncitori!

HUNGARIAN

Felhivás az alkalmazottakhoz!

By Order

W. C. REILLY

General Superintendent

Language Challenges. By the early 20th century, so many immigrants of various backgrounds worked in the mills that management had to develop methods of communication to reach all of them. At right is a sign from the Youngstown Sheet & Tube Company (YS&T) from around 1920, translated into six languages, including Italian (top left), advising employees to notify their supervisors about any misuse or deliberate damage to mill property—under threat of dismissal. Many large companies encouraged their foreign-born employees to learn English. To that end, they sponsored English-language classes, like the one pictured below at YS&T. (Both, courtesy of OHC-YHCIL.)

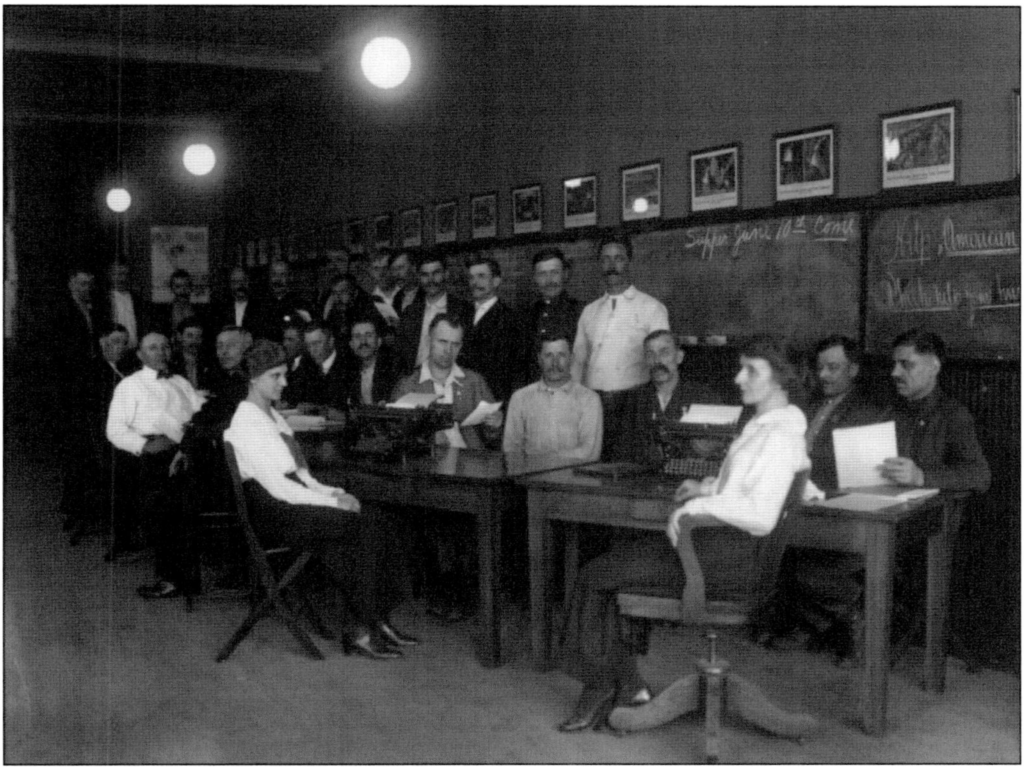

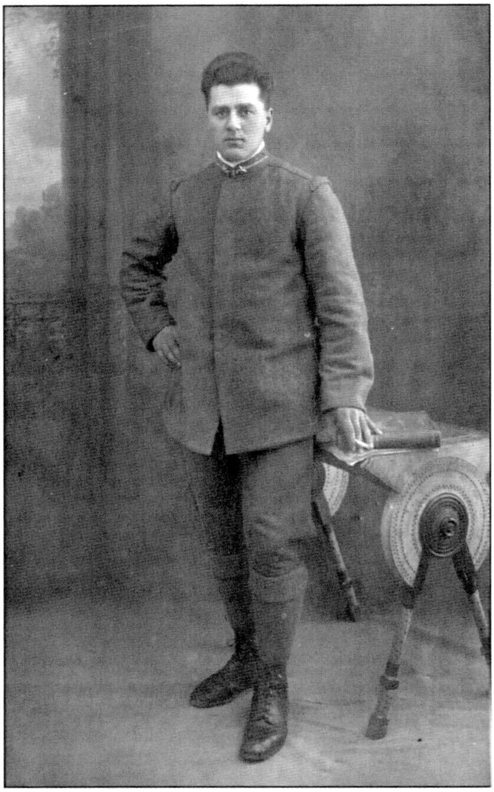

World War I. Italian Americans proved their loyalty to the United States by serving in its armed forces. When World War I began in 1914, most Americans wanted nothing to do with what they saw as a largely European conflict. By 1917, however, it was a different story. Germany engaged in what the American government saw as hostile activities when its U-boats began sinking neutral vessels without warning, pushing the United States into the war on the side of the Allies in April 1917. Leopold Didonato (left), who emigrated to the United States from Rivisondoli in southern Italy, registered for the draft in 1918. The nation financed the war through a series of bond drives, called Liberty Loans. On September 22, 1918, Italian Americans, representing the Sons of Italy in Trumbull County, participated in the Fourth Liberty Loan Drive (below). They are standing in front of the National McKinley Birthplace Memorial in downtown Niles. (Left, courtesy of Carl and Edith Ritch; below, courtesy of Joe Merlo.)

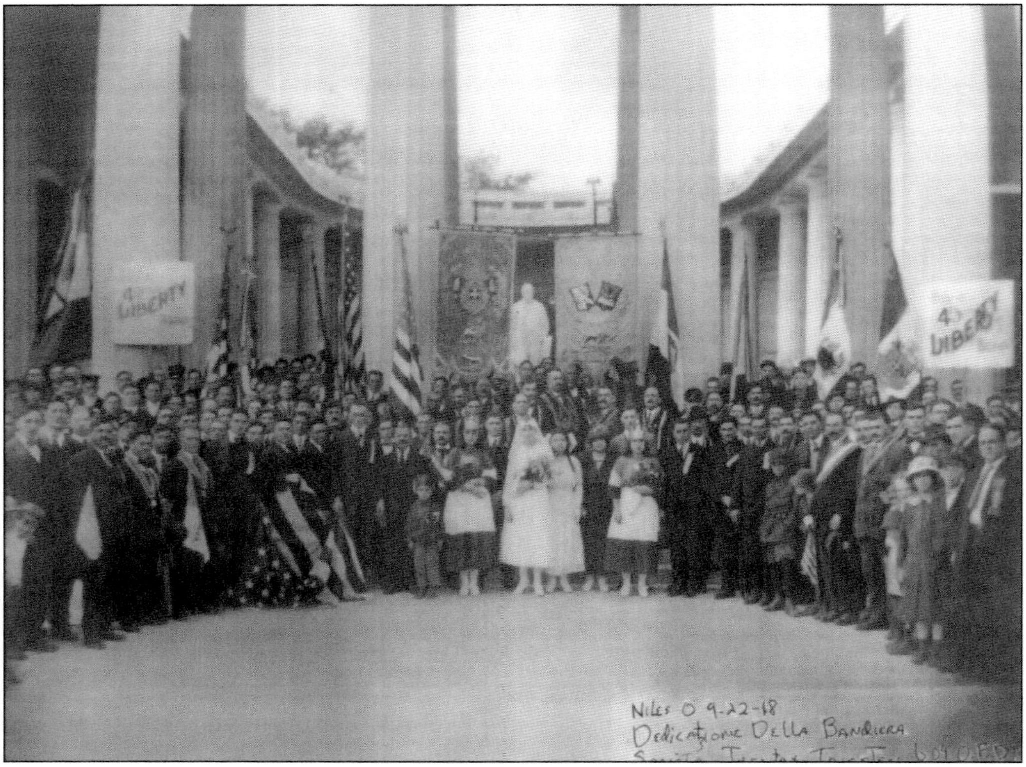

World War II. World War II offered another opportunity for Italian Americans to exhibit their patriotism. As with World War I, when the conflict started on September 1, 1939, most Americans wanted to remain neutral. Franklin D. Roosevelt understood the threat of fascism and slowly nudged public opinion in the direction of aiding the Allies. With the Japanese bombing of Pearl Harbor on December 7, 1941, the nation quickly mobilized. As part of its mobilization, the United States called up men who had already registered or volunteered. Italian Americans, such as Geno Pasquinelli (right), heeded the call to service. Born in 1921, Pasquinelli served in the Pacific as a US Marine during the war. He later completed a second tour of duty as a trainer during the Korean conflict. Similarly, Frank Listorti (below) of Lowellville served in both North Africa and on the Italian peninsula. (right, courtesy of Rosanne Pasquinelli Dando; below, courtesy of Frank Pape.)

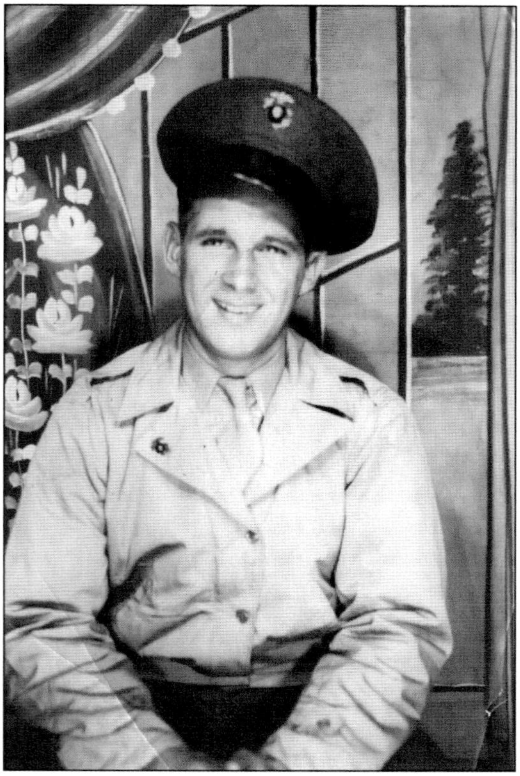

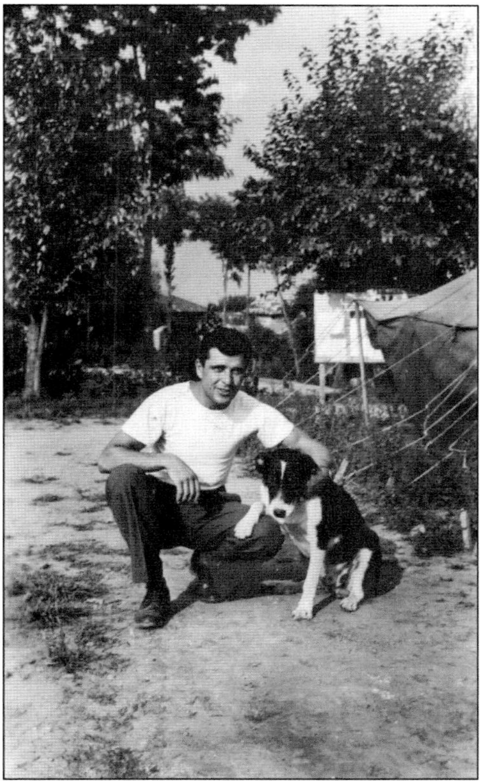

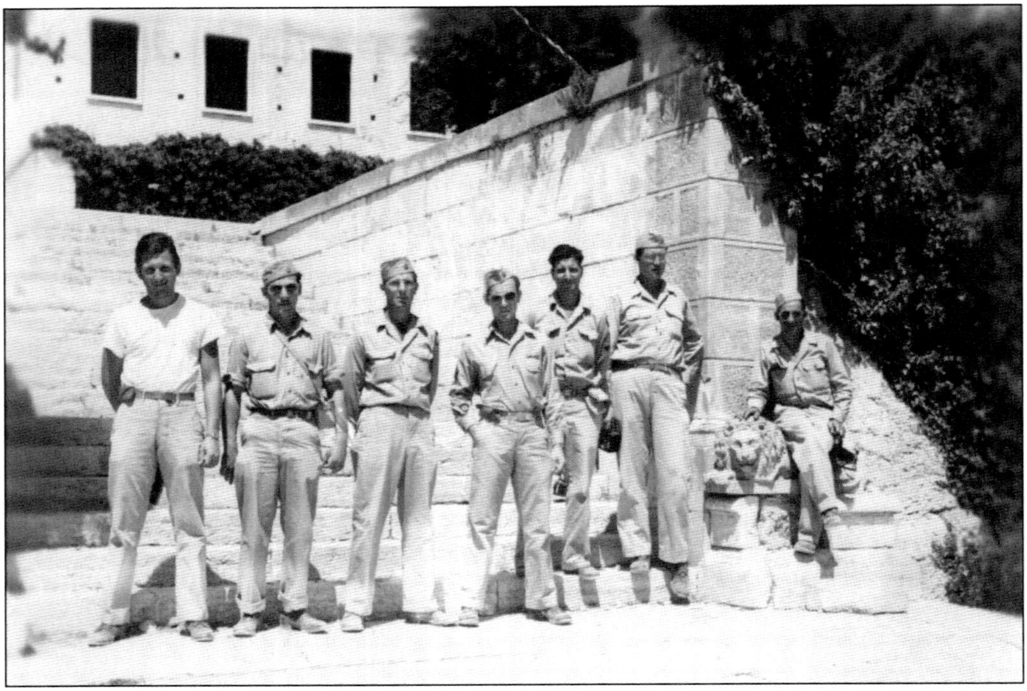

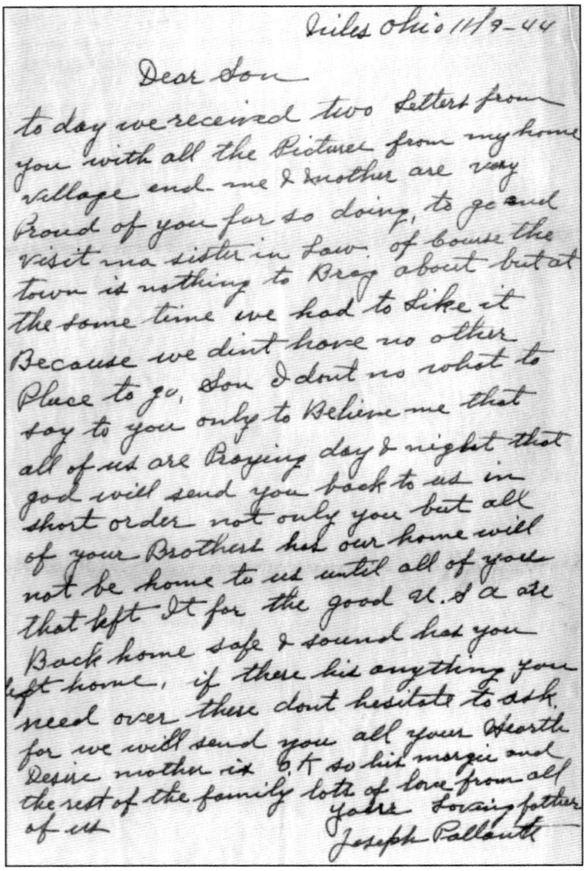

Niles Ohio 11/9-44

Dear Son

to day we received two Letters from you with all the Picture from my home village end me & mother are very Proud of you for so doing, to go and visit ma sister in Law, of course the town is nothing to Brag about but at the same time we had to like it Because we dint have no other Place to go, Son I dont no what to say to you only to Believe me that all of us are Praying day & night that god will send you back to us in short order not only you but all of your Brothers has our home will not be home to us until all of you that left It for the good U.S A are Back home safe & sound has you left home, if there his anything you need over there dont hesitate to ask, for we will send you all your Hearth Desire mother is O.K so his margie and the rest of the family lots of love from all of us

Yours Loving father

Joseph Pallante

Writing Home. Communication with loved ones back home was important to the soldiers and their families. The above photograph, which was sent home, shows a group of American soldiers in the town of St. Angelo in southern Italy. It was taken in 1944, after the Allied invasion. Shown are, from left to right, soldiers Gittleman, Genaslaw, Smith, E.H., Pallante, Roberts, and Boris. Larry Pallante received the letter at left from his father. In the letter, dated December 9, 1944, Joseph Pallante reassures his son that the family is well but they all miss him and his three brothers enormously. Joseph says, "all of us are praying day and night that God will send you back to us in short order. Not only you, but all of your brothers, as our home will not be home to us until all of you that left it for the good of the USA are back home."

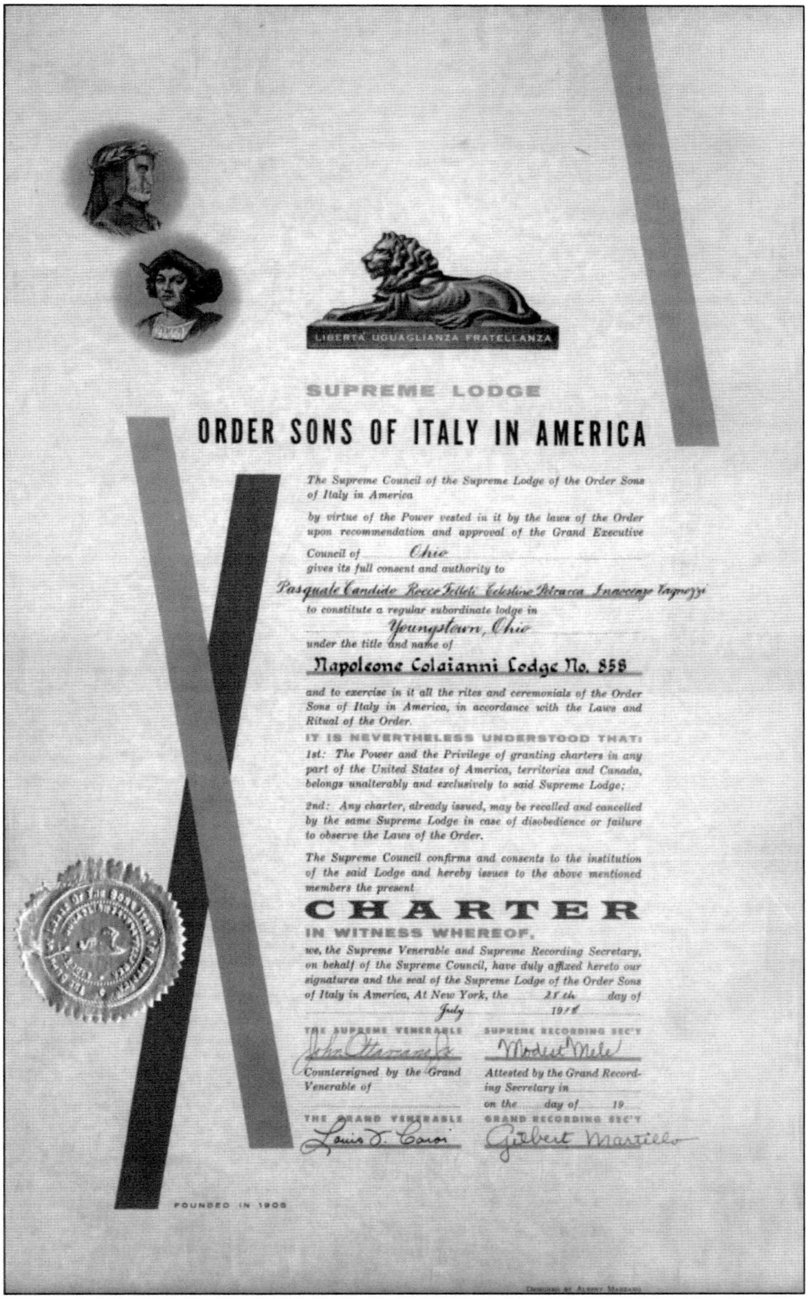

LIBERTÀ UGUAGLIANZA FRATELLANZA

SUPREME LODGE

ORDER SONS OF ITALY IN AMERICA

The Supreme Council of the Supreme Lodge of the Order Sons of Italy in America

by virtue of the Power vested in it by the laws of the Order upon recommendation and approval of the Grand Executive

Council of Ohio

gives its full consent and authority to

Pasquale Candido Rocco Felleti Celestine Petrarca Innocenzo Vagnozzi

to constitute a regular subordinate lodge in

Youngstown, Ohio

under the title and name of

Napoleone Colaianni Lodge No. 858

and to exercise in it all the rites and ceremonials of the Order Sons of Italy in America, in accordance with the Laws and Ritual of the Order.

IT IS NEVERTHELESS UNDERSTOOD THAT:

1st: The Power and the Privilege of granting charters in any part of the United States of America, territories and Canada, belongs unalterably and exclusively to said Supreme Lodge;

2nd: Any charter, already issued, may be recalled and cancelled by the same Supreme Lodge in case of disobedience or failure to observe the Laws of the Order.

The Supreme Council confirms and consents to the institution of the said Lodge and hereby issues to the above mentioned members the present

CHARTER

IN WITNESS WHEREOF,

we, the Supreme Venerable and Supreme Recording Secretary, on behalf of the Supreme Council, have duly affixed hereto our signatures and the seal of the Supreme Lodge of the Order Sons of Italy in America, At New York, the 25th *day of* July 1918

THE SUPREME VENERABLE — SUPREME RECORDING SEC'Y

Countersigned by the Grand Venerable of

Attested by the Grand Recording Secretary in ______ on the ____ day of ______ 19__

THE GRAND VENERABLE — GRAND RECORDING SEC'Y

Gilbert Martillo

FOUNDED IN 1905

Sons of Italy Charter. In 1918, the Order of the Sons of Italy in America granted a charter to the newly formed Napoleone Colaianne Lodge No. 858 in Youngstown, Ohio. The founding members were Pasquale Candido, Rocco Felleti, Celestine Petrarca, and Innocenzo Vagnozzi. At the time the charter was granted, Candido was a patrolman at the YS&T Company, and Felleti was a barber. Petrarca worked as a laborer, but by 1921, he was the publisher of the local Italian-language newspaper, *Il Cittadino Italo-Americano*. Vagnozzi was a businessman engaging in various roles, including hotel proprietor, realtor, interpreter, and insurance agent. The charter granted the new lodge the right "to exercise all the rights and ceremonials of the Sons of Italy in America, in accordance with the Laws and Rituals of the Order." (Courtesy of Sons of Italy in America.)

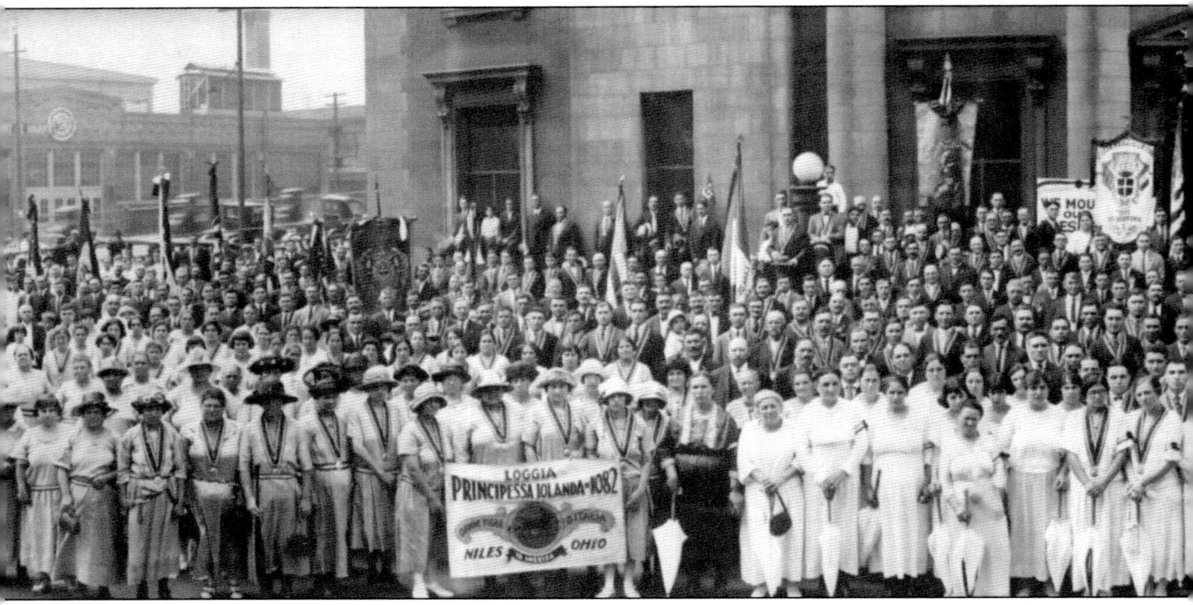

SONS OF ITALY MEETING. Established on June 22, 1905, the Order of the Sons of Italy in America started out as a benevolent society, providing immigrants with vital services such as insurance and death benefits. One of its major goals was to assist Italians in becoming Americans, with English-language classes and other educational opportunities. During World War I, the Sons made an all-out effort to support the United States, with lodges, as the local chapters were

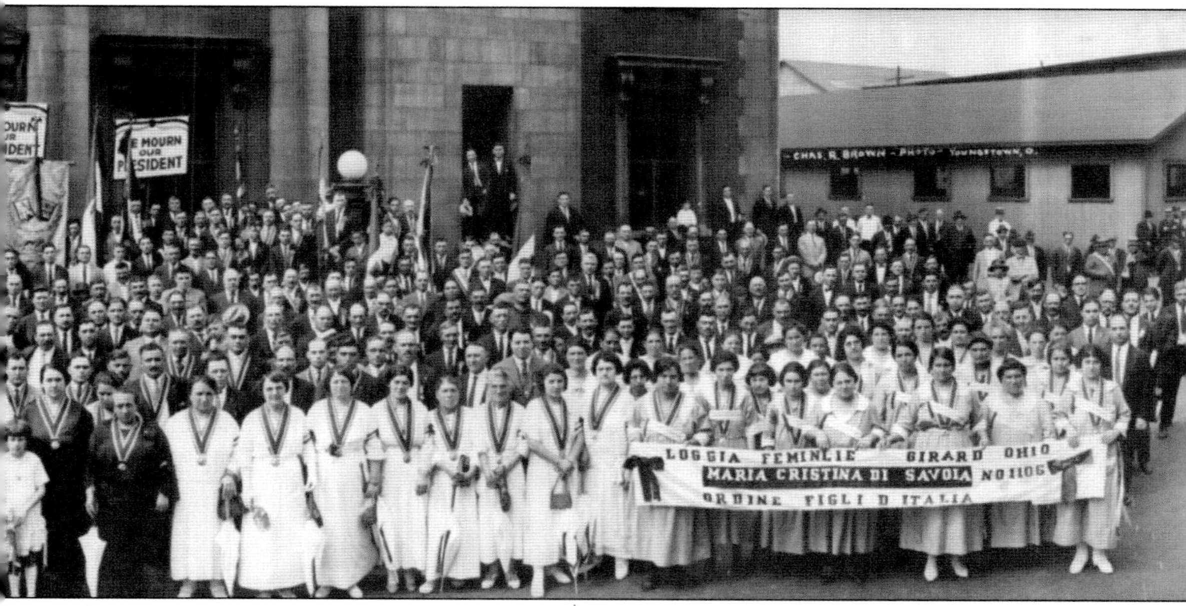

called, competing with each other to raise funds for the war effort. In 1923, the Ohio Lodge of the Sons of Italy held its annual convention in Youngstown. Women's lodges were also a part of the organization. Note the sign, "We Mourn our President." This refers to Warren G. Harding, who died on August 2, 1923. (Courtesy of Sons of Italy in America.)

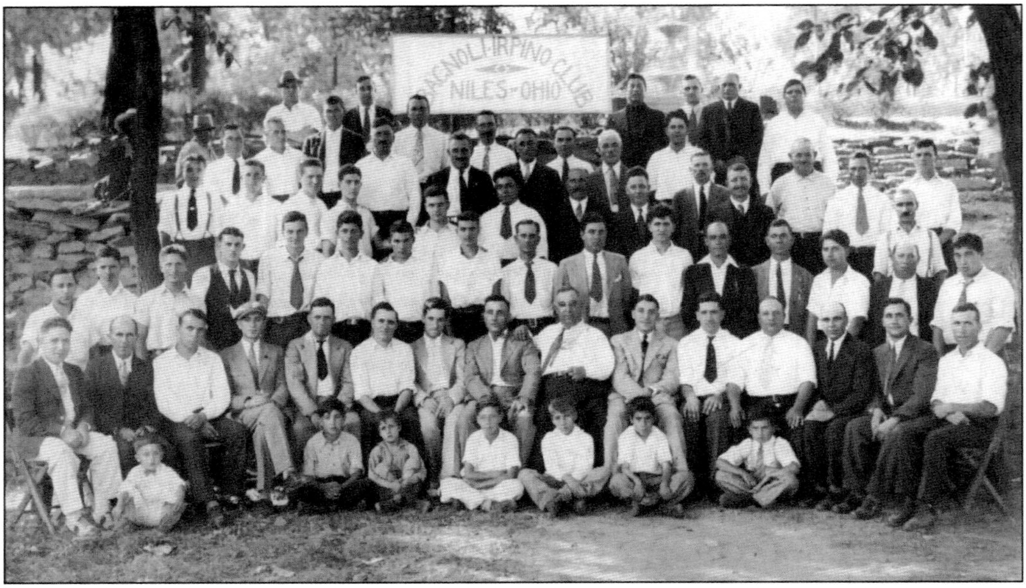

Bagnoli Irpino Club. Established in 1932, the Bagnoli Irpino Club, located in Niles, Ohio, served two purposes: one, social, and the other, educational. It was a place where the men from Bagnoli and their sons could bond over food, drink, and conversation, as well as winemaking. The organization also provided a path to becoming American, offering English-language and literacy classes in addition to instruction for naturalization.

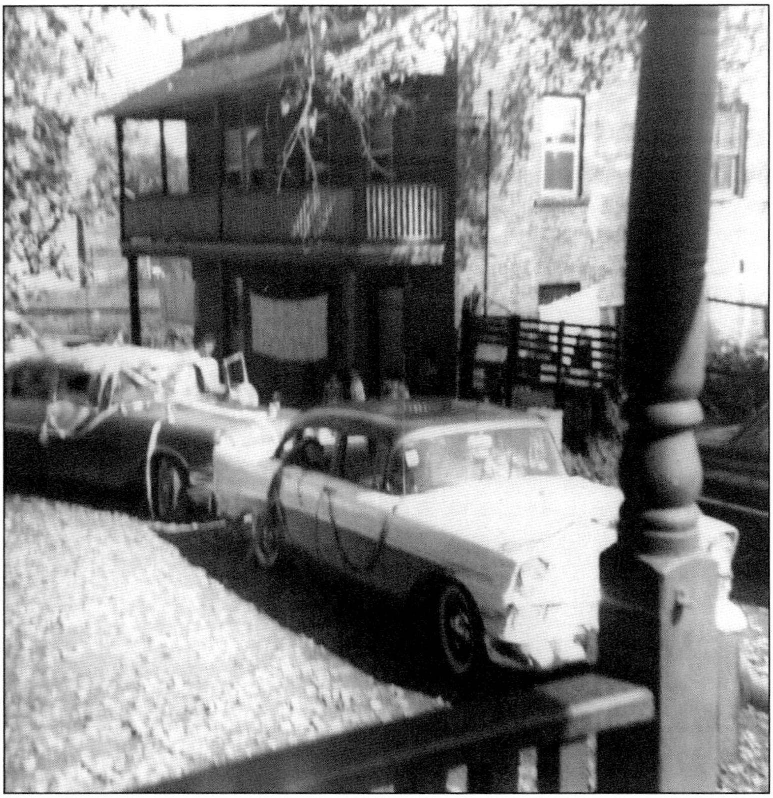

Golden Eagles Club. Formed in the 1930s, the Golden Eagles Club provided a place for young men to socialize, engage in sports, and participate in other leisure activities. The name was suggested by Youngstown parks commissioner John Chase. The young men liked the name, particularly since the eagle was an American national symbol. The original clubhouse (pictured) was in Smoky Hollow on Walnut Street. (Courtesy of Anthony Worrelia.)

SCHOOL DAYS. Unlike in most larger communities, the Mahoning Valley's Italian Americans did not demonstrate the same disdain for education, because, in the steel industry, there were few jobs that children could do, so they rarely worked there. Venturina Porfirio (right) lived in Smoky Hollow and attended the Wood Street School, located on the corner of Wood Street and Summit Avenue. Venturina arrived in Youngstown in 1904 at the age of six. She quickly learned to read and write in English, keeping up with her classmates. Her report card (below) shows her promotion to the seventh grade.

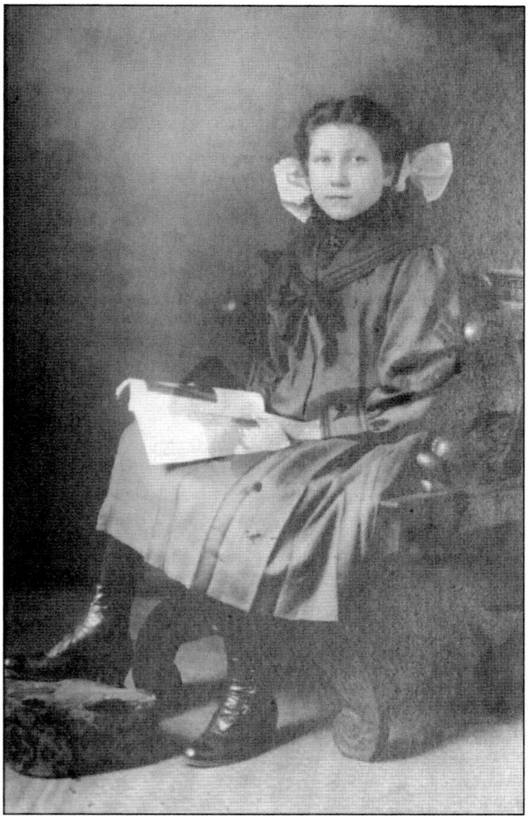

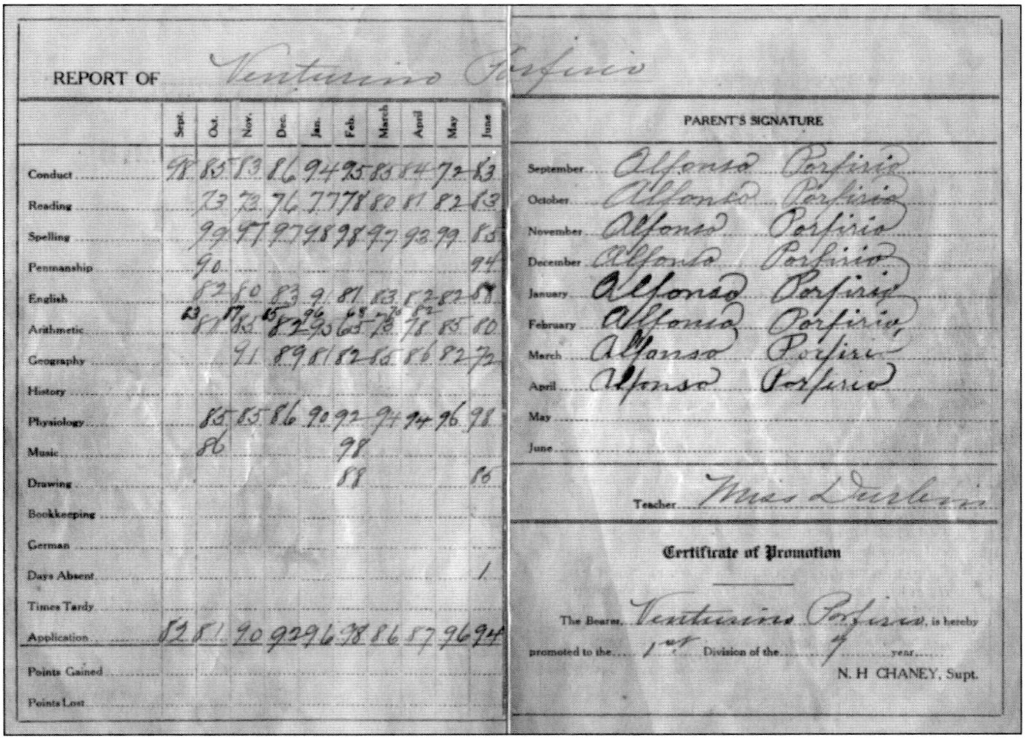

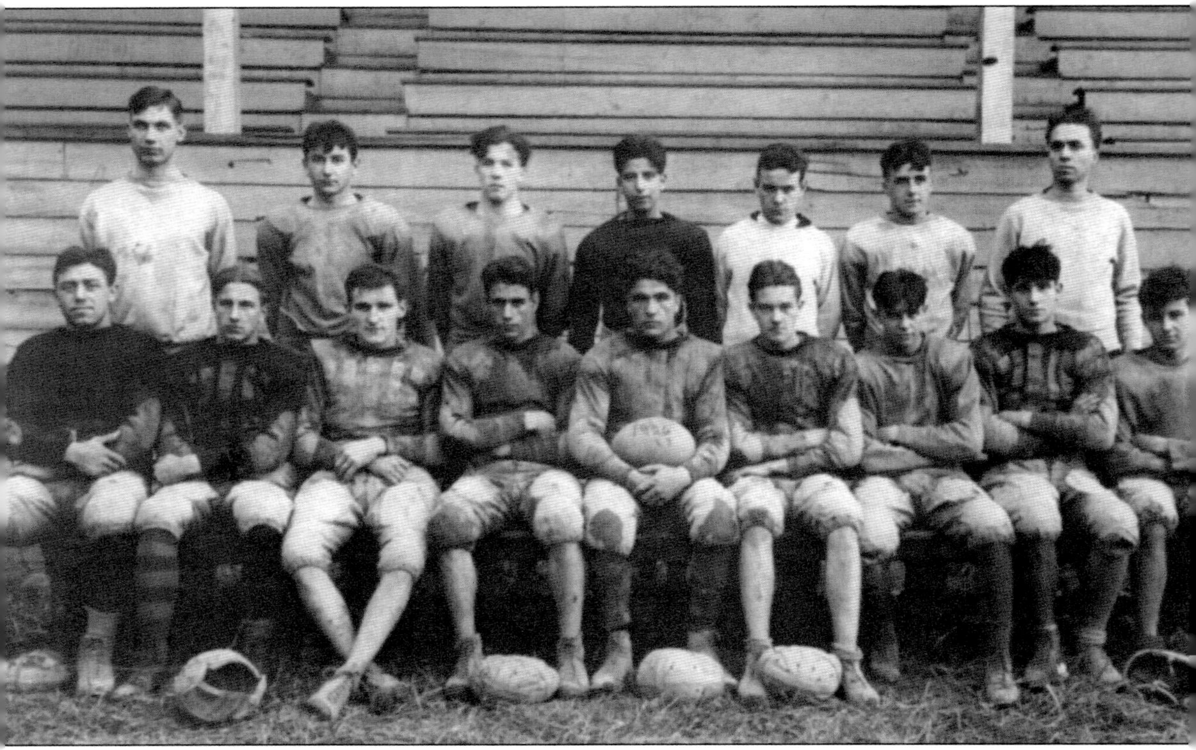

Niles Football Team. Sports, like education, has always acted as an agent of Americanization. In this case, the presence of three Italian Americans on the 1926 Niles McKinley High School football squad is symbolic of the educational aspirations of their families. By the 1920s, a high school education was becoming more widespread, but it was still not common in immigrant communities. The Mahoning Valley challenged the national norms when it came to education for Italian Americans beyond the eighth grade. Shown here are, from left to right, (first row) Frank Lutz, Omar Stien, Paul Lewis, Abie Sundie, John DeChristafaro, Bill Orr, P. Parker, Stan Wilder, and Monk Williams; (second row) assistant coach Hall, Joe Kovic, Bill Bohne, Larry Pallante, Harold Humphries, Mac McGowan, and head coach Collier.

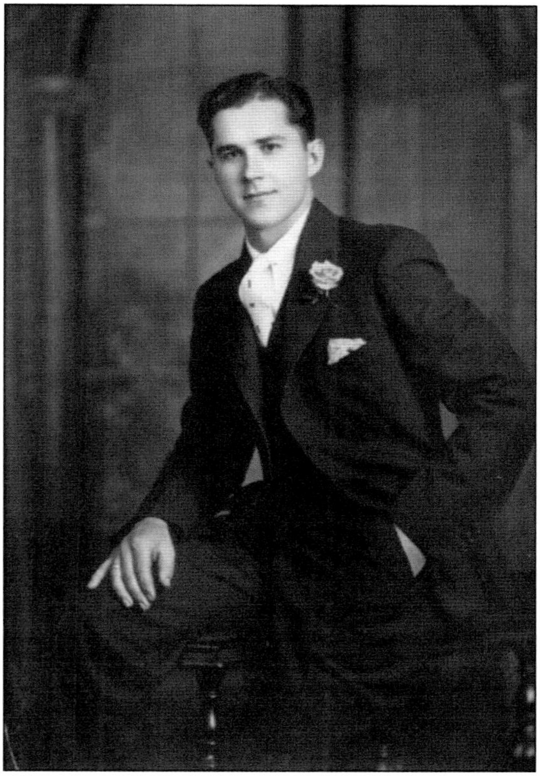

High School Graduation. Like most people, Italian Americans were proud of their children's accomplishments. They regarded education as a way out of the working class and into jobs that were not backbreaking or dangerous. Unlike what is usually ascribed to Italian Americans, they educated both their sons and their daughters. Albert Bartoli (right) graduated from high school around 1927. By 1930, he was a salesman in his father's grocery store, the Milano Market. Edith D'Altorio (below) was a member of the class of 1947 at Warren G. Harding High School in Warren, Ohio. (Right, courtesy of Rosanne Pasquinelli Dando; below, courtesy of Carl and Edith Ritch.)

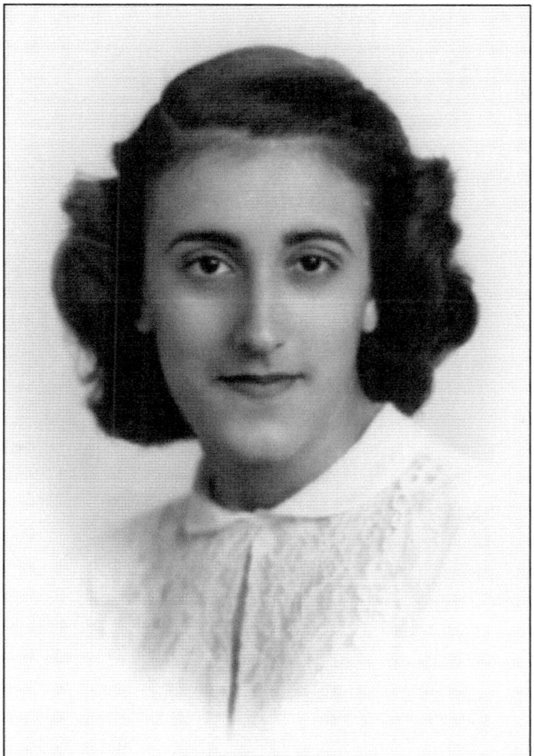

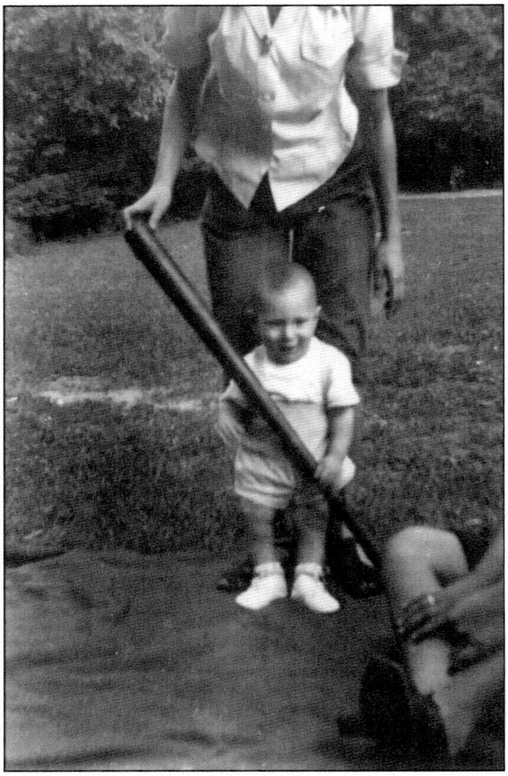

AMERICAN FUN. Italian American children, because of their relationships forged outside of the family, perhaps in school, often Americanized much faster than their elders. Baseball was America's pastime. At left, the DiLallo family's baby, seen here around 1940, was trained at a very young age how to properly hold a baseball bat. In Italy, Halloween is a religious holiday, the eve before All Saint's Day. In the United States it is a secular event, filled with spooky costumes and lots of tricks and treats. Seen below in 1958, Rosanne Pasquinelli (left) is dressed as a gypsy, and Angela Pasquinelli is much scarier as a skeleton. (Left, courtesy of Anthony Worrelli; below, courtesy of Rosanne Pasquinelli Dando.)

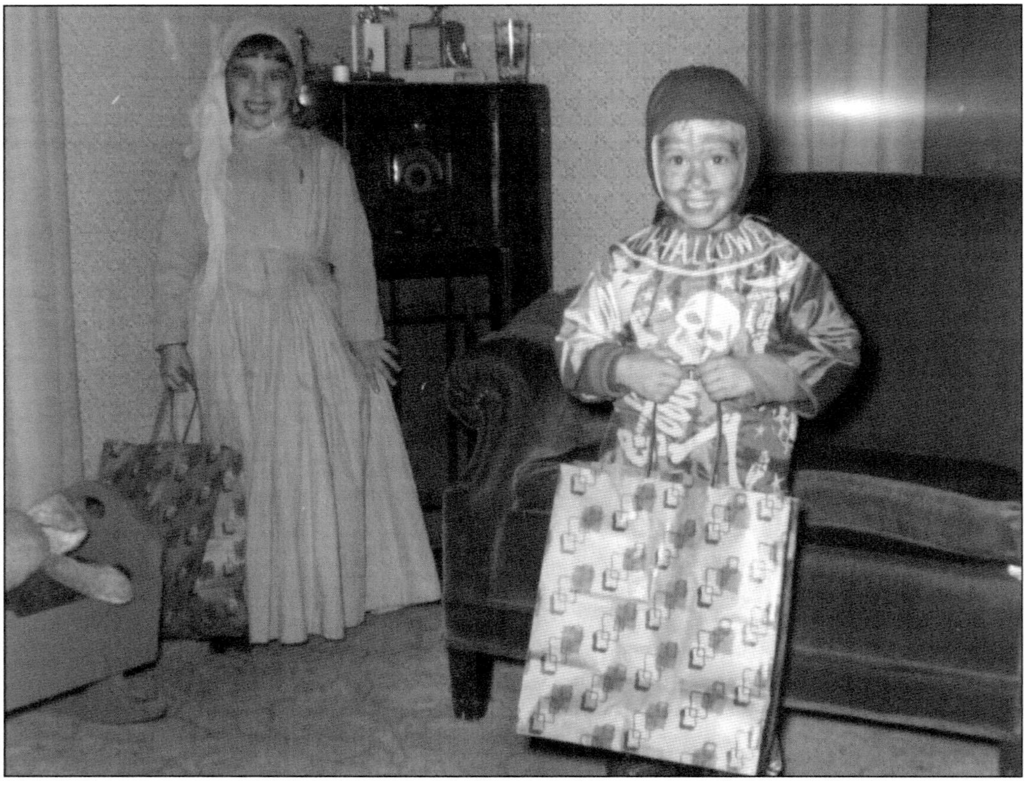

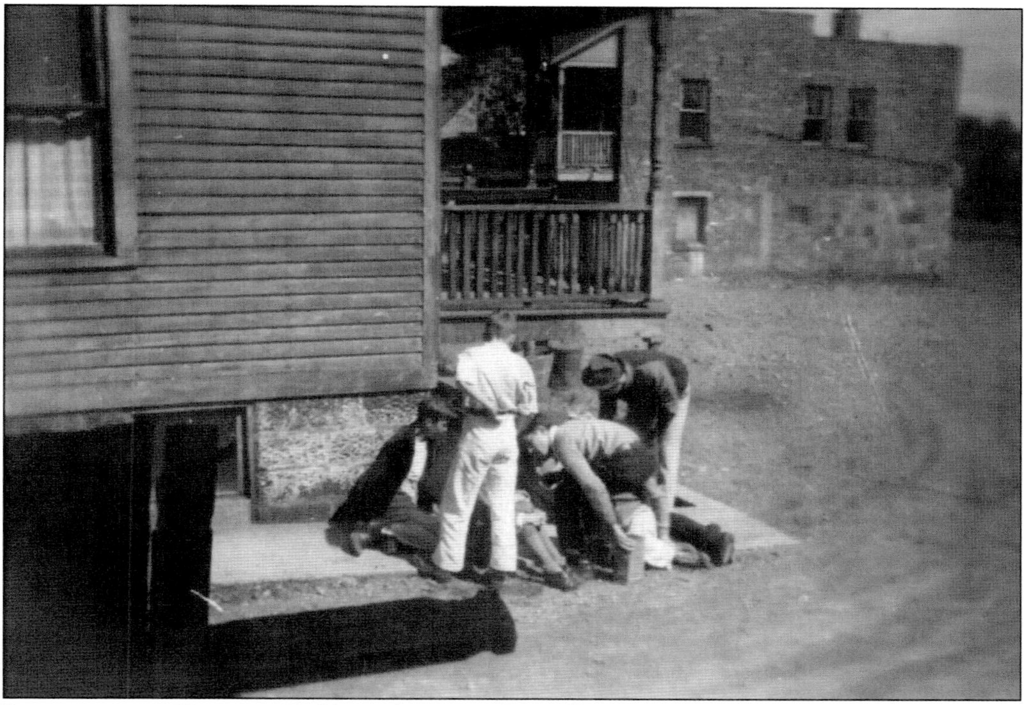

PLAYING IN THE HOLLOW. Children play in Smoky Hollow around 1935. While Italian and Italian American children played games from the old country, they soon engaged in activities common in the United States. Some of the children seen here, possibly shooting marbles, are members of the Worrellia family and their friends. They are on Walnut Street; the building housing the Golden Eagles Club is in the background on the right. (Courtesy of Anthony Worrellia.)

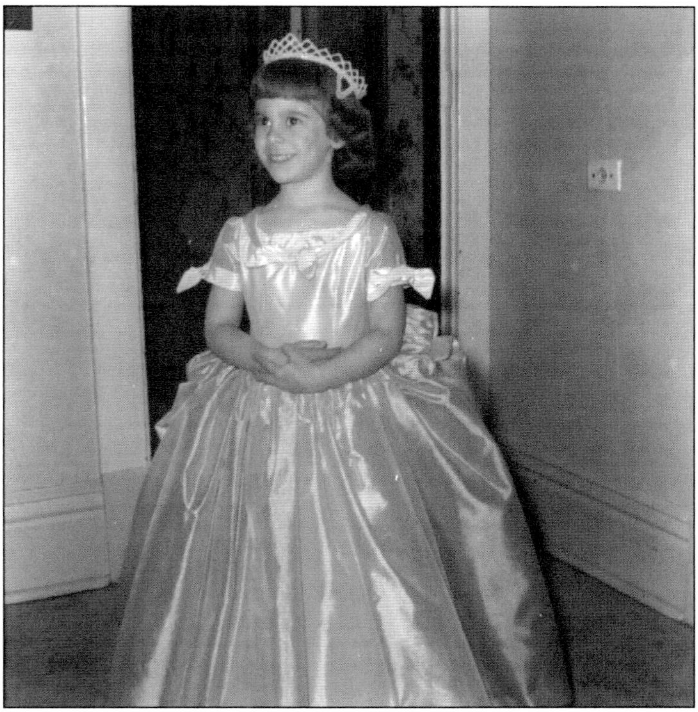

LITTLE PRINCESS. Homecoming is a very American celebration, prevalent in both high schools and colleges. Youngstown State University has held homecoming events for much of its history. In the late 1950s, Rosanne Pasquinelli was a member of Youngstown University's homecoming queen's court, carrying the queen's crown. She is seen here in the princess dress that she wore during homecoming celebrations. (Courtesy of Rosanne Paquinelli Dando.)

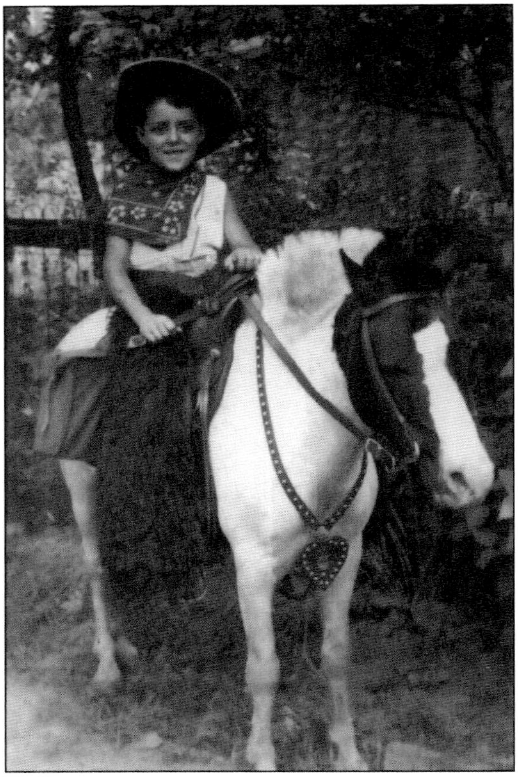

Playing Cowboy. Richard Cagna (left) of Youngstown is dressed in his full cowboy gear, including chaps and a 10-gallon hat. Cagna, who was born in 1934, posed for this photograph in the early 1940s. Shown below are two "cowboys" from the DiLallo family in Smoky Hollow. According to local lore, a man went around the city with the pony, giving children rides on the animal and taking photographs. The cowboy was a potent American symbol that children especially admired and tried to emulate, thanks largely to motion pictures—and, later, television shows—set in the American West. These children of Italian immigrants absorbed American popular culture as they pretended they were riding the range in the Old West. (Left, courtesy of Rosanne Pasquenelli Dando; below, courtesy of Anthony Worrellia.)

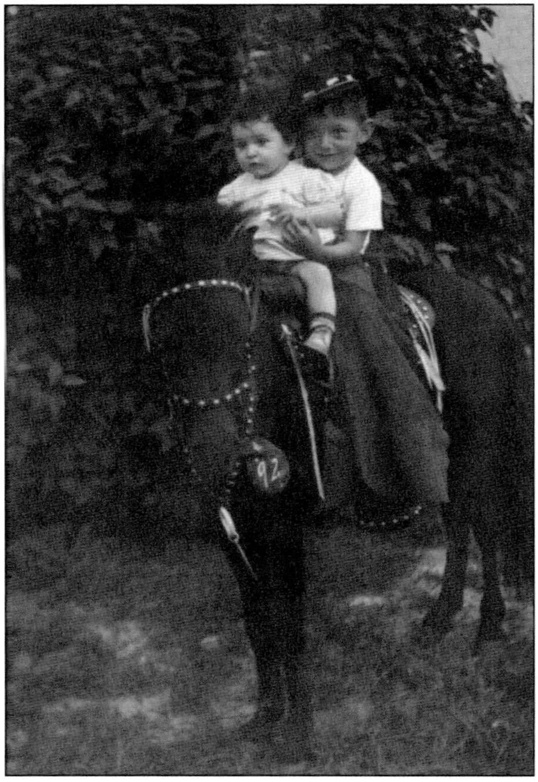

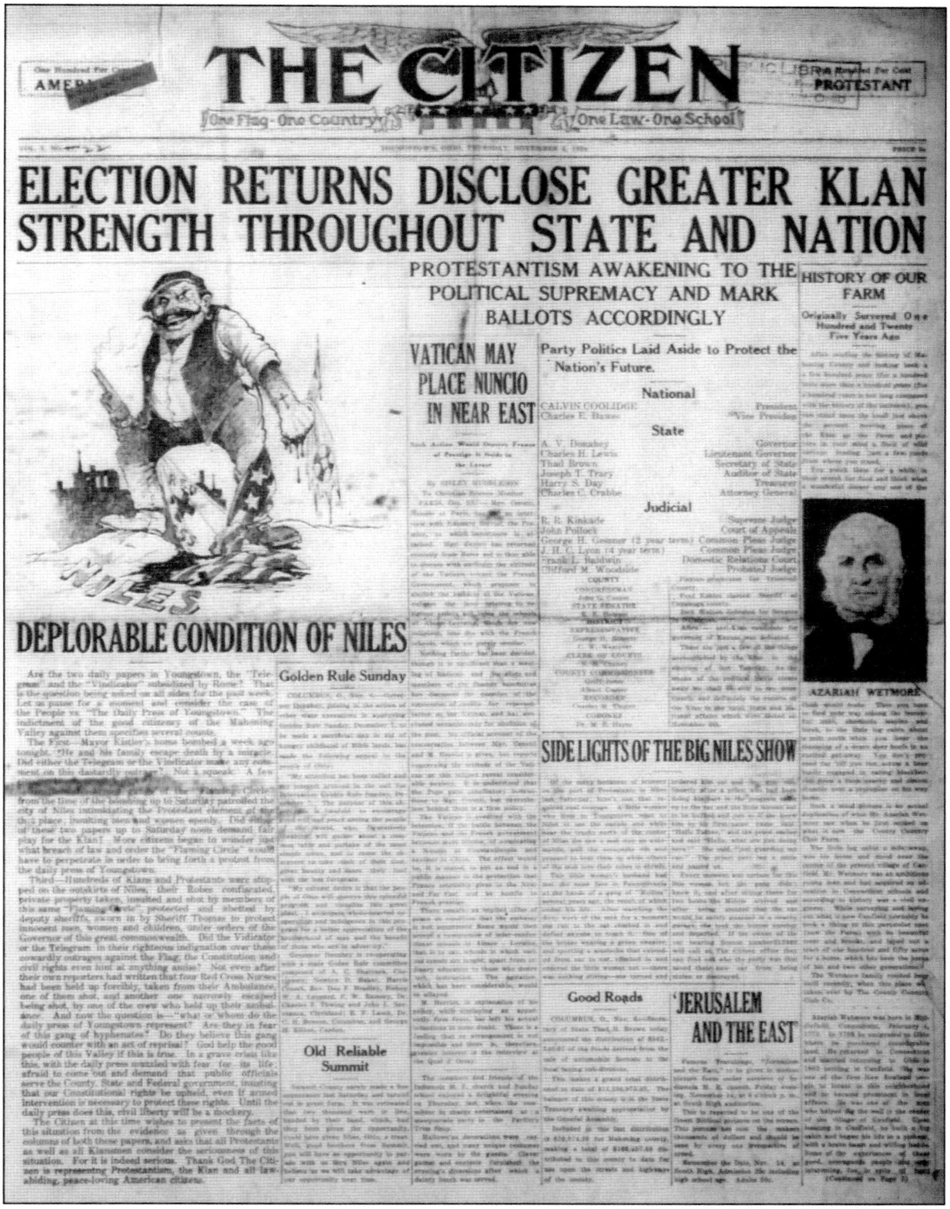

THE CITIZEN

One Flag - One Country

One Law - One School

One Hundred Per Cent PROTESTANT

ELECTION RETURNS DISCLOSE GREATER KLAN STRENGTH THROUGHOUT STATE AND NATION

PROTESTANTISM AWAKENING TO THE POLITICAL SUPREMACY AND MARK BALLOTS ACCORDINGLY

HISTORY OF OUR FARM

Originally Surveyed One Hundred and Twenty Five Years Ago

VATICAN MAY PLACE NUNCIO IN NEAR EAST

Party Politics Laid Aside to Protect the Nation's Future.

National

CALVIN COOLIDGE	President
Charles E. Dawes	Vice President

State

A. V. Donahey	Governor
Charles H. Lewis	Lieutenant Governor
Thad Brown	Secretary of State
Joseph T. Tracy	Auditor of State
Harry S. Day	Treasurer
Charles C. Crabbe	Attorney General

Judicial

DEPLORABLE CONDITION OF NILES

Golden Rule Sunday

SIDE LIGHTS OF THE BIG NILES SHOW

Good Roads

'JERUSALEM AND THE EAST'

Old Reliable Summit

AZARIAH WETMORE

INTOLERANCE. Not every native-born American welcomed immigrants from Southern and Eastern Europe in the early 20th century. Some turned their prejudices into efforts to "Americanize" the newcomers and developed ways to help them adjust to life in the New World. Others were less benign. In 1915, the Ku Klux Klan, which in the 1860s and 1870s terrorized African Americans, re-emerged and focused its animosity against new groups: Catholic and Jewish immigrants. By the 1920s, many middle-class Americans either joined the Klan or were sympathetic toward it. In the Valley, the Klan was so influential that it elected many of its own to political offices. In 1923 and 1924, the Klan engaged in several demonstrations, including cross burnings, near Niles. On November 1, 1924, Catholics fought back, rioting over a rumor that the KKK was going to storm the convent of the Humility of Mary Sisters. Seen here is the front page of the local Klan newspaper, *The Citizen*, which denounced the successful rebuff of the Klan parade, including a blistering editorial cartoon characterizing Italians as brutish, gun-toting thugs. (Courtesy of OHC-YHCIL.)

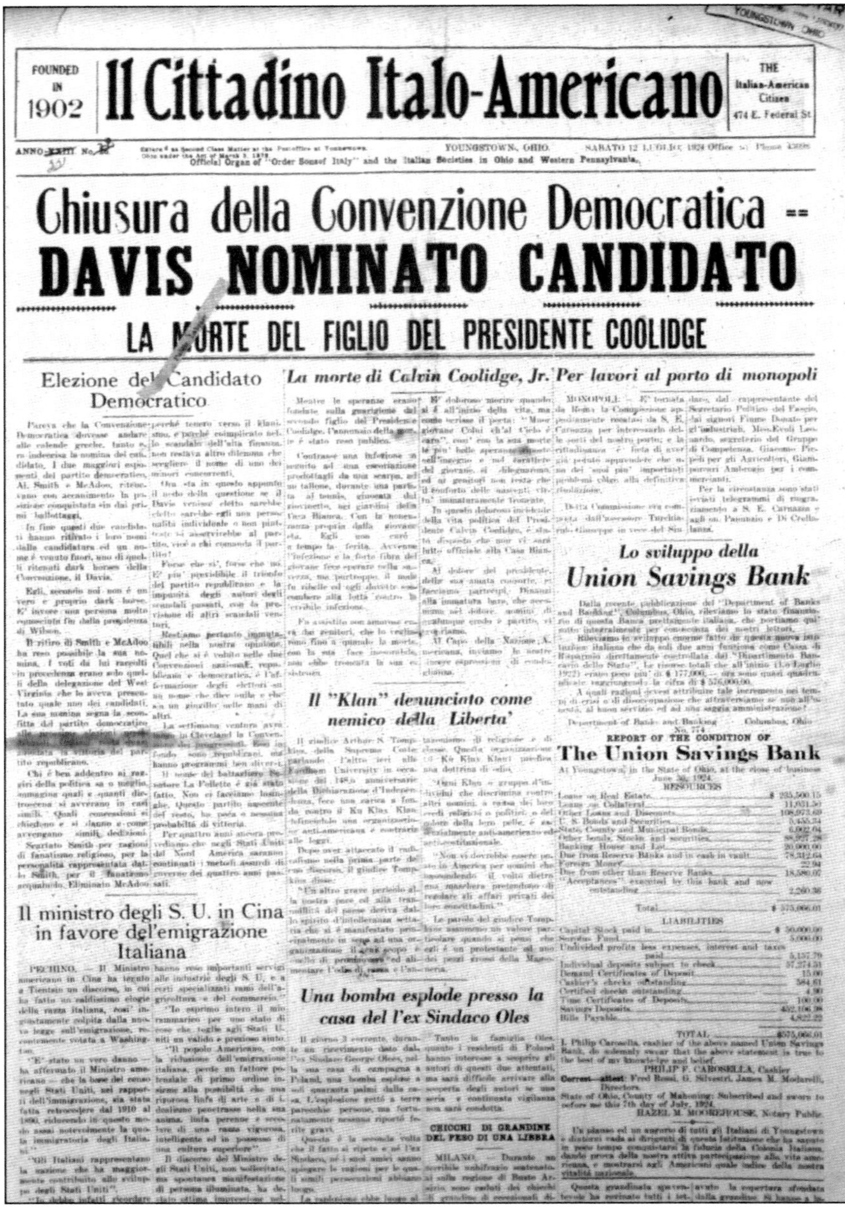

FOUNDED IN 1902

Il Cittadino Italo-Americano

THE Italian-American Citizen 474 E. Federal St.

YOUNGSTOWN, OHIO.

Official Organ of "Order Sons of Italy" and the Italian Societies in Ohio and Western Pennsylvania.

Chiusura della Convenzione Democratica ==

DAVIS NOMINATO CANDIDATO

LA MORTE DEL FIGLIO DEL PRESIDENTE COOLIDGE

Elezione del Candidato Democratico

La morte di Calvin Coolidge, Jr.

Per lavori al porto di monopoli

Lo sviluppo della Union Savings Bank

Il "Klan" denunciato come nemico della Liberta'

REPORT OF THE CONDITION OF

The Union Savings Bank

Il ministro degli S. U. in Cina in favore dell'emigrazione Italiana

Una bomba esplode presso la casa del l'ex Sindaco Oles

CHICCHI DI GRANDINE DEL PESO DI UNA LIBBRA

Il Cittadino. With the arrival of so many people from Southern and Eastern Europe, one of the most crucial institutions these newcomers developed was newspapers in their native languages. By 1917, there were 1,323 foreign-language newspapers in the United States, including 163 in Italian. Beginning in 1903, the Mahoning Valley had its own Italian-language newspaper, *Il Cittadino Italo-Americano* (*The Italian American Citizen*). The newspaper, which by 1920 was published by Celestino Petrarca, promoted political involvement and citizenship as the means for Italians to get ahead. With the rise of the KKK, *Il Cittadino* vigorously protested its actions and became a voice defending Italian Americans. In the July 12, 1924, issue (pictured) its editor states: "Any Klan or group of individuals that discriminates against all men, because of their religious or political beliefs, or because of the color of their skin, is especially anti-American and anti-Constitutional. There should not be a place in America for men who hide their face behind a mask claiming to regulate the private affairs of their fellow citizens." (Courtesy of OHC-YHCIL; translation courtesy of Ashley M. Zampogna.)

Three

Community/Neighborhoods

Upon arrival in the Mahoning Valley, Italians, like other newcomers, usually settled with people from their homeland. The ethnic enclaves were normally located within walking distance of workplaces; these men and women lived in the shadow of the steel mills that dominated the skyline of the Mahoning Valley. There was a level of comfort in residing with people who spoke the same language, had the same customs, worshipped in the same church, and faced the same problems. Many families took in boarders to supplement their incomes. Since many Italian immigrants were single men, this was a convenient living arrangement. Often, the men boarded with their *paesani*—people from their hometown in Italy. Once the rest of the family came over or the man married here, the boarder moved into his own place. Indeed, contrary to larger communities, Italians in the Mahoning Valley were fairly quick to become homeowners.

In Youngstown, two areas were known as "Little Italy:" Smoky Hollow and Brier Hill. Campbell (originally East Youngstown), Struthers, and Lowellville also boasted large Italian populations. In Trumbull County, Niles had a very high percentage of Italians, many of whom settled on the east side. In the early 20th century, the houses available to working-class people were relatively small, usually two stories, one room wide and two deep. There was a front room and kitchen on the first floor and two bedrooms upstairs. Later, the homeowners added rear ells to include an indoor bathroom. The lots were small, but nearly every Italian family boasted a bountiful garden, supplying fresh fruits and vegetables, and many also raised chickens. There was also an outdoor wood-fired oven, keeping the kitchen cool in the summer. In later years, people who grew up in these neighborhoods often recalled the smell of fresh-baked bread that permeated the area. Over time, as Italian Americans became more integrated in American life, they left their old neighborhoods in search of more prosperous surroundings and modern amenities.

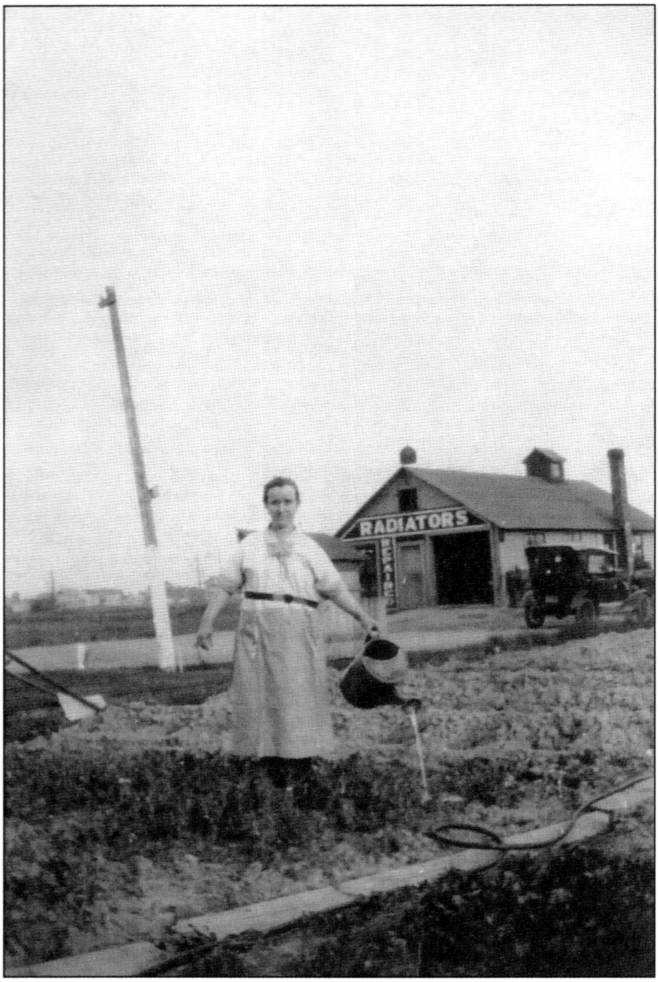

Italians in Warren. At left, Maria Ferrara D'Altorio poses around 1916 on West Market Street in Warren, Ohio. Koby's Radiator, which is still a going concern, is in the background. Born in 1882, D'Altorio immigrated to the United States in 1915 with her husband and children and first settled on West Market Street. Shown below in the mid-1940s are, from left to right, Carmella Caniglia (on steps), Emedio D'Altorio, John Falcione (in uniform), Amelia Gesue, Corinne D'Altorio, and Maria D'Altorio. The family is standing on the sidewalk next to their home on Highland Avenue. In the background is a streetscape of Highland Avenue, showing the types of houses in the neighborhood. (Both, courtesy of Carl and Edith Ritch.)

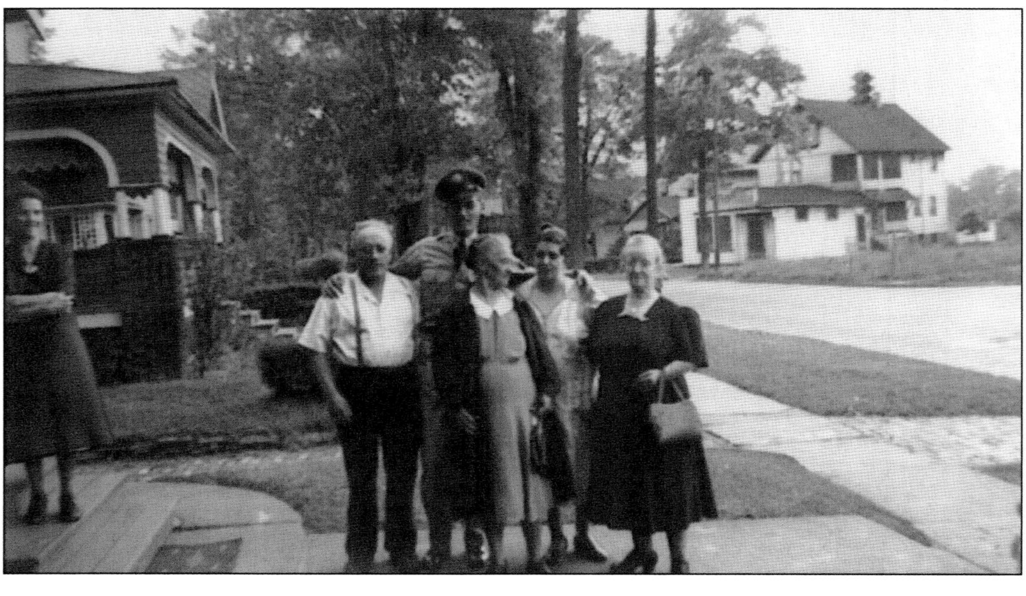

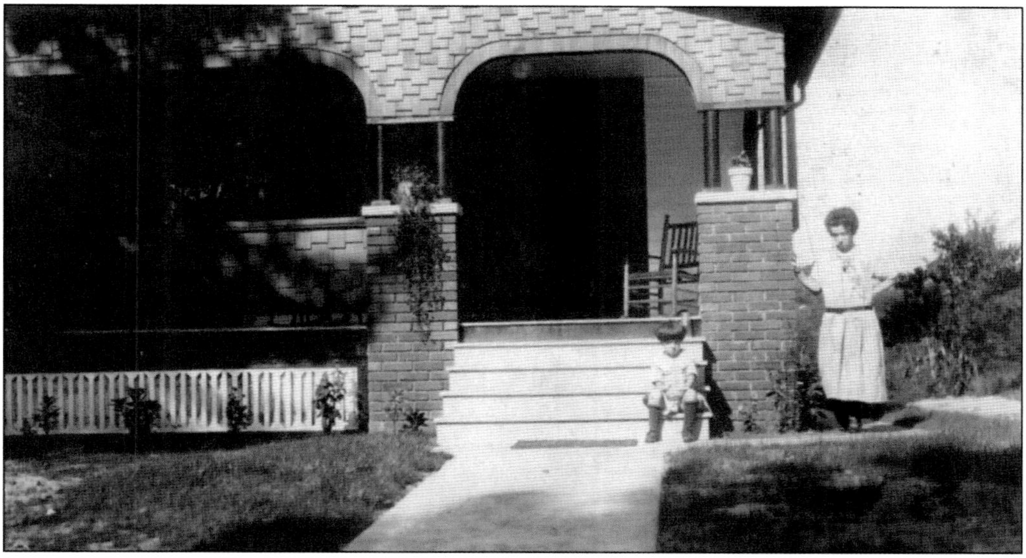

Living on Highland Avenue. By the late 1920s, the D'Altorio family lived at 806 Highland Avenue. Above, sisters Emily (on steps) and Ida D'Altorio pose in front of the home. Ida was born in Italy in 1909, and Emily was born in the United States in 1920. At right, Corinne D'Altorio stands in the driveway at 806 Highland Avenue in March 1944. Born in 1909, Corinne was the daughter of Antonia and Francesco Bevilaqua, who settled in Ravenna, Ohio. In 1926, she married Emideo D'Altorio and moved to Warren. The residents were an extended family, including Emideo's parents, Maria and Patsy D'Altorio, as well as his and Corinne's children. (Both, courtesy of Carl and Edith Ritch.)

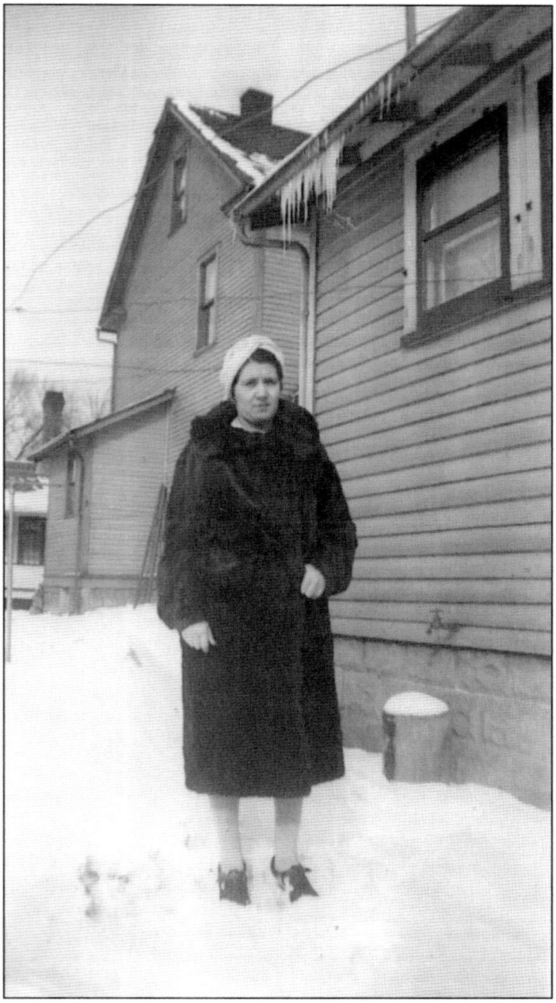

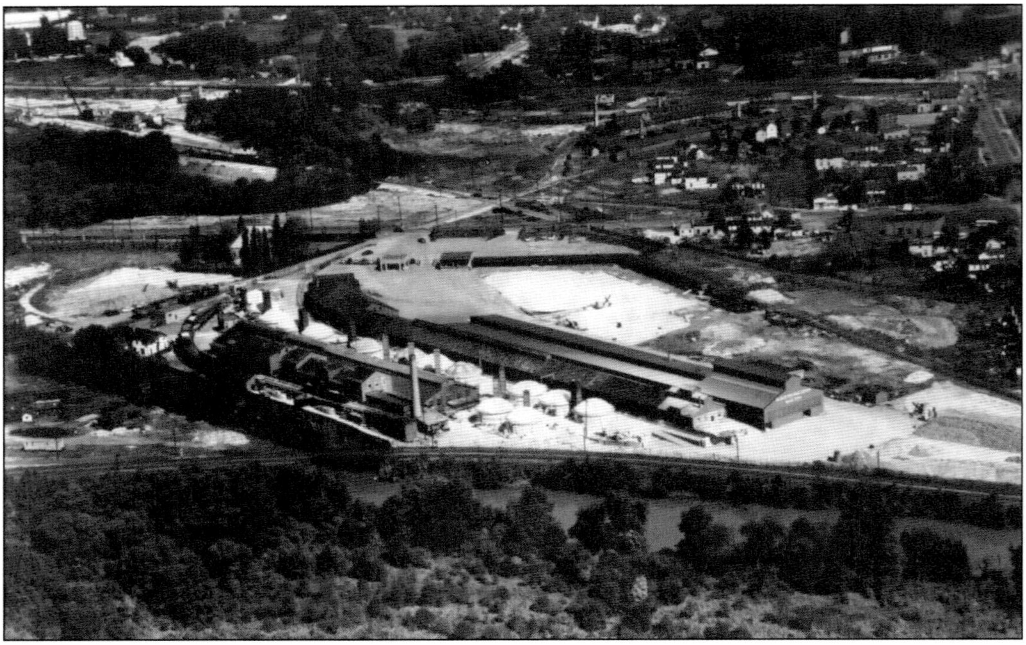

NFB AND HOUSING. Niles Fire Brick had a large immigrant workforce, primarily Italian Americans, who needed housing. In the early 20th century, most working-class people had to live within walking distance of their place of employment. Few could afford cars or spend precious money on public transportation. The above photograph provides an aerial view of the Niles Fire Brick Company in 1953. At top right, clustered along Langley Street, are the homes of many NFB employees. Many of the homes were company-built structures, which NFB had to sell in the 1940s. Note the Mahoning River along the southern edge of the plant. Shown below are workers' houses on Langley Street. These typify the two-story, four-room residences common in the Mahoning Valley.

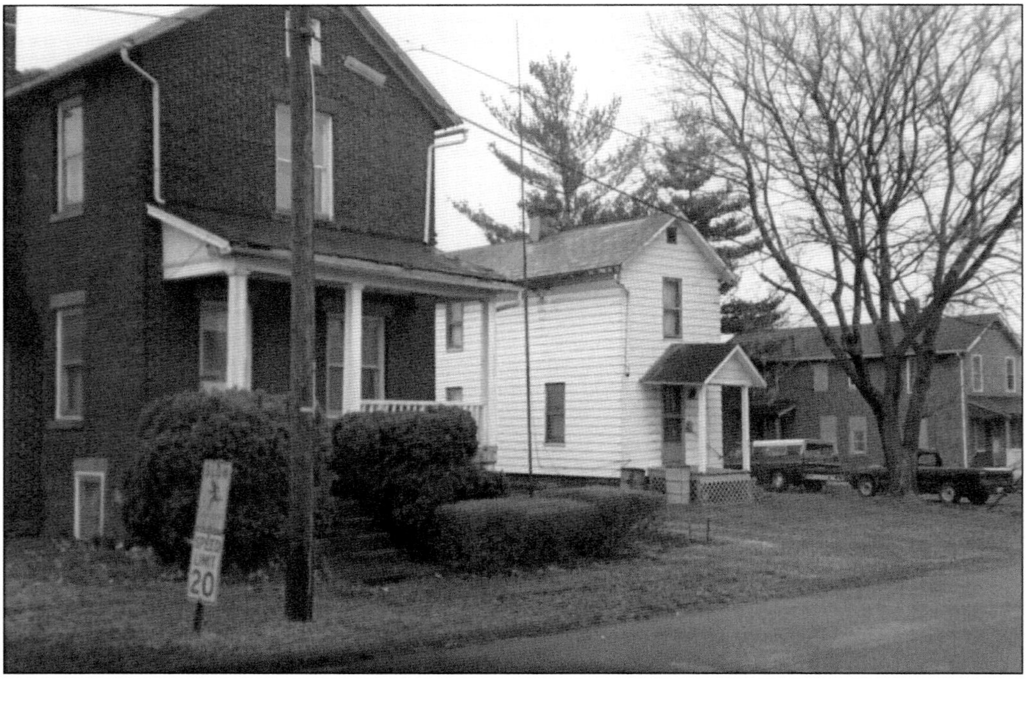

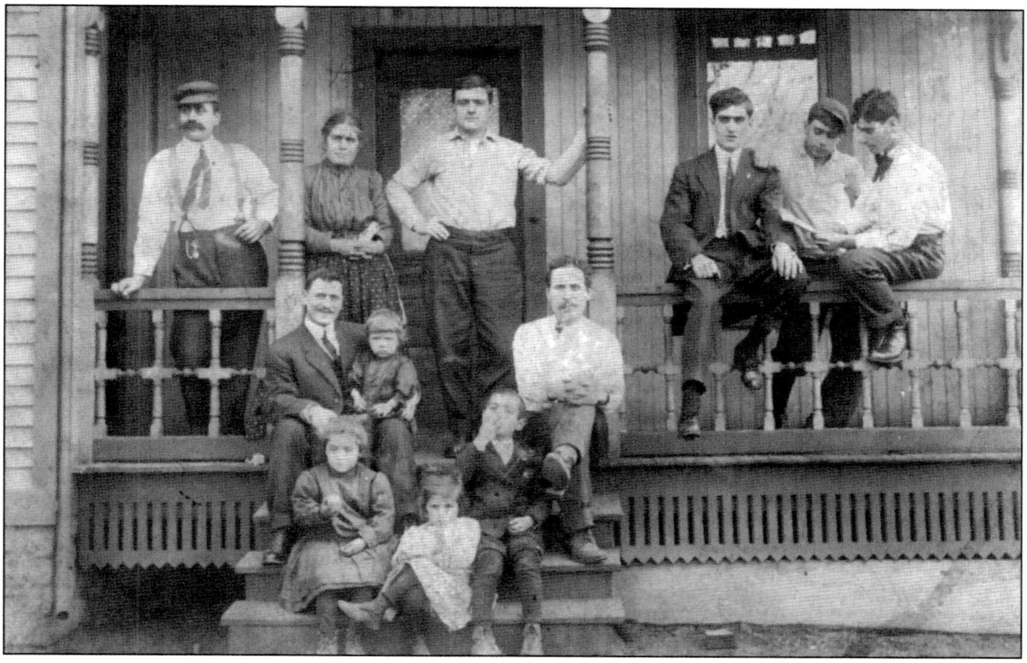

Niles Neighborhoods. Above, the Scarnecchia family poses on their front porch at 449 Mason Street around 1915. The patriarch, Pasquale, started work as a laborer, and by 1915 had opened his own business, Pasquale Scarnecchia & Sons Bakers of Fine Bread, located behind the home. Below, Lucia Pallante relaxes on her front porch, reading the newspaper in 1955. The house, which the family built around 1918, was located at 710 Warren Avenue. It was a working-class neighborhood, but few Italians lived there. The wood-frame house across the street was typical of the neighborhood; the Pallante house, in comparison, was a solid brick structure. (Above, courtesy of Toni and Dom D'Urso.)

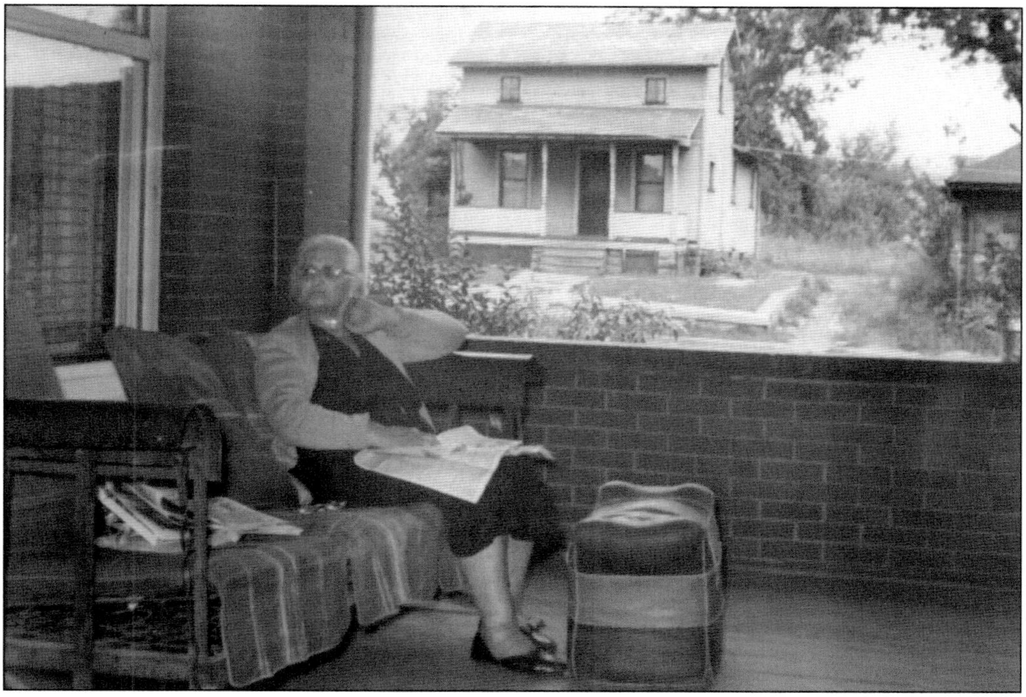

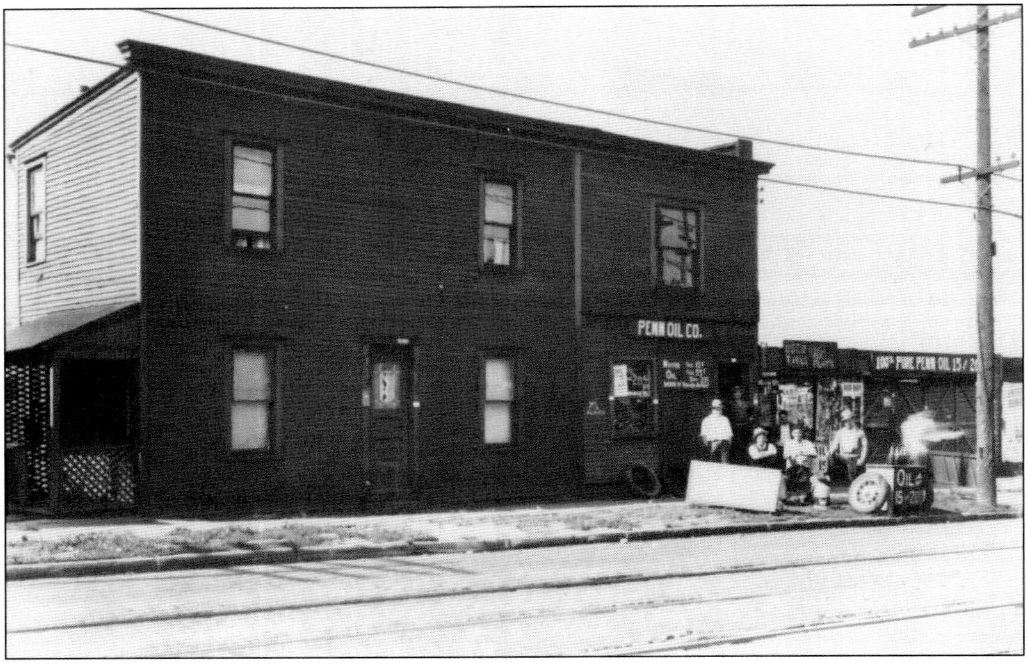

BRIER HILL. Located on Youngstown's north side, Brier Hill was originally a part of the Tod family holdings. David Tod served as Ohio's governor during the Civil War. By the mid-19th century, rich deposits of coal were found here, which contributed to the growth of the local iron industry and provided jobs for immigrants from Wales, Germany, and Ireland. With the boom in the steel industry in the 1890s, the earlier settlers moved out, and immigrants from Southern and Eastern Europe took their places. Italians were one of the largest groups to settle there. The area became a thriving community, with residential, commercial, and civic properties abounding. These two photographs show commercial areas around 1923. (Both, courtesy of OHC-YHCIL.)

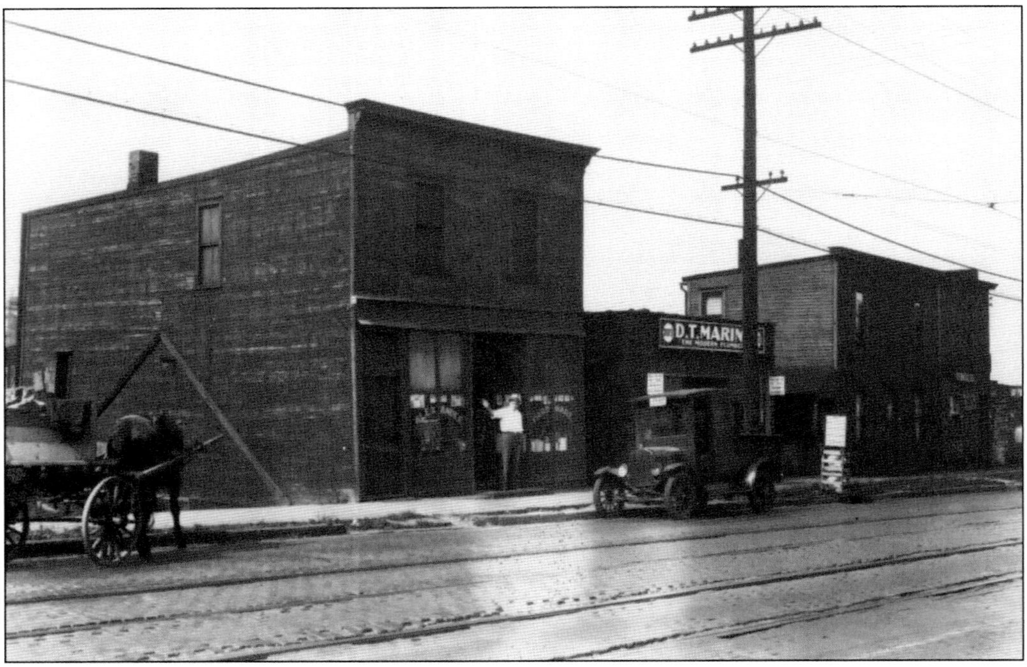

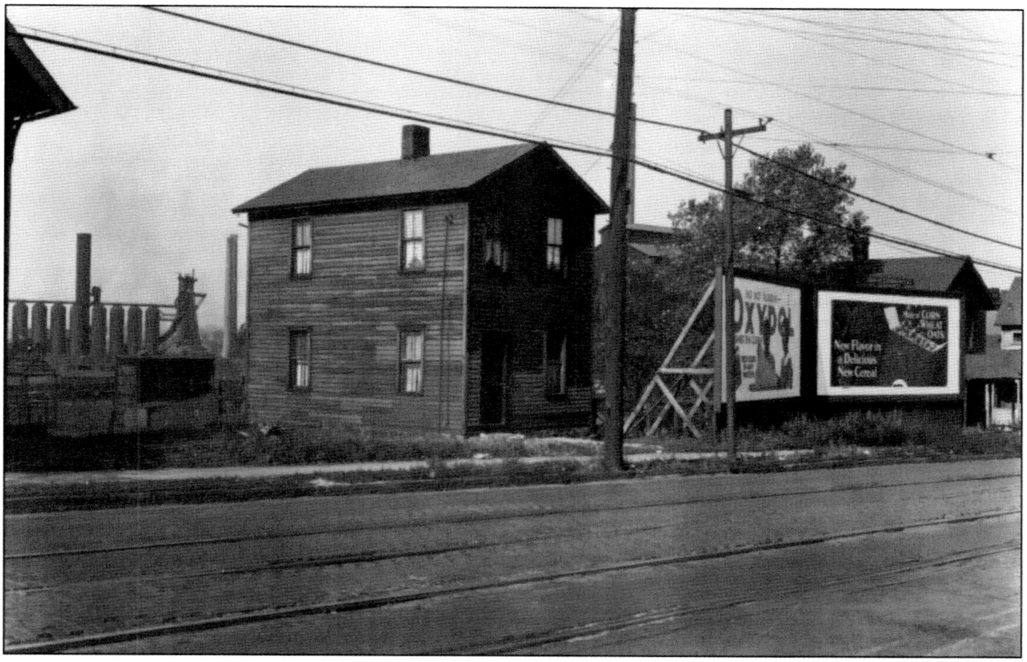

LIVING IN BRIER HILL. These two photographs show residences in Brier Hill in the early 20th century. The houses shown above were typical of worker housing in the Mahoning Valley—two stories, two rooms deep, with the front and back doors aligned. This type of house existed in working-class neighborhoods throughout the Valley. The builders of the residence shown below took advantage of the hillside, deftly inserting the structure to conform to the landscape. In both photographs, the mill can be seen in the background. Established in 1912, the Brier Hill Steel Company was absorbed by the YS&T Company (YS&T) in 1923. At the time of the acquisition, Sheet & Tube took these photographs of the neighborhood. (Both, courtesy of OHC-YHCIL.)

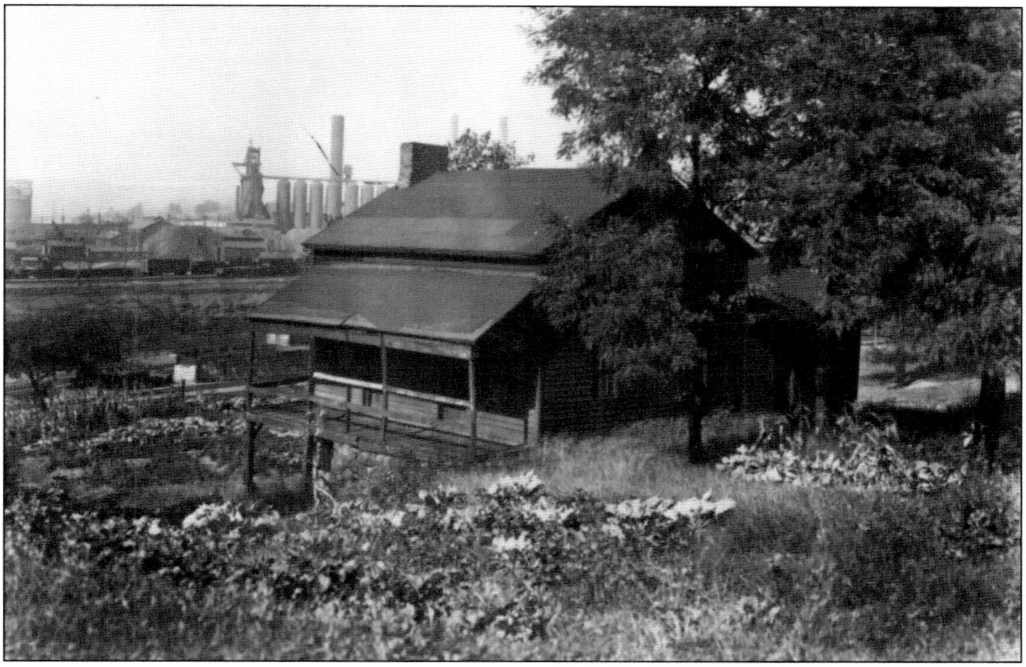

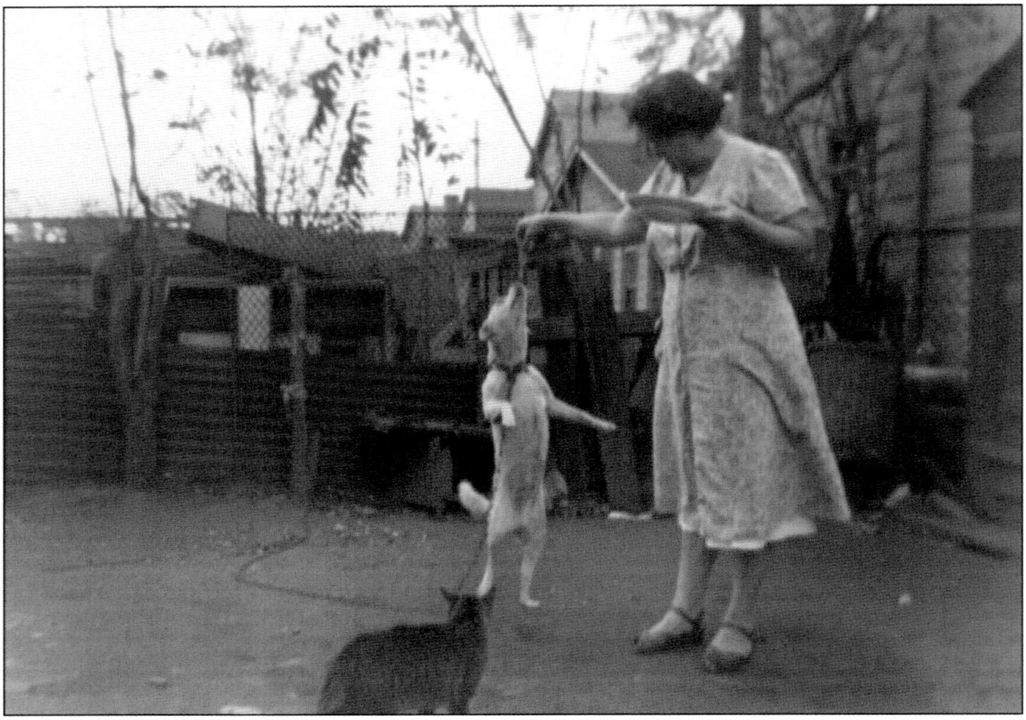

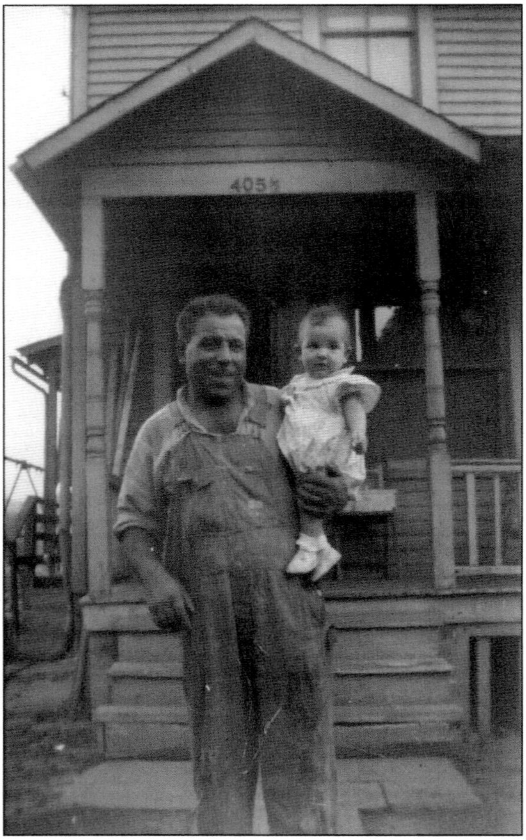

Smoky Hollow. Platted in 1900, Smoky Hollow, located on Youngstown's near northeast side, originally belonged to the wealthy Wick family. The rapid growth of the city in the early 20th century, due in part to immigration, meant that new neighborhoods had to be developed. In the Hollow's early years, there were few Italian Americans. According to the census, by 1910, many had moved into the area; by 1930, they were over one third of the population. These photographs show members of the DiLallo family, who lived at 407 North Walnut Street. Above is Philomena DiLallo, born in 1899 in Colletorto, Campobasso, Italy. She came to the United States in 1910 and, in 1923, married Attilio DiLallo, shown at left holding his baby daughter, Rose. (Both, courtesy of Anthony Worrellia.)

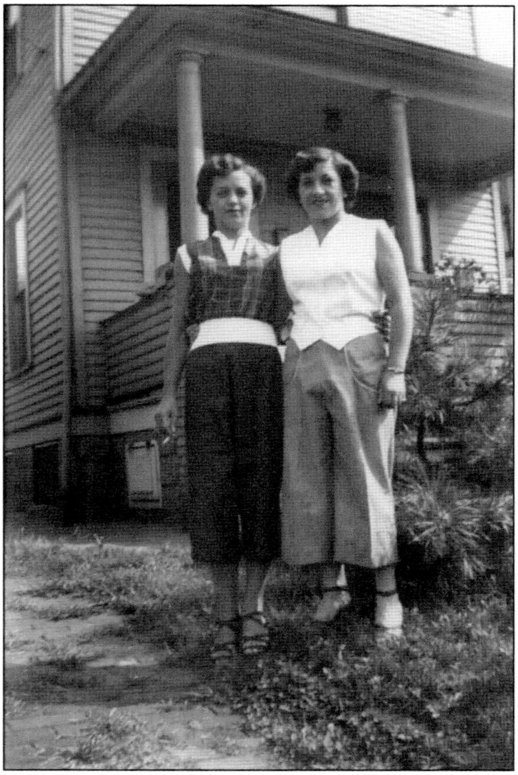

Life in the Hollow. Smoky Hollow got its name because it was in a small valley that was a magnet for the dust and smoke from the nearby steel mills. Like Brier Hill, the Hollow was often referred to as "Little Italy," and its residents took great pride in their neighborhood. These two photographs were taken on Emerald Street in the early 1950s. At right, sisters-in-law Helen Maxin DiLullo (left) and Jean DiLullo pose in front of the family home at 306 Emerald Street. Below, an unidentified baby rests on a blanket in the front yard, surrounded by bushes, which were present on many lots in the Hollow. Note the massing of the houses in the background, with their steeply pitched roofs facing the street.

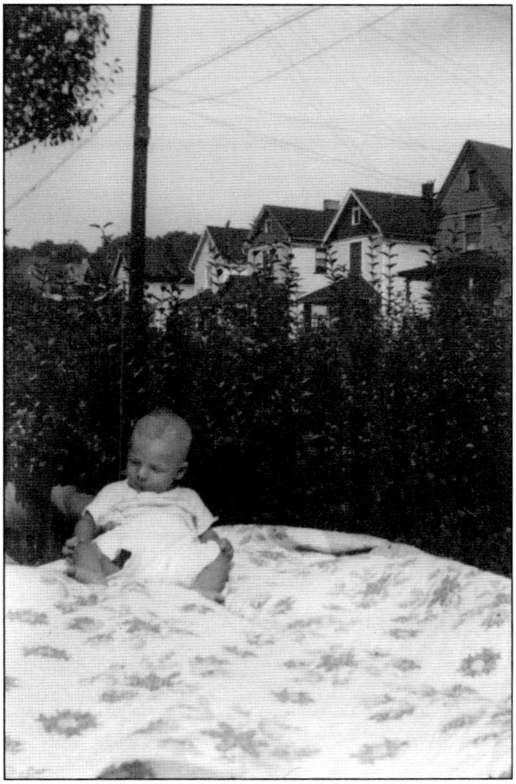

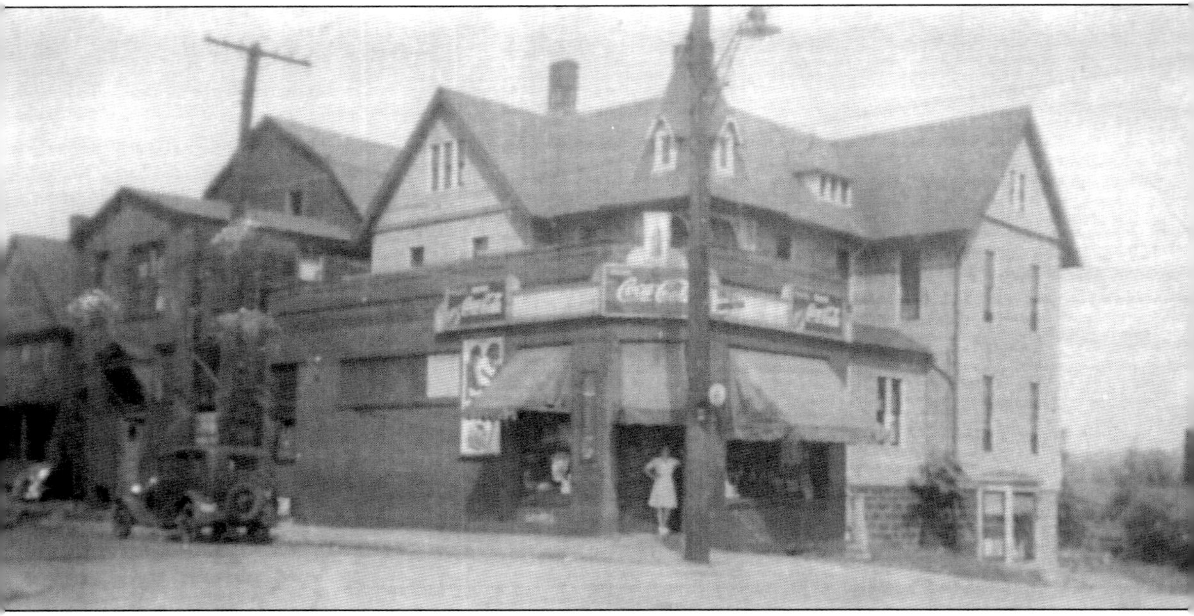

Smoky Hollow Streetscape. Taken around 1930 at the corner of Walnut Street and East Rayen Avenue, this photograph of Smoky Hollow depicts the juxtaposition of commercial and residential properties. On the corner is Labate's Grocery Store. Farther down the hill was the entrance to "Benny the Barber" Caruso's shop. While the Hollow was predominately Italian, other ethnic groups also settled in the neighborhood. To the left of the grocery is the home of Benjamin and Pearl Warner. These Jewish immigrants from Poland were the parents of the four men who founded the famous Warner Brothers Studio: Jack, Sam, Albert, and Harry. While the brothers eventually moved on to Hollywood, the parents lived out their lives in Youngstown. Jack Warner always considered the Steel City his hometown. (Courtesy of the Cassese family.)

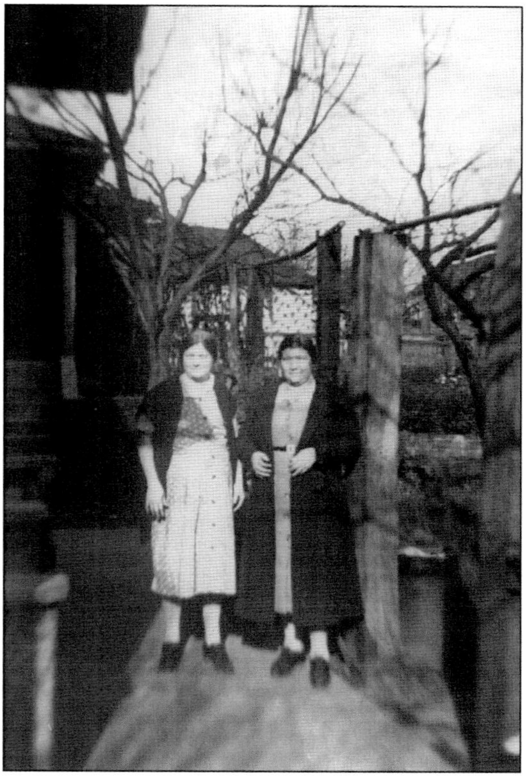

CAMPBELL. Originally known as East Youngstown, Campbell was renamed in 1926 in honor of the longtime president of the YS&T Company, James A. Campbell. Because of its proximity to the mill, many immigrants, including a large number of Italians, made their homes there. At right are Maria De Rochis Piccoli (right) and her sister Rose Campione at Maria's home at 295 Twelfth Street in Campbell. Maria Piccoli immigrated from Patrica, Frosinone, Italy, in 1913. Below, family and friends celebrate the 50th wedding anniversary of Carolina Moccia and Vitale DeBlasio in 1956. The couple poses with their young grandson Vito. Vitale came to the United States in 1920; Carolina and her youngest daughter, Ermelinda, arrived in Campbell in 1937. Their three sons, Alessio, Feruccio, and Andrea, did not arrive until after the end of World War II. The DeBlasio home was located on Jefferson Street. (Right, courtesy of Noreen Modarelli.)

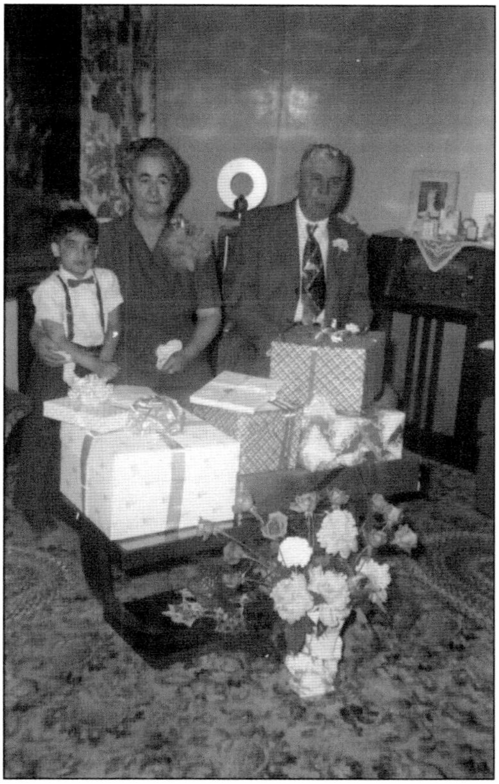

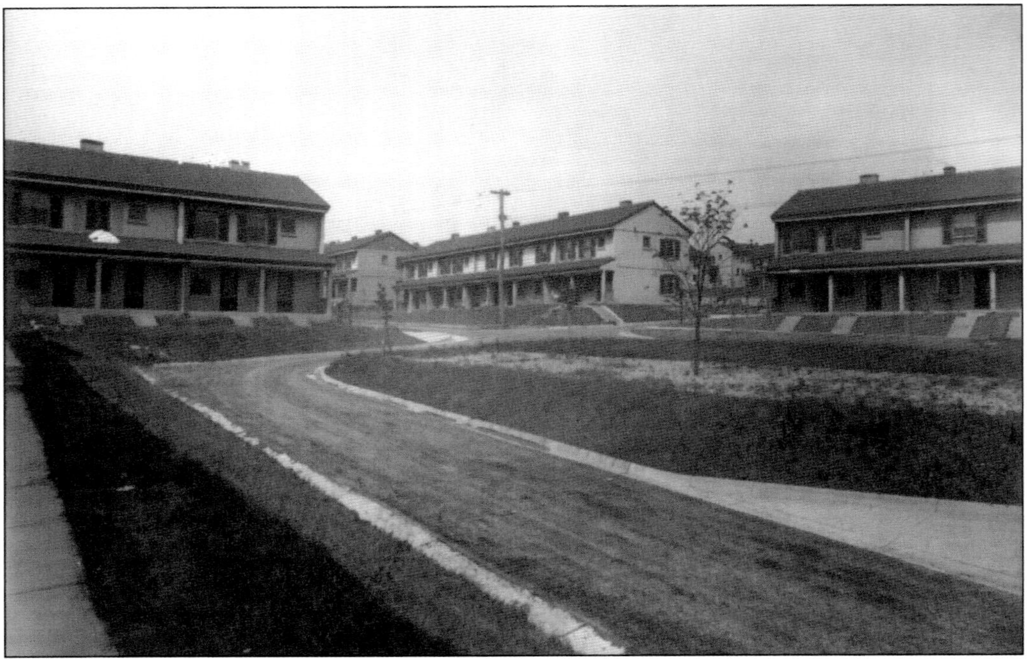

Blackburn Plat. Following a 1916 strike at its flagship East Youngstown plant, the YS&T Company instituted "welfare capitalism" to instill loyalty to the company and forestall unionization. One aspect of the program included the construction of housing for employees. In 1919, YS&T began building company housing. At Blackburn Plat, located in East Youngstown, homes were designed for immigrant and African American workers. The row houses were built of reinforced concrete, making the units vermin-proof and practically indestructible. Each had one or two bedrooms, a full basement, indoor plumbing, central heating, and electricity—and they were available for rent only. The company made them small to discourage boarders. These two photographs show Blackburn Plat just as construction was completed. (Both, courtesy of OHC-YHCIL.)

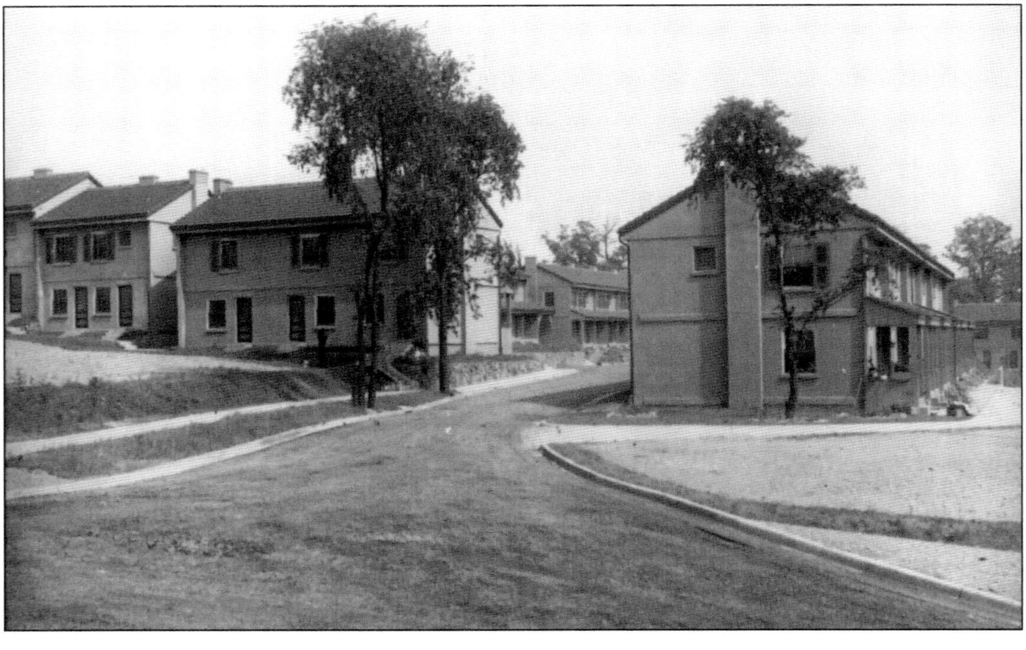

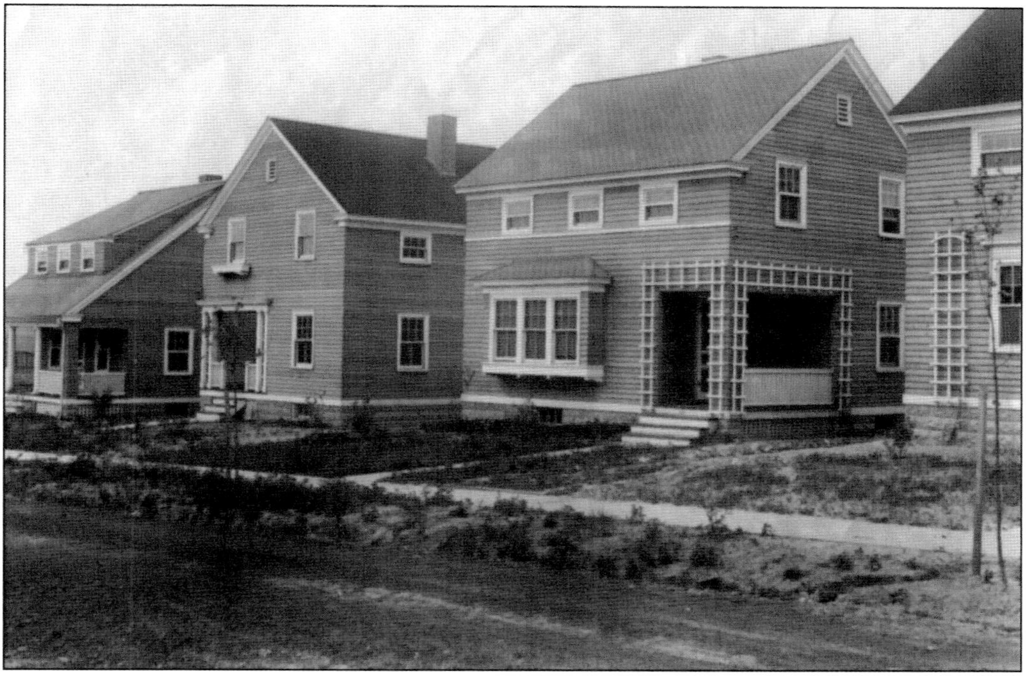

Highview Plat. YS&T developed three other plats for its workers. Overlook, in Struthers, consisted of duplexes for rent to white, American-born workers only. Loveland Farms, in Youngstown near Struthers, was comprised of detached, single-family homes for sale to white, American-born workers only. The third (pictured) was Highview Plat in Struthers, providing detached, single-family houses for immigrant workers who had "proven themselves to be good company men," for purchase or rent. All of the YS&T housing properties were controlled through a subsidiary called the Buckeye Land Company. The city of Struthers had a significant Italian American population, many of whom lived in Highview. (Both, courtesy of OHC-YHCIL.)

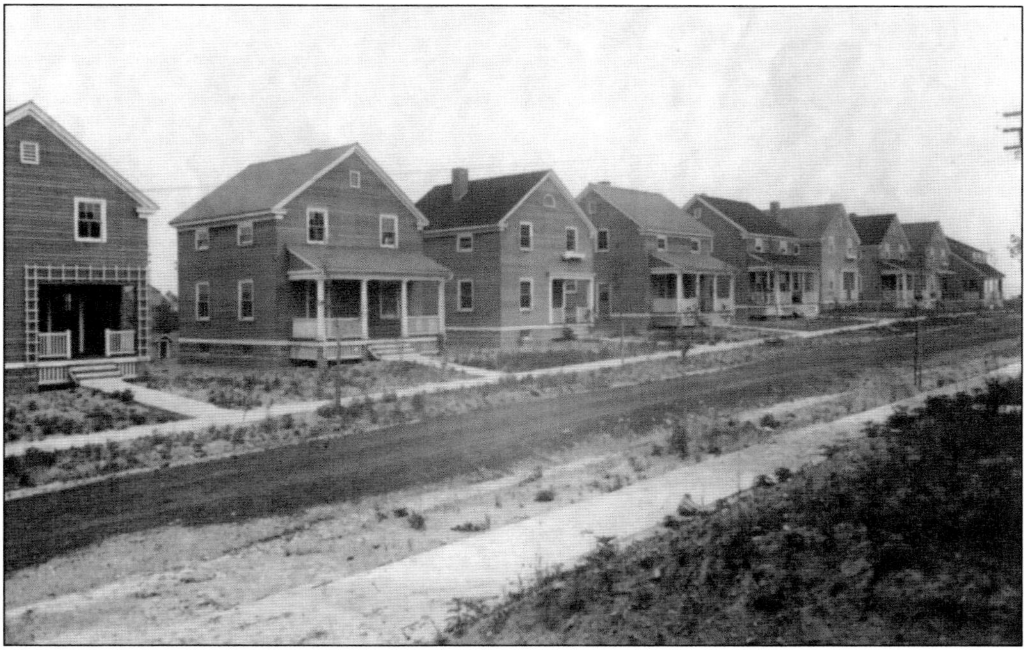

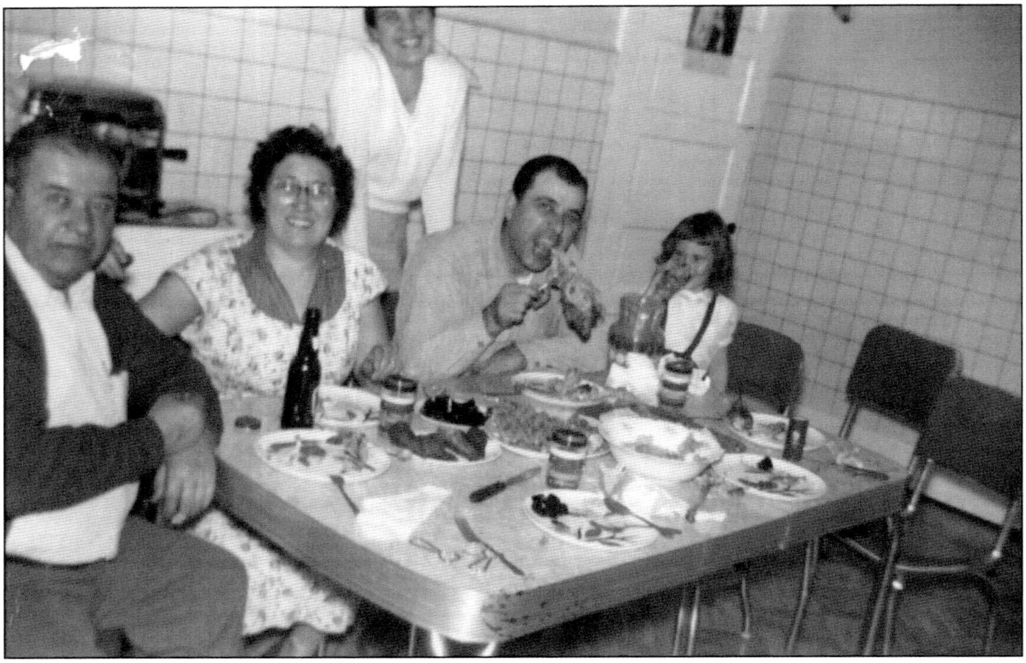

LISTORTI FAMILY. Frank Listorti was born on February 23, 1920, in Castelbottaccio, Italy. He came to the United States in 1934 at the age of 14. He married Helen Cinque, also from Castelbottaccio, on April 24, 1940. He served in the US Army from 1941 to 1946 as a private first class, first in North Africa and then in the invasion of Italy. After returning from the service, he worked at Sharon Steel, Lowellville Works, from 1946 to 1948. He later owned a neighborhood grocery store in Lowellville (1949–1965) and Frank's Barber Shop in Poland, Ohio, for three years. He died on July 2, 1971, at 51. Above, the Listorti family gathers for dinner. Frank is seated next to the little girl at right. Below, Frank poses with his wife, Helen. Both photographs are from the mid-1950s. (Both, courtesy of Frank Pape.)

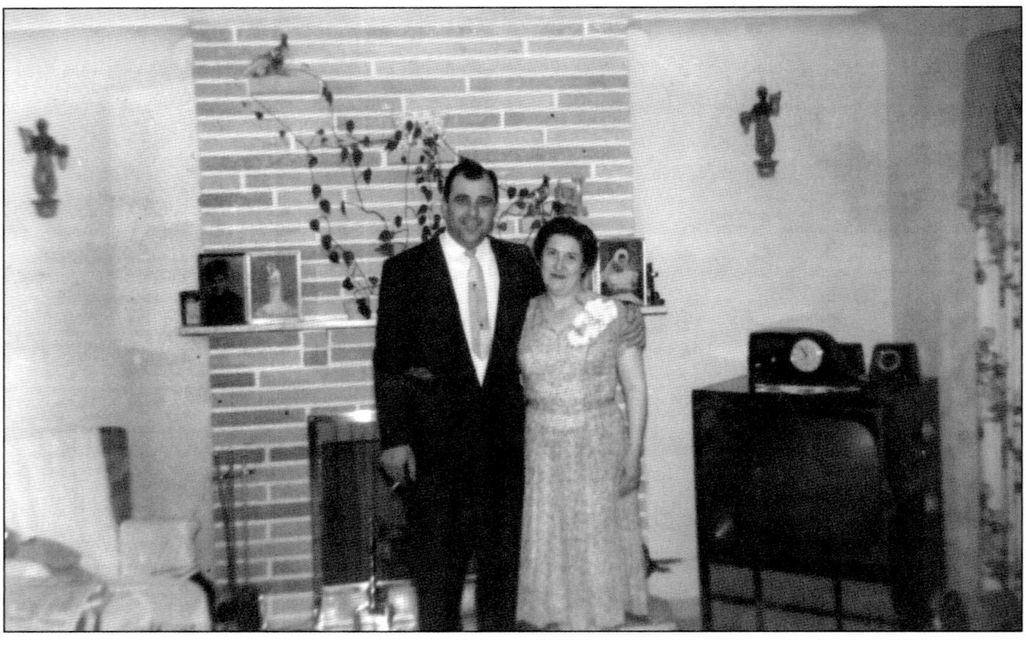

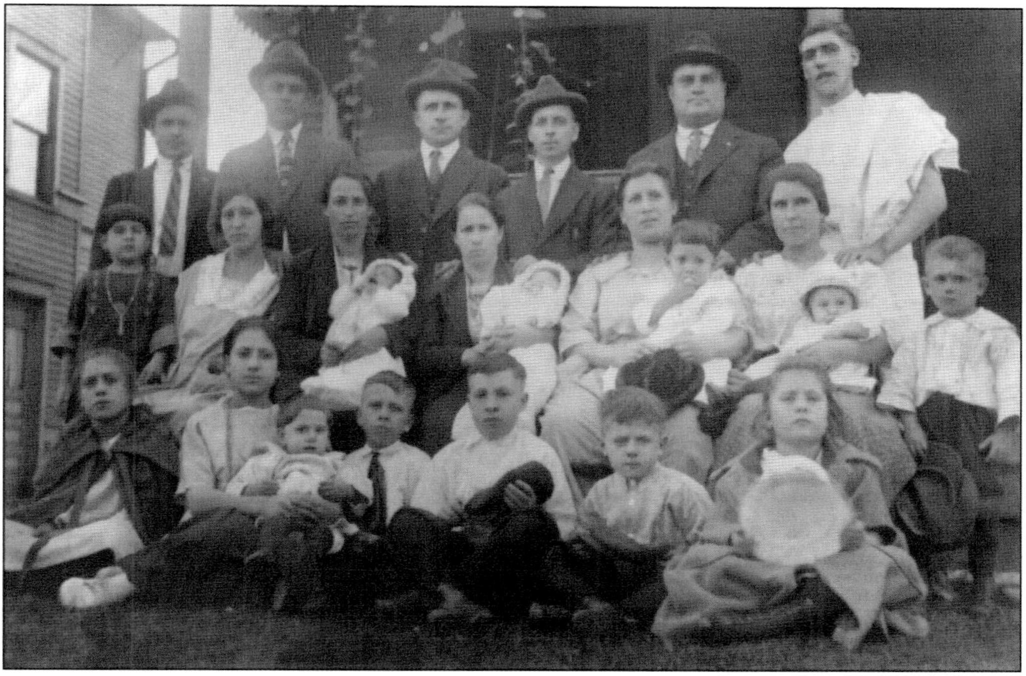

The East Side. Many Italian Americans called the east side of Youngstown home. Nearby industrial facilities, including Republic Rubber and the Trussed Concrete Company (later Truscon Steel), provided jobs. Above, immigrants from Capricotta, Abruzzi region, are seen in front of their home on Charlotte Street, off Garland Avenue near Oak Street. Below, members of the Joseph (Giuseppe) Lariccia family, including his brothers Angelo and Gennaro, are in front of their home on Thorn Hill Road. Joseph Lariccia was born in 1880 and came to the United States in 1924. The Lariccias became successful grocers; Joseph and Gennaro started a store on East Rayen Avenue. (Both, courtesy of Ben Lariccia.)

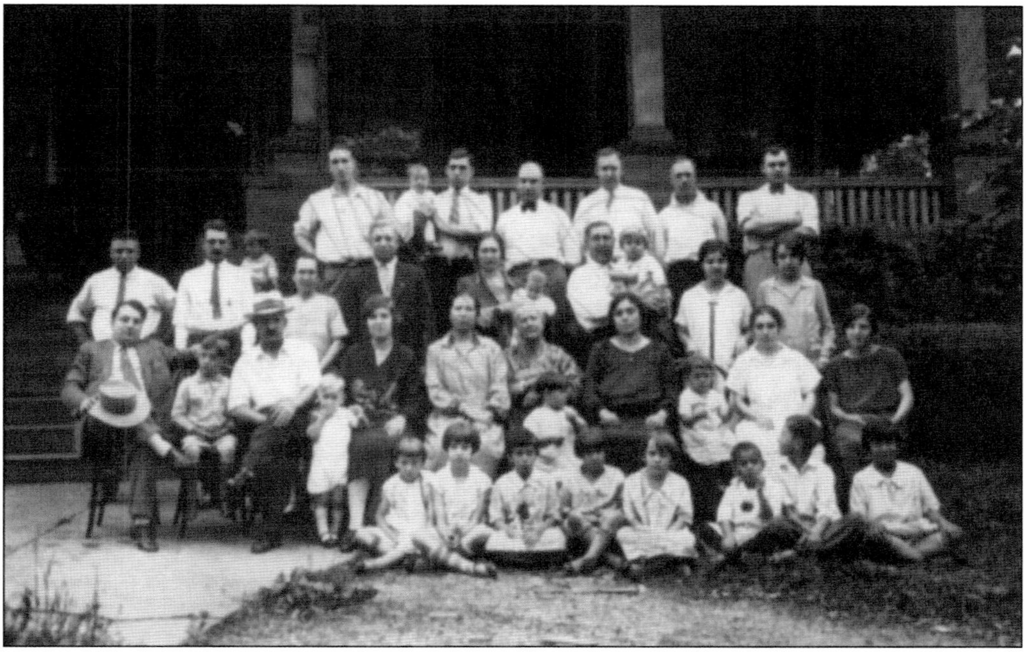

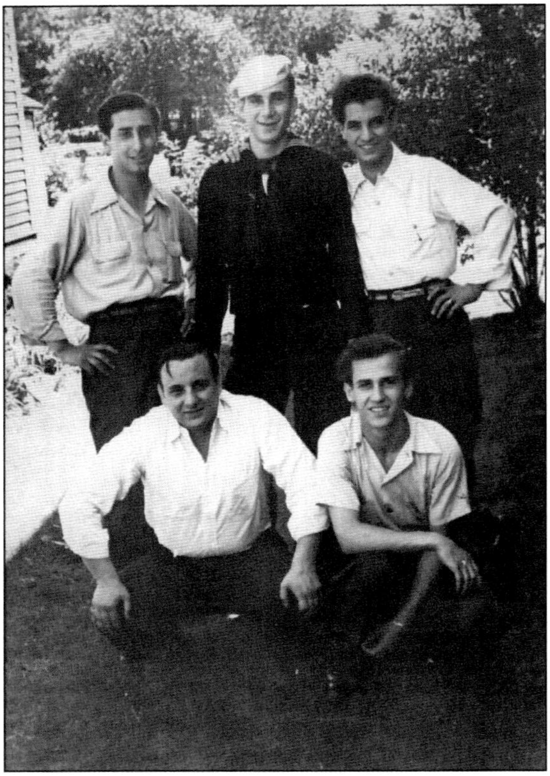

East Side Men. Joseph Mendozzi served in the US Navy during World War II. He grew up on Quinn Street on Youngstown's east side, between North Garland and North Truesdale Avenues. At left, he poses in uniform in his driveway with friends, celebrating his return from the service. Following his tour of duty, Mendozzi had a career as a model for Strouss Department Store in Youngstown. He is seen below in a newspaper advertisement for the men's department at Strouss. (Both, courtesy of Ben Lariccia.)

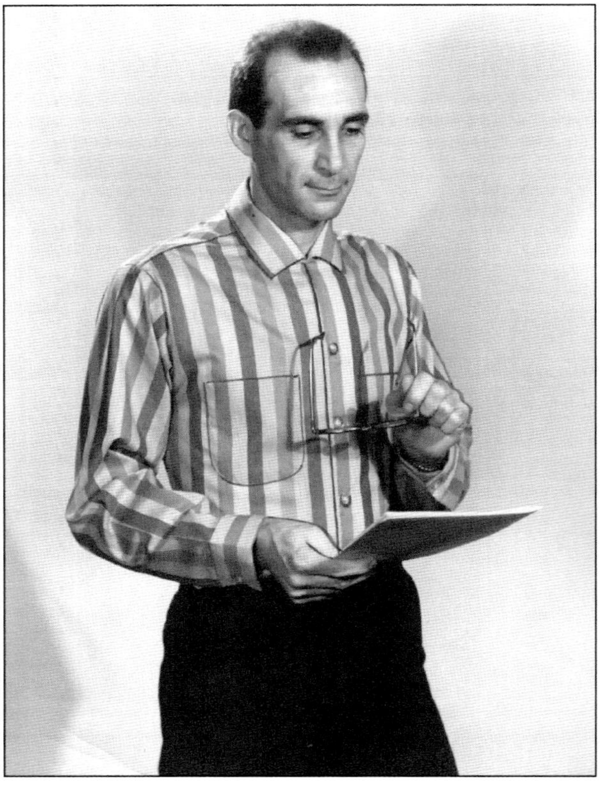

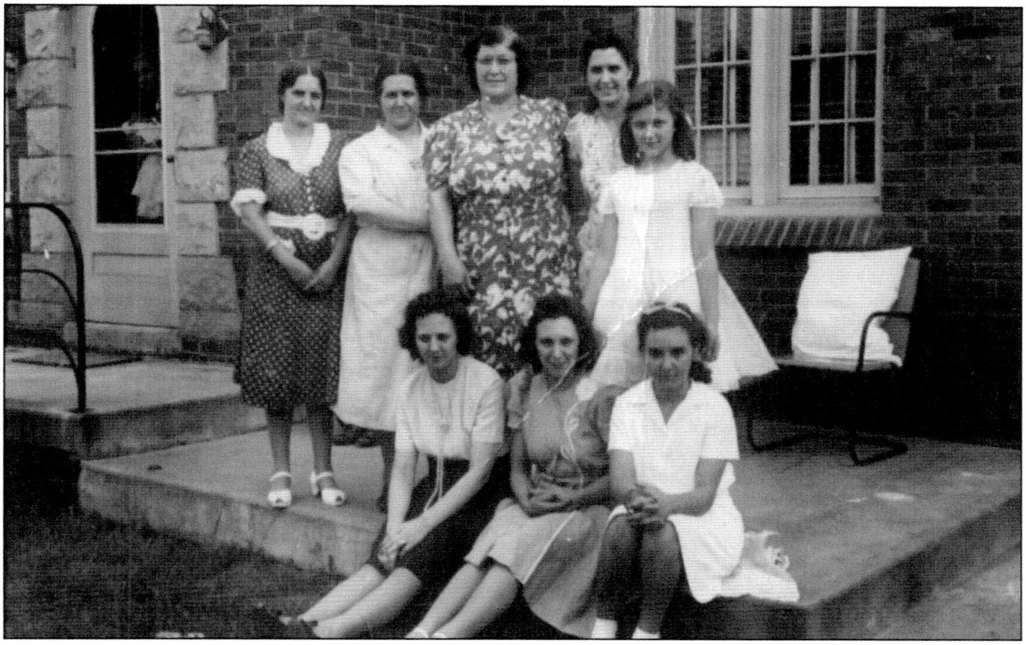

Moving Up. As Italian Americans grew more prosperous, they began to move out of their original working-class neighborhoods. This was not always easy; restrictive covenants forbidding the sale of real estate to certain groups, including Southern and Eastern Europeans and African Americans, were in place following World War II. As these restrictions eased, Italian Americans moved away from the city center and into first-ring suburbs with larger homes and more amenities. Above, women relax on Vermont Avenue on the south side. They are, from left to right, (seated) Linda Pasquinelli, Stella Pasquinelli, and Sylvia Mariani; (standing) Ida Cagna, Blanche Pasquinelli, Nell Marsch, Edith Marsch, and Eleanor Pasquinelli. Below, Adalea Marsch Moritz, age one, poses as a hood ornament on her family's Dodge on Vermont Avenue. (Both, courtesy of Adalea Marsch Moritz.)

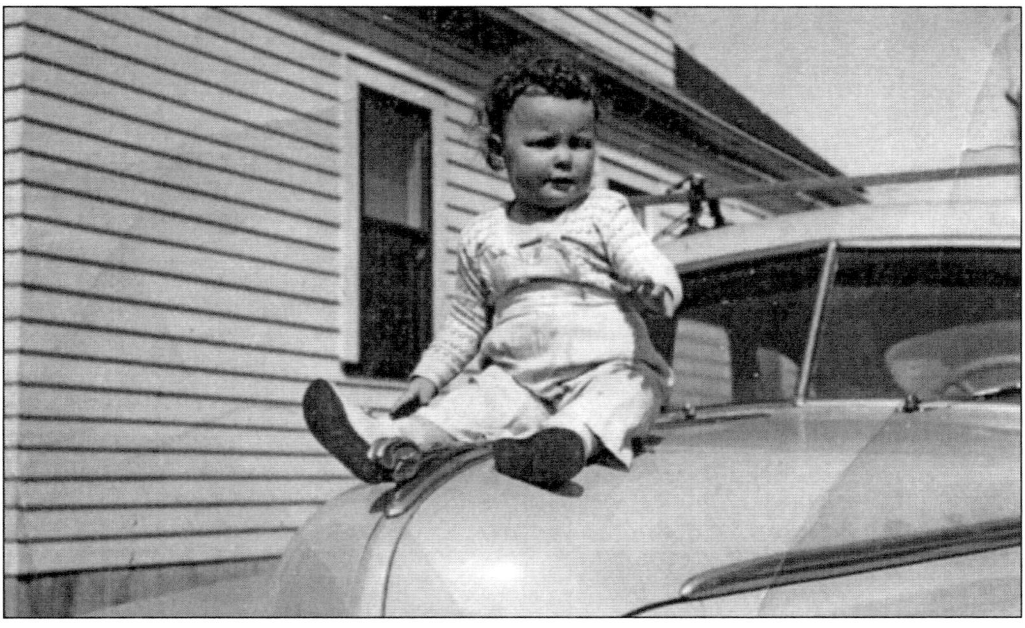

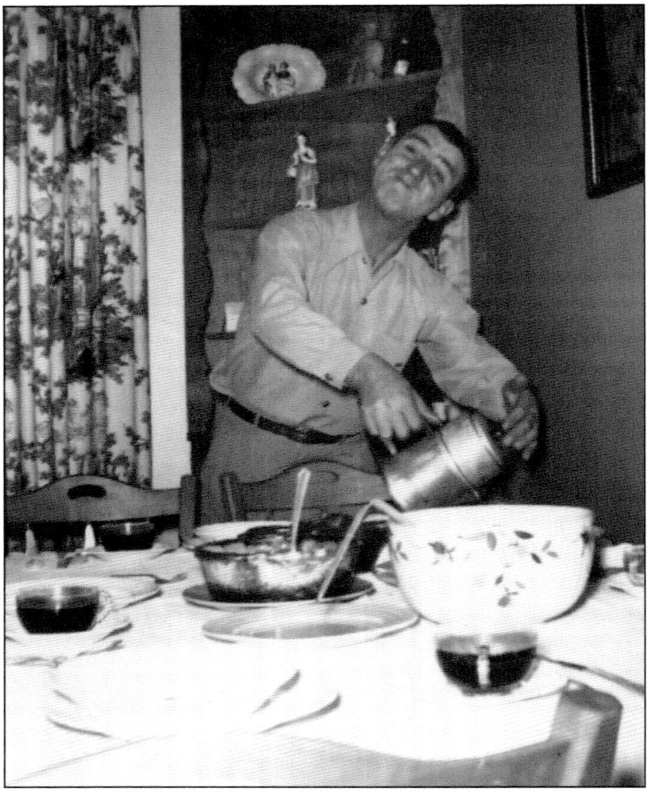

Moving Out. By 1950, Italian Americans in Niles began moving to newly opened subdivisions in areas generally not previously accessible to them. At left, Louis Marinelli entertains in the dining room of his home on Stepney Street. He was originally from Smoky Hollow in Youngstown and met his wife, Ann, through relatives and family friends. Marinelli, who was a builder for the Edward J. DeBartolo Corporation, did most of the work on his new house. Below, Mary Bernard stands in the doorway between her dining room and kitchen in her house at 21 Hogarth Avenue. Note the Youngstown Steel Kitchen that graced her house. This company built steel kitchens for residential properties, the latest word in Midcentury Modern design.

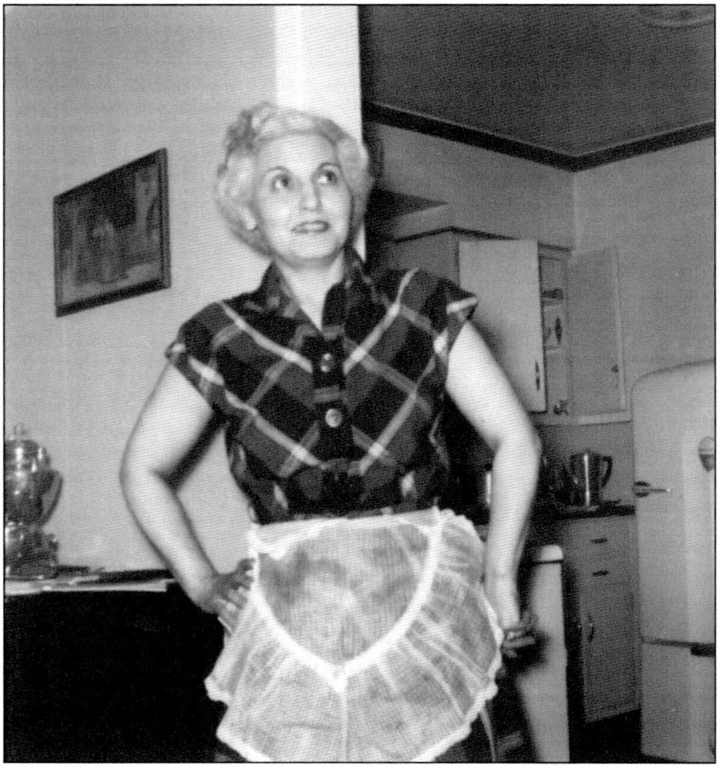

Four

Steel Magnets

By the beginning of the 20th century, the Mahoning Valley was well on its way to becoming a leading steel manufacturer. Although iron production was well established by the mid-19th century, these firms were relatively small and employed mostly skilled and semiskilled men. The mass production of steel, on the other hand, requires a large workforce, much of which is unskilled. By 1923, there were three large firms in the Mahoning Valley: YS&T, Carnegie Steel (US Steel), and Republic Iron & Steel. Jobs in the mills were a magnet for immigrants, as well as for African American migrants. The work was hard, the hours long, the pay low, and the environment dangerous. Still, thousands of newcomers flocked to the mills. Eventually, with the successful introduction of collective bargaining in the 1930s, working conditions improved, and many steelworkers made enough to better their lives and join the middle class. The Mahoning Valley also housed a number of ancillary industries that supplied needed products for the steel industry. The Niles Fire Brick Company, for example, made the refractory brick used to line the furnaces and boasted a large Italian workforce. Women were not excluded from factory work, especially during World War II, when Italian American women joined thousands of other "Rosie the Riveters" on the shop floor.

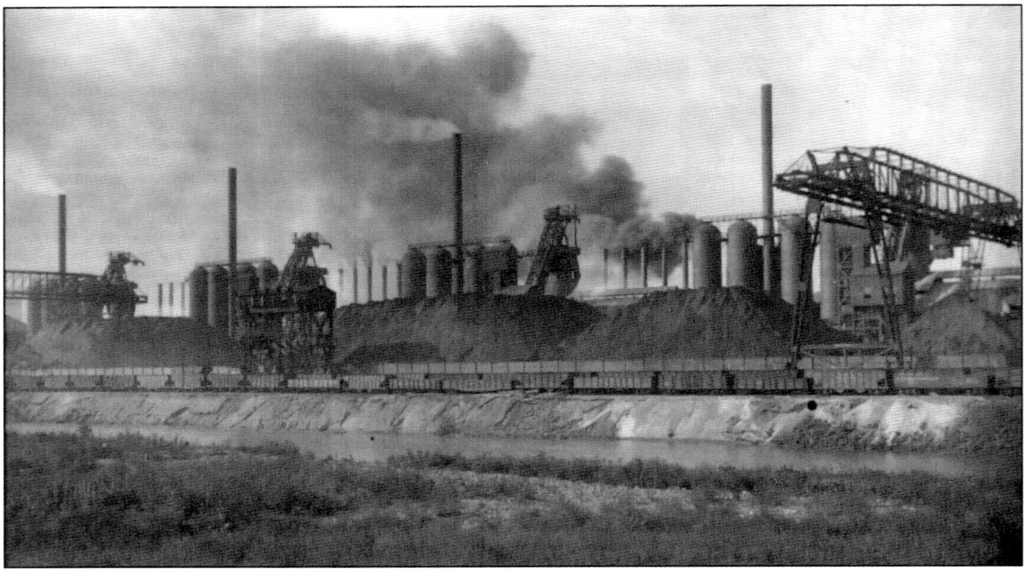

YS&T Company. Founded in 1901, the company was originally known as the Youngstown Iron Sheet & Tube Company. Recognizing the growing importance of steel, the word "iron" was dropped in 1907. The first plant was located in East Youngstown, at a site where a number of railroad tracks converged. Since the Mahoning River was not navigable, local industries relied on railroads to bring raw materials in and take finished goods out. Sheet & Tube grew quickly, buying up coal mines and other interests in Ohio and other areas. The year 1923 was a banner one, when Sheet & Tube acquired the Brier Hill Steel Company as well as the Steel & Tube Company in East Chicago and Indiana Harbor, making it the nation's fifth-largest steel company. The above photograph shows the Campbell Works along the Mahoning River, including its four blast furnaces. Below, men are casting at the blast furnace. (Both, courtesy of OHC-YHCIL.)

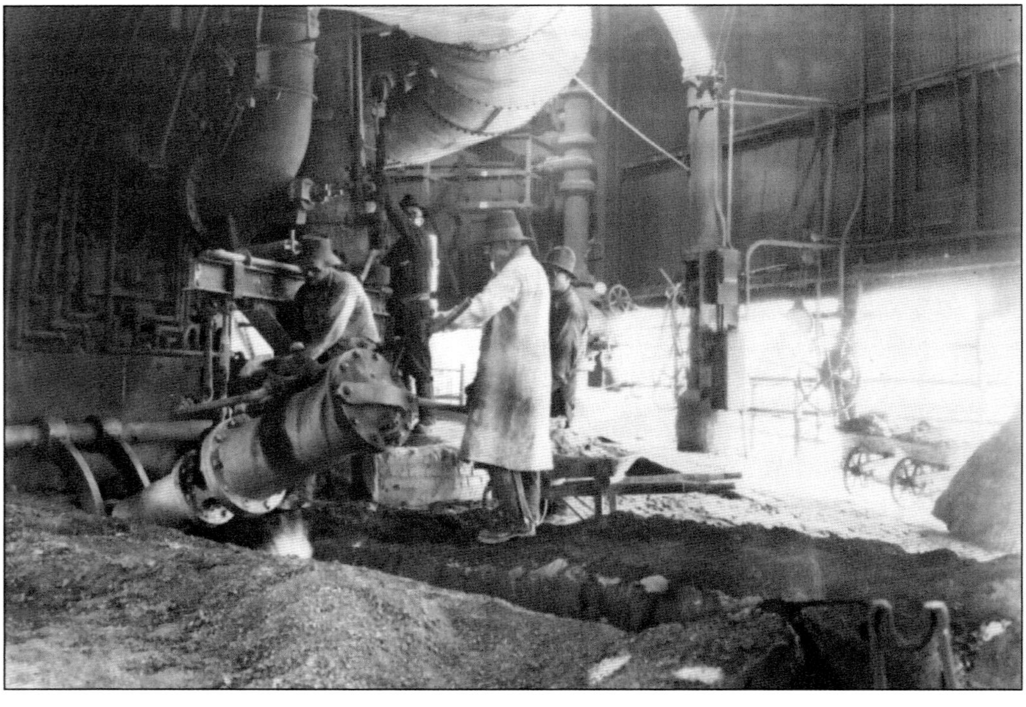

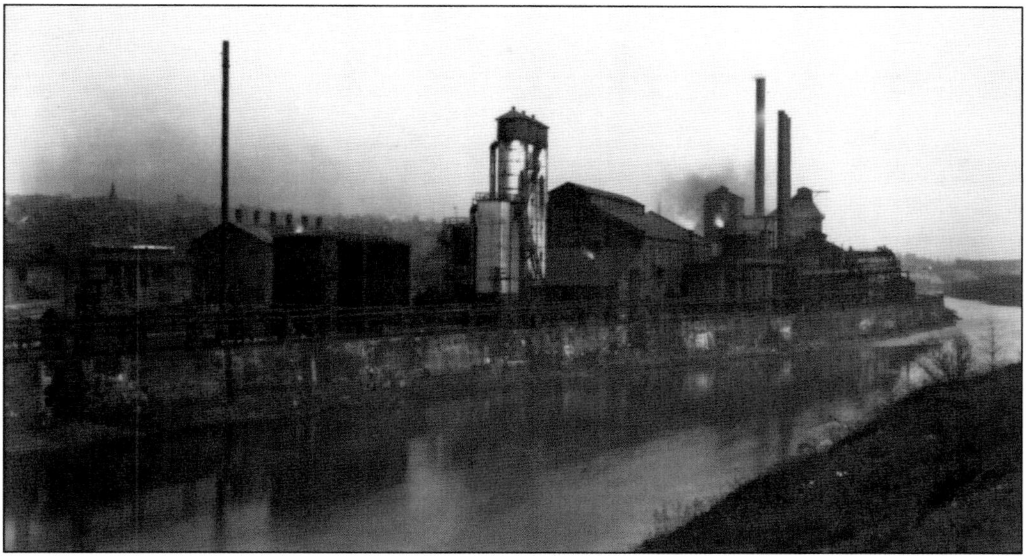

BRIER HILL STEEL. Founded in 1912, Brier Hill Steel provided employment for new immigrants, especially those who settled in the neighborhood just to the east of the plant. The company had two blast furnaces, Grace and Jeanette, named for the owner's daughters. Shown above is the Brier Hill Steel coking operation. The most abundant coal in the United States, bituminous, or soft coal, has many impurities that have to be removed or "coked" before use in the blast furnace. The below photograph, taken around 1912, shows Brier Hill Steel employees and their families in the neighborhood. (Both, courtesy of OHC-YHCIL.)

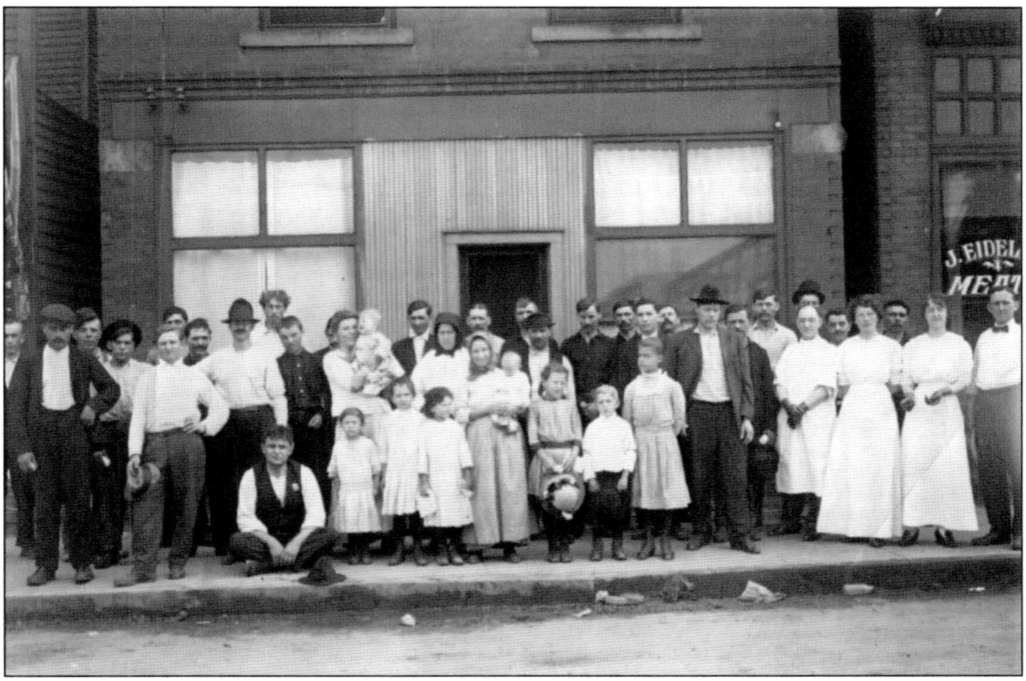

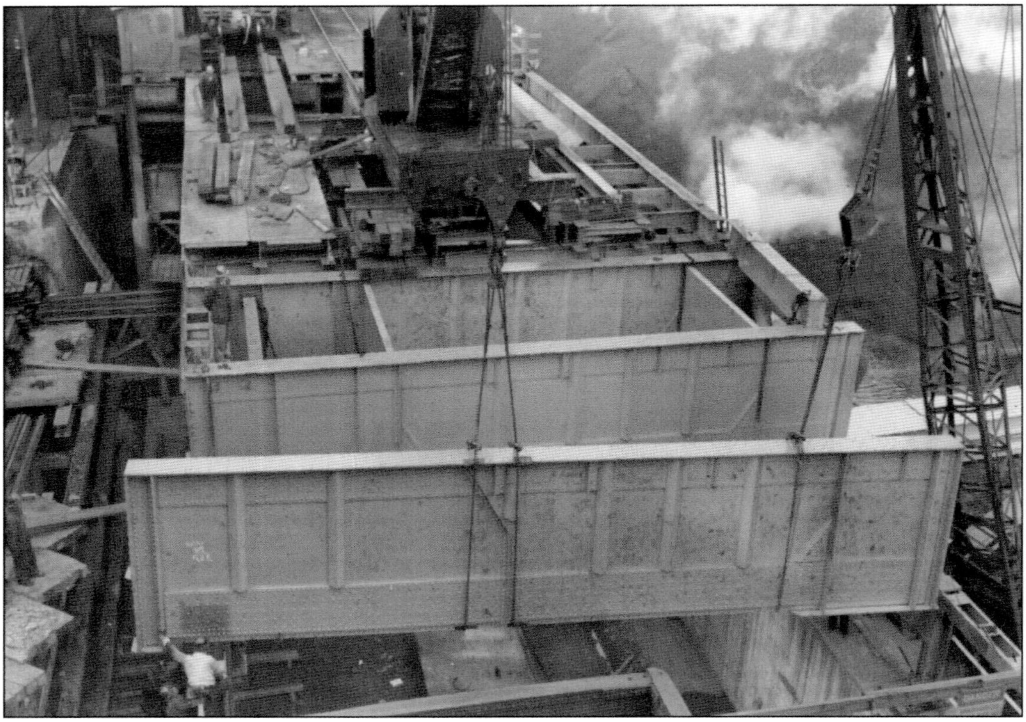

Carnegie Steel. In 1895, the Ohio Steel Company poured the Mahoning Valley's first Bessemer Process steel. In 1899, National Steel bought out Ohio Steel and another local business, Union Iron & Steel, operating them as the American Steel Hoop Company. Andrew Carnegie sold his interests to financier J.P. Morgan in 1901, forming the world's first billion-dollar corporation, US Steel. Two years later, US Steel absorbed both National Steel and American Steel Hoop. The giant company operated its Youngstown plant under Carnegie Steel, which later became Carnegie-Illinois Steel. Shown above is the trestle of a blast furnace under construction. Below, bricklayers, who were often Italians, prepare to reline the furnace with refractory brick. (Both, courtesy of OHC-YCHIL.)

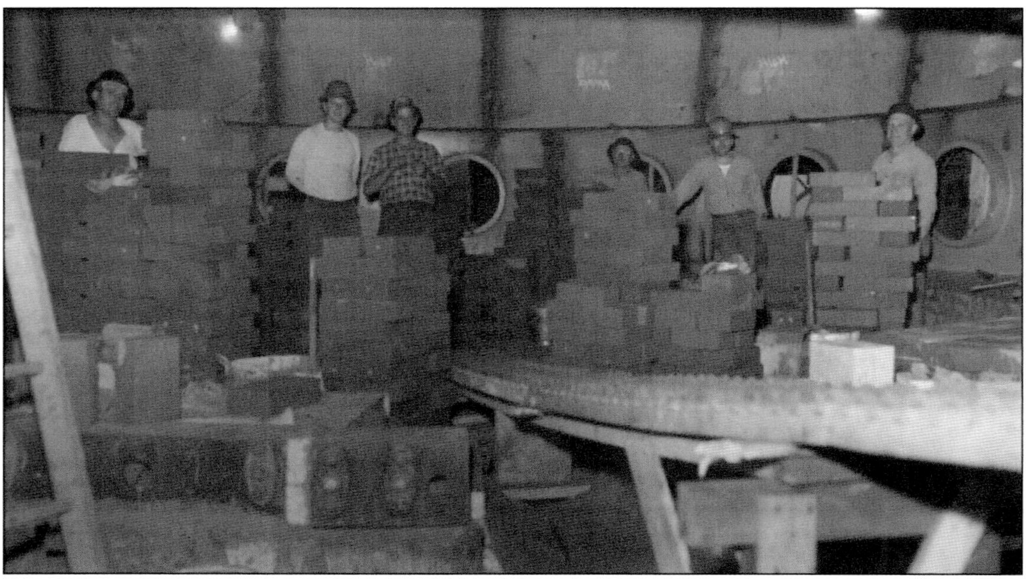

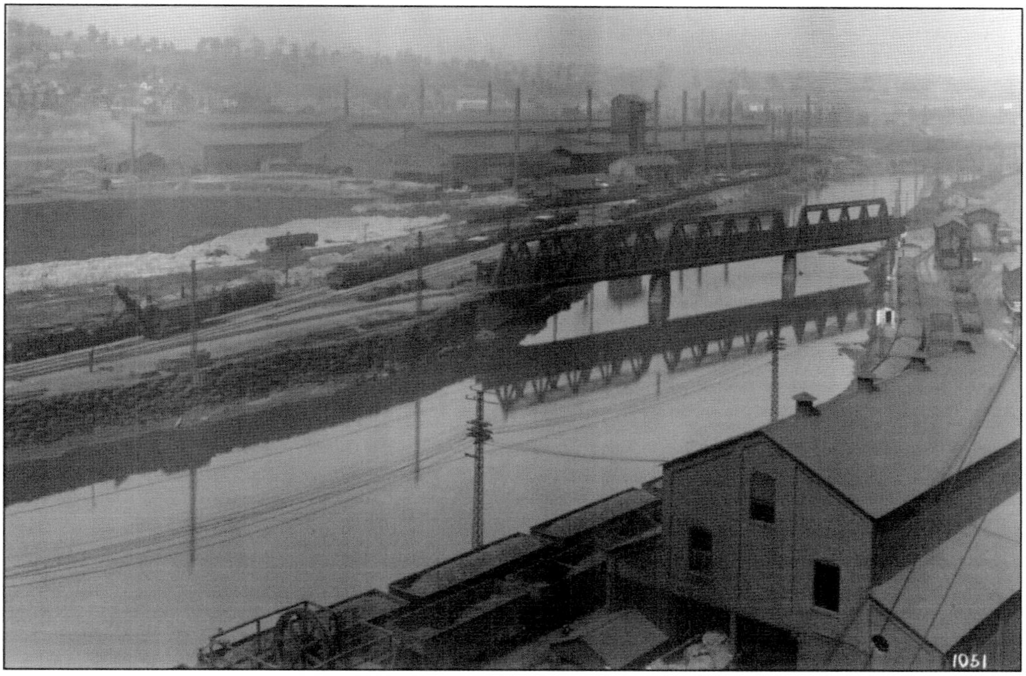

Republic Iron & Steel. A conglomeration of several iron and steel companies in the Midwest, Republic Iron & Steel purchased several Youngstown firms, including Brown, Bonnell & Company, Andrews Brothers & Company, and Mahoning Valley Iron Company in 1899. Republic's original headquarters in Pittsburgh was moved to Youngstown in 1911. In the early 1930s, the company headquarters moved to Cleveland, and the name was changed to Republic Steel Corporation. The above photograph shows the tube works; seen below is the 90-inch plate mill. (Both, courtesy of OHC-YHCIL.)

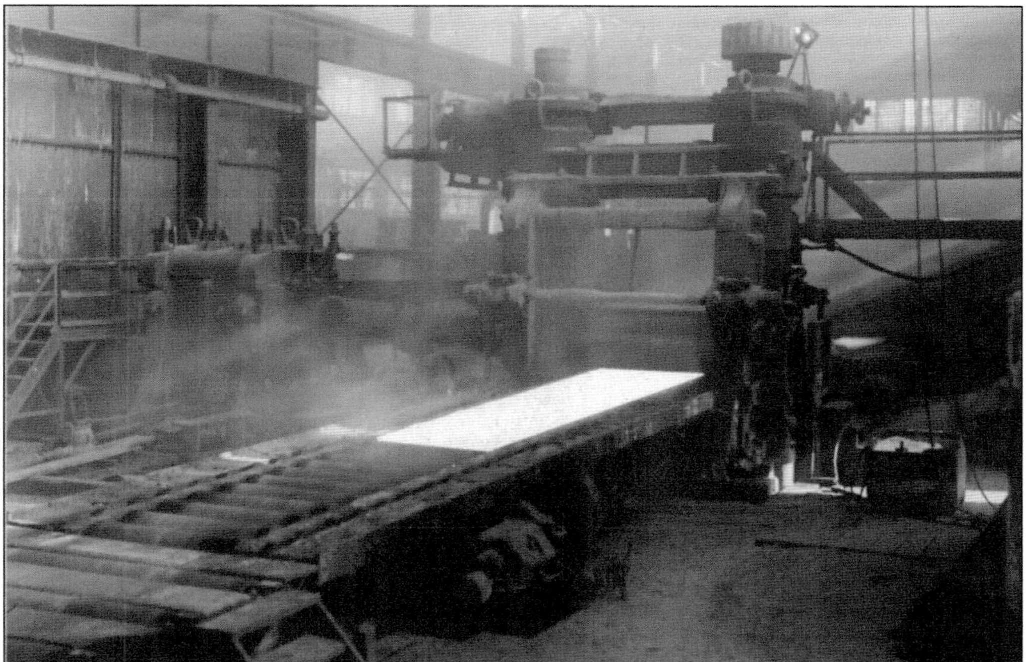

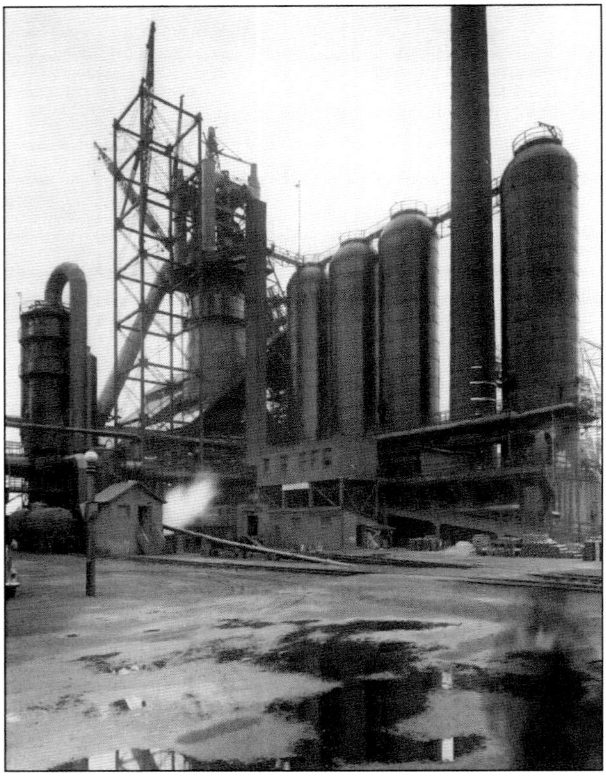

Republic Steel in Warren. Besides its large operations in Youngstown, Republic Steel extended its reach into Warren, purchasing the Trumbull Steel Company in 1928. Trumbull Steel was organized in 1912 and began operations the following year. In 1922, Trumbull Steel built a new blast furnace, the largest in the world, with a 60-ton daily capacity. When Republic combined this plant with the Niles and Youngstown facilities, the entire operations were renamed the Youngstown District. In the 1980s, LTV Steel purchased Republic; the Warren plant was purchased by the Renco Group and operated under several different names, including WCI Steel and RG Steel. The plant closed for good in 2012. These photographs show the blast furnace being rebuilt in 1939 (left) and the interior of the tin plate mill (below). (Both, courtesy of OHC-YHCIL.)

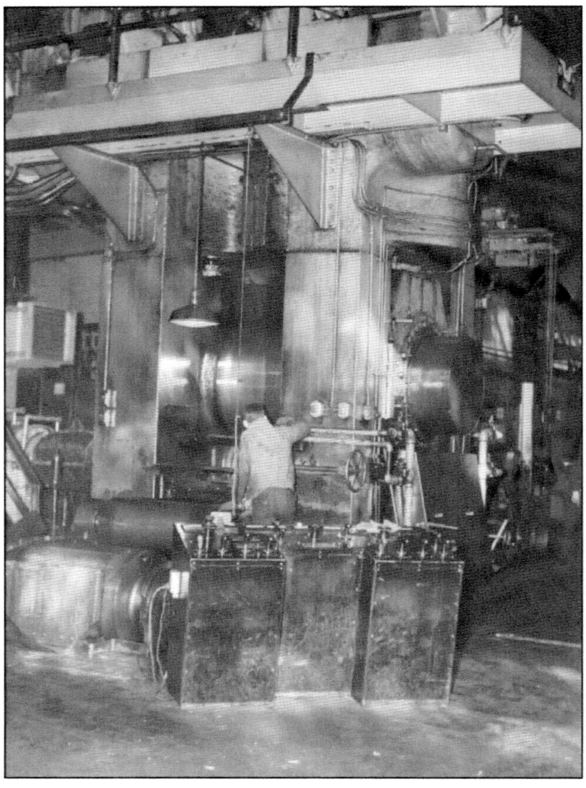

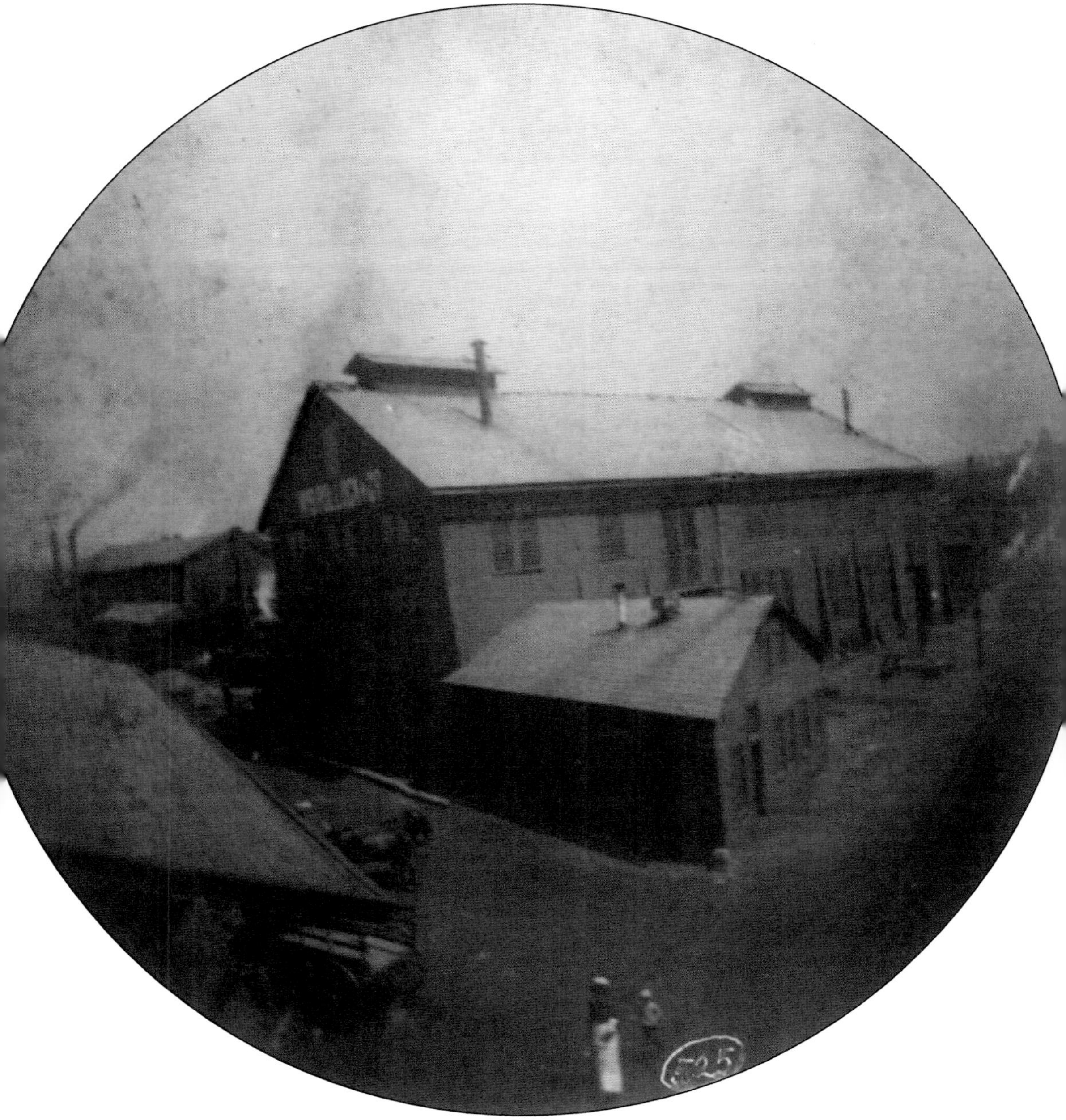

POLLOCK COMPANY. An old Youngstown business, the William B. Pollock Company was formed in 1863. William Pollock started as a blast-furnace operator. With his practical, hands-on experience, he formed a company to build blast furnaces. The original shop was on Basin Street near downtown Youngstown; in 1881, Pollock built a new plant on Market and Front Streets. After a fire destroyed that facility in 1900, the Pollock Company built a new plant at East Federal Street and Andrews Avenue, on the edge of Smoky Hollow. The company added other product lines including ladle cars, torpedo cars, and other large pieces of equipment used by the steel industry. The Pollock Company supplied steel concerns not just in the United States but all over the world. Seen here is the William B. Pollock Company plant on Andrews Avenue around 1905. (Courtesy of OHC-YHCIL.)

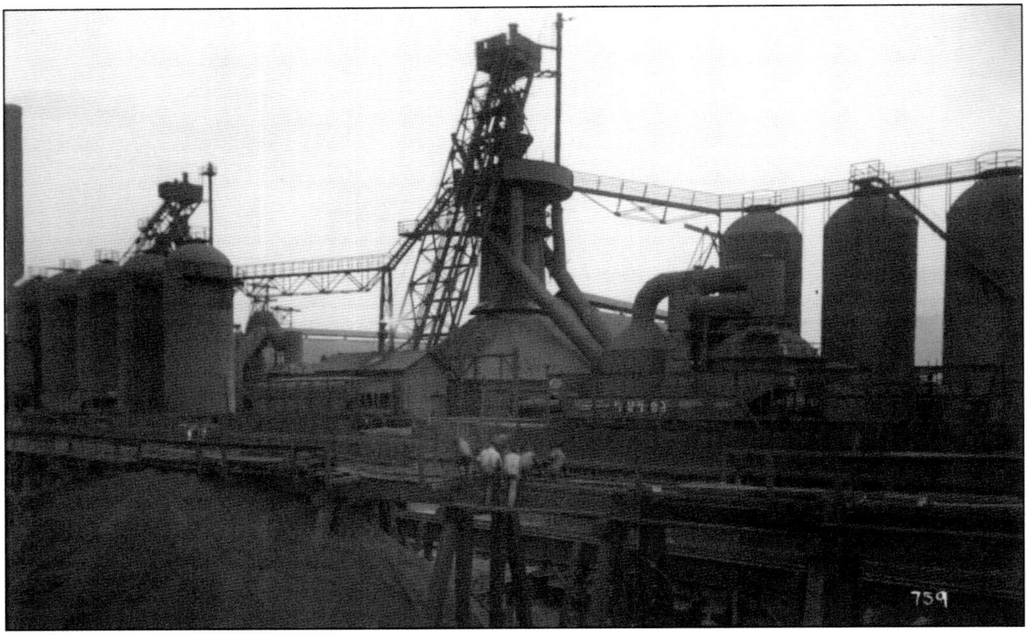

Hubbard Furnace. One of the sights that greeted Italian immigrants who arrived in Hubbard, east of Youngstown, was the Hubbard Furnace. The factory was one of numerous magnets for new immigrants seeking employment. The Hubbard Furnace (above) and its cast house (below) were originally owned by the Andrews & Hitchcock Iron Company. In 1916, the YS&T Company purchased this concern, which the *Iron Trade Review* hailed as one of the most important industrial acquisitions in months. The Hubbard Furnace gave YS&T an adequate supply of pig iron, which it desperately needed with the onset of World War I. The Hubbard Furnace was one of the last in the Valley to produce pig iron. (Both, courtesy of OHC-YHCIL.)

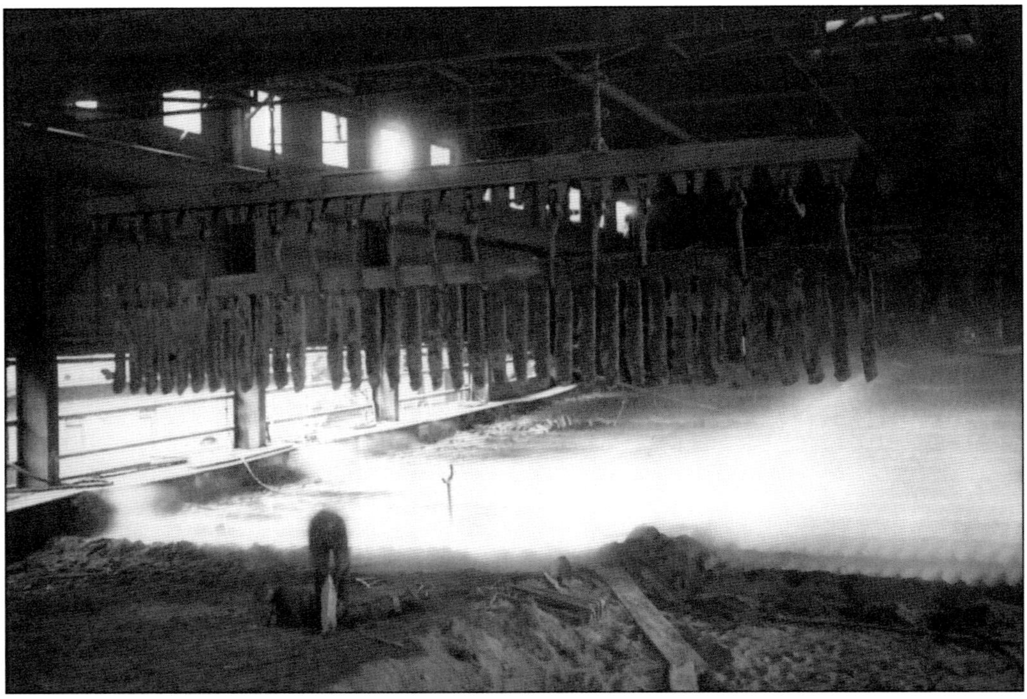

WORKING AT YS&T. Bernardo Piccoli, seen at right with his wife, Maria De Rochis Piccoli, worked at the YS&T Company's Campbell Works. The family lived near his place of work, on Twelfth Street in Campbell. Bernardo worked in various departments in the mill as a laborer. In 1944, Piccoli received the letter shown below, along with a pin for 25 or more continuous years of service to YS&T. The company's general superintendent, A.S. Glossbrenner, who signed the letter, noted that YS&T would not hold "a gathering of Old Timers for a personal presentation of the pin," because of World War II. (Both, courtesy of Noreen Modarelli.)

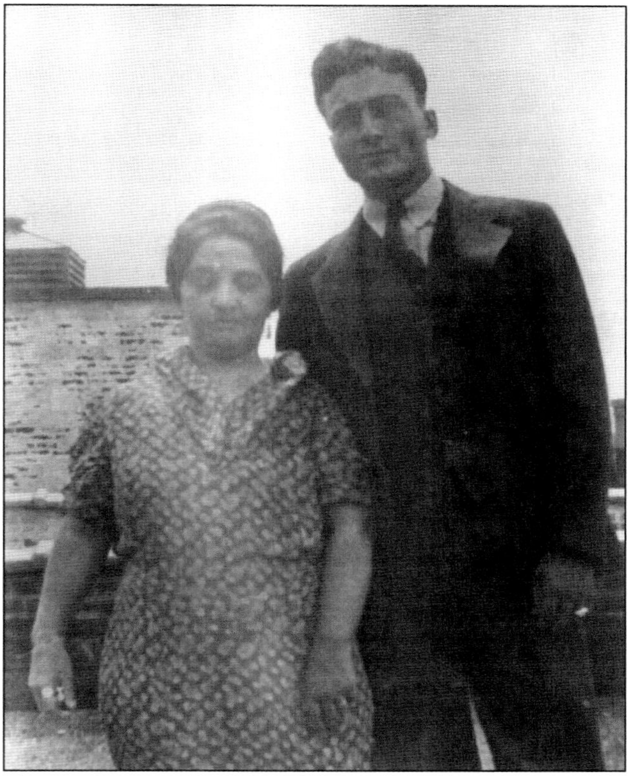

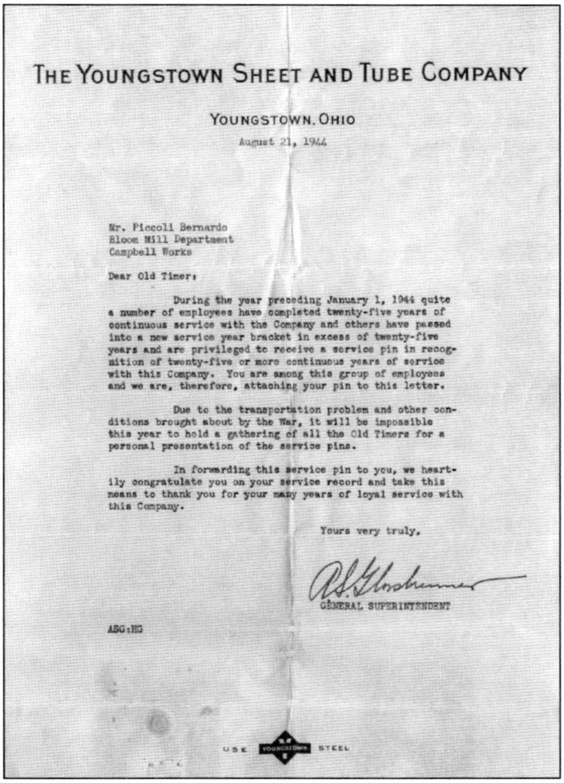

THE YOUNGSTOWN SHEET AND TUBE COMPANY

YOUNGSTOWN, OHIO

August 21, 1944

Mr. Piccoli Bernardo
Bloom Mill Department
Campbell Works

Dear Old Timer:

During the year preceding January 1, 1944 quite a number of employees have completed twenty-five years of continuous service with the Company and others have passed into a new service year bracket in excess of twenty-five years and are privileged to receive a service pin in recognition of twenty-five or more continuous years of service with this Company. You are among this group of employees and we are, therefore, attaching your pin to this letter.

Due to the transportation problem and other conditions brought about by the War, it will be impossible this year to hold a gathering of all the Old Timers for a personal presentation of the service pins.

In forwarding this service pin to you, we heartily congratulate you on your service record and take this means to thank you for your many years of loyal service with this Company.

Yours very truly,

A.S. Glossbrenner
GENERAL SUPERINTENDENT

ASG:HG

USE YOUNGSTOWN STEEL

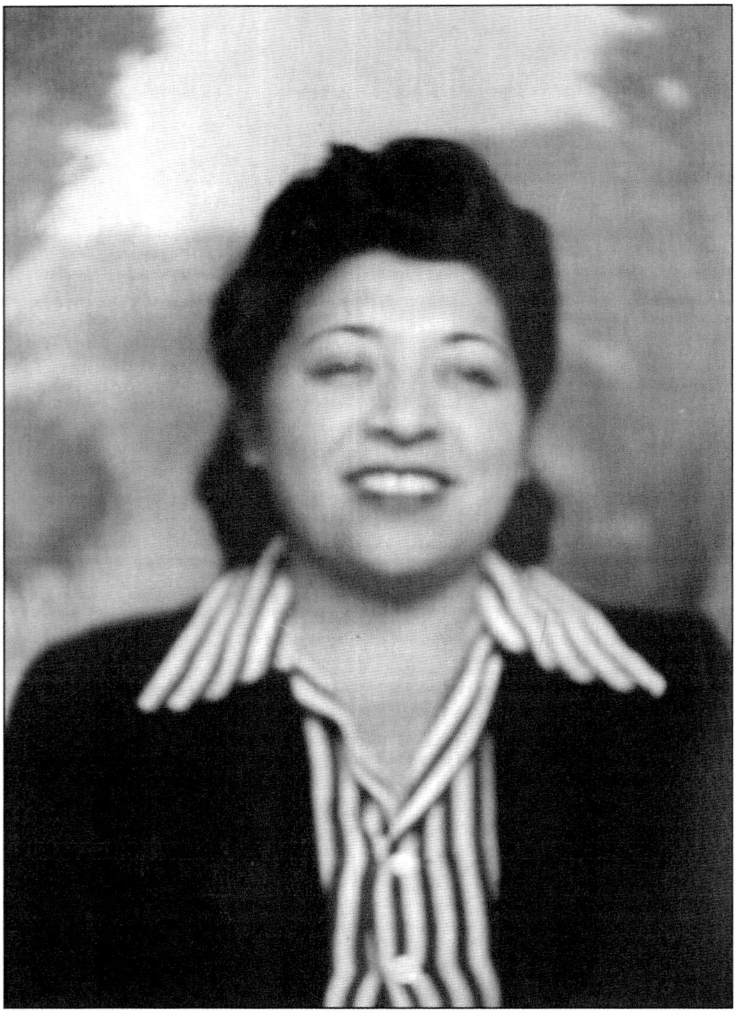

ROSIE THE RIVETER. With America's entry into World War II in 1941, women entered the workplace, including the shop floor, replacing the men who left to serve their country. Italian American women answered the call and played a vital role in the war effort. Clotilda DiLullo (left) was one of the thousands of Rosie the Riveters who shed their high heels and dresses for overalls and steel-toed shoes. DiLullo first worked at the Ravenna Arsenal, then later got a job closer to her home in Smoky Hollow, at Truscon Steel, where she checked welds. Shown below is her pay stub from Truscon for April 28, 1948.

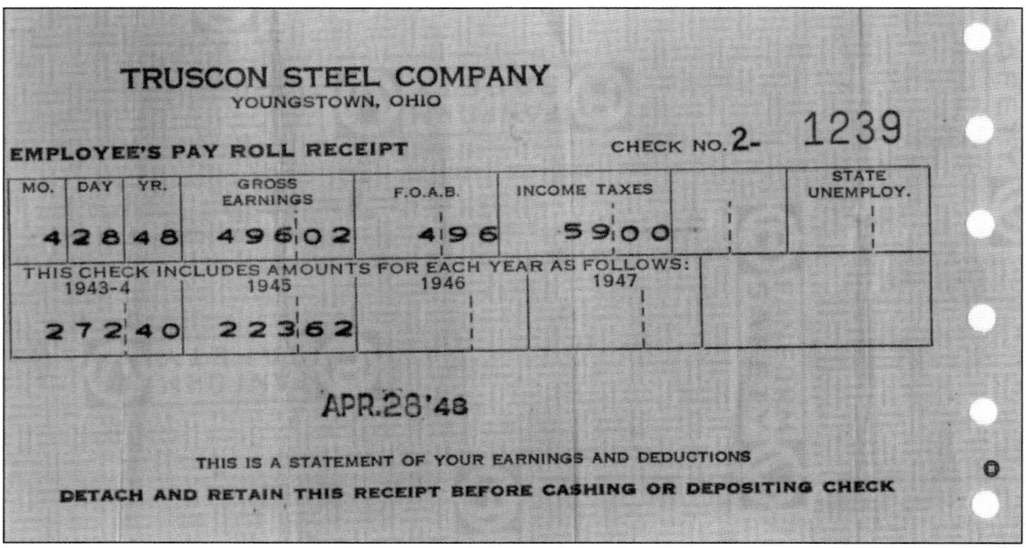

TRUSCON STEEL COMPANY
YOUNGSTOWN, OHIO

EMPLOYEE'S PAY ROLL RECEIPT — CHECK NO. 2- 1239

MO.	DAY	YR.	GROSS EARNINGS	F.O.A.B.	INCOME TAXES		STATE UNEMPLOY.
4	28	48	496.02	4.96	59.00		

THIS CHECK INCLUDES AMOUNTS FOR EACH YEAR AS FOLLOWS:

1943-4	1945	1946	1947
272.40	223.62		

APR.28'48

THIS IS A STATEMENT OF YOUR EARNINGS AND DEDUCTIONS

DETACH AND RETAIN THIS RECEIPT BEFORE CASHING OR DEPOSITING CHECK

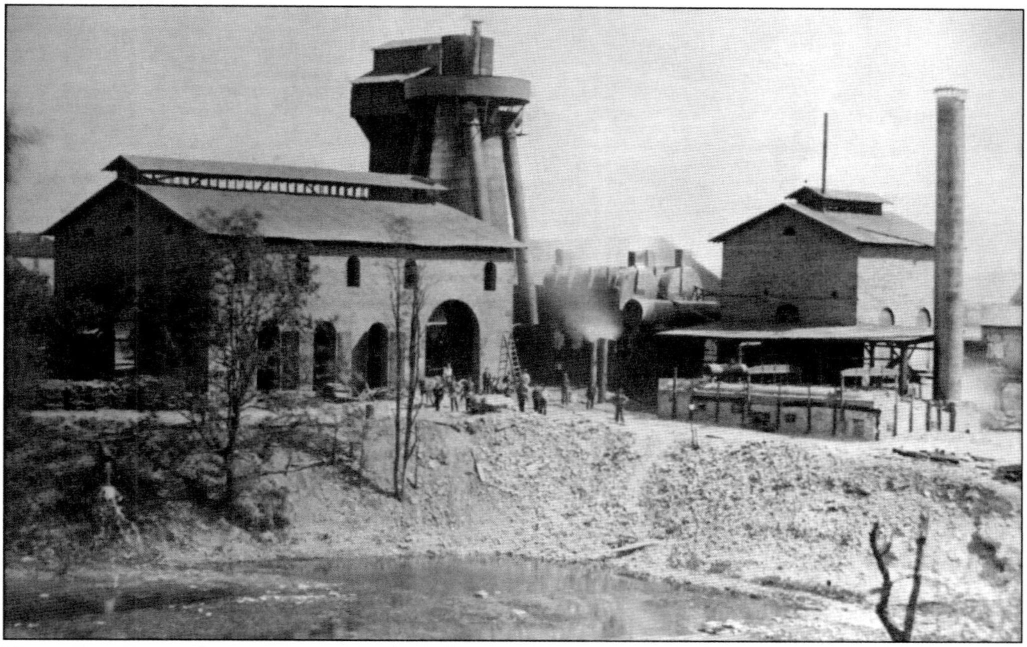

Niles Fire Brick Company. Iron and steel companies, besides acting as a magnet for immigrants, attracted subsidiary companies, such as the Pollock Company and United Engineering & Foundry. One of the most significant was the Niles Fire Brick Company (NFB), owned and operated by the J.R. Thomas family. By 1890, John Rhys Thomas recruited a small group of Italians, highly skilled in the firing of ceramic products, to work at his refractory brick operations. The company operated between 1872 and 1972. Until the mid-1920s, it recruited much of its labor force from southern Italy. The above photograph, taken around 1895, depicts the Thomas Iron Works on the left and the NFB on the right. Below is its second plant, shown shortly after construction in 1905. The company expanded to meet the needs of the changing local steel industry and flourished in the Valley as long as steel did.

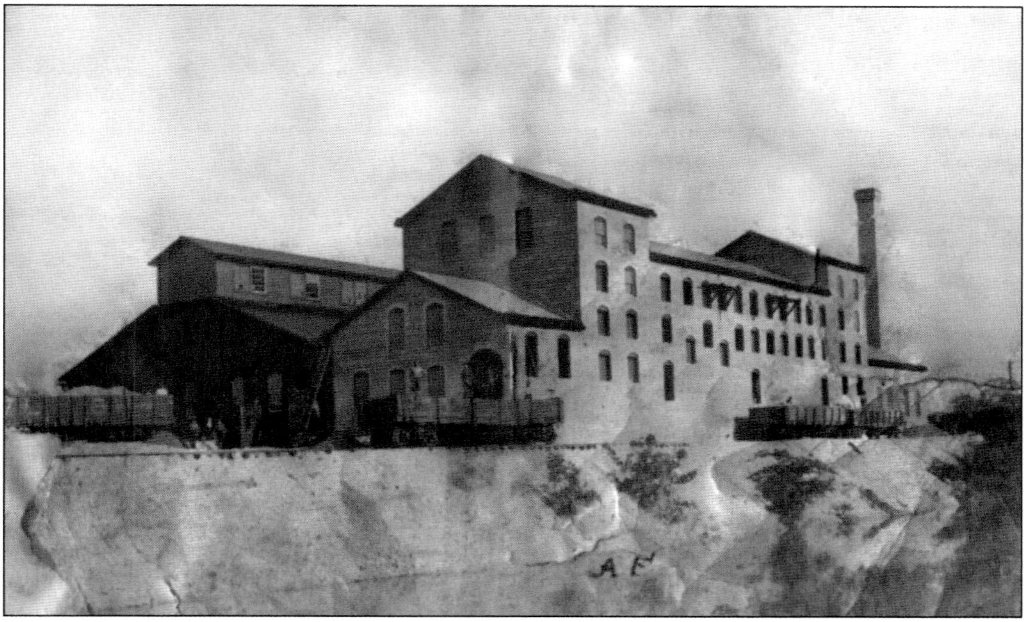

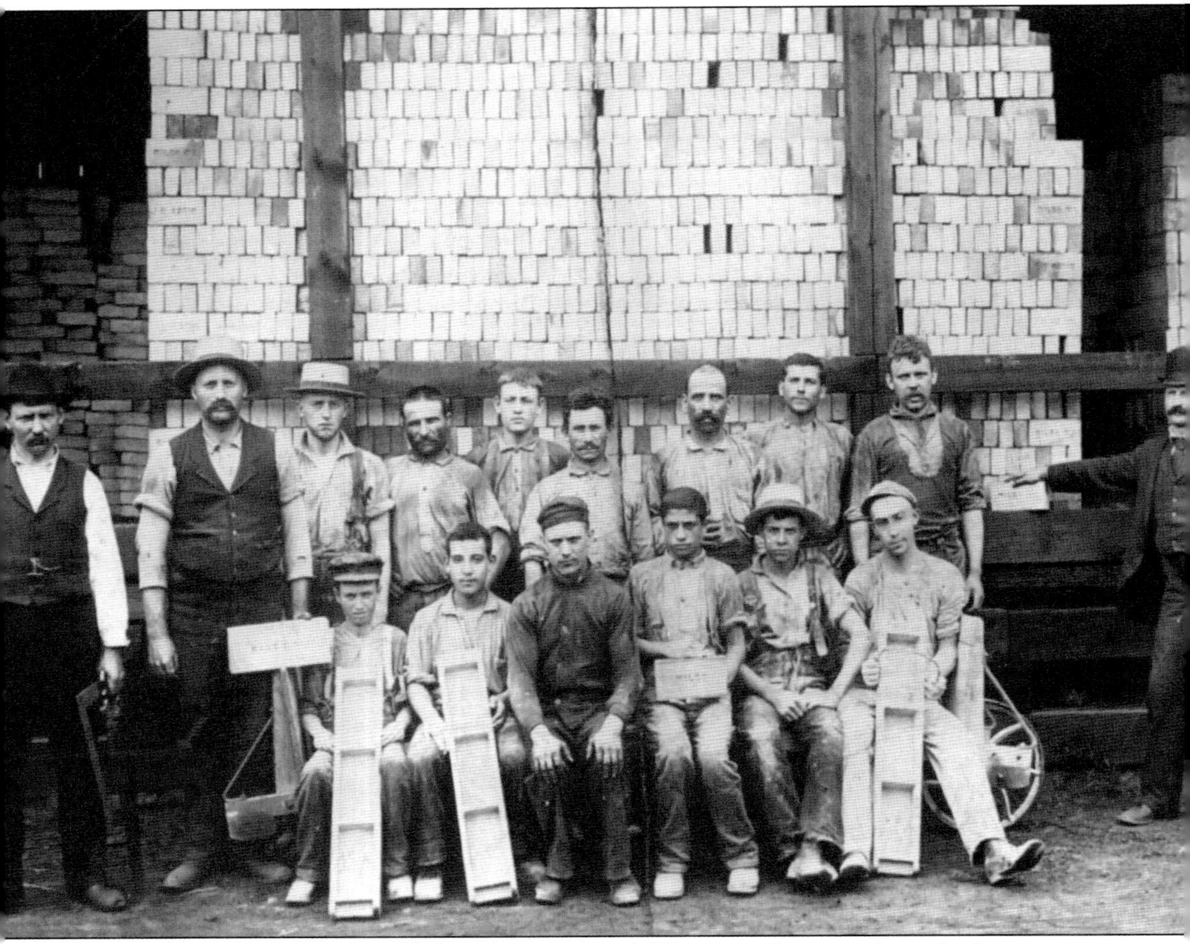

Working at NFB. Most of the workers at the NFB originally came from the home country of the Thomas family, Wales. Then, changing conditions made immigration to America less attractive, and the Thomases sought their labor elsewhere. The nucleus of their Italian workforce can be seen here around 1895. At far right is T.E. Thomas, son of the owner. Standing at far left is J. Rosensteel. Next to him is P.J. Sheehan. Of the remaining thirteen workers, four are Italian: seated second from left is Joseph Pallante, and standing are Carmel Laborial (fourth from left), Michael Infante (sixth from left), and Lorenzo Pallante (seventh from left). Note the presence of teenage boys as part of the workforce. There were no laws forbidding child labor at the dawn of the 20th century.

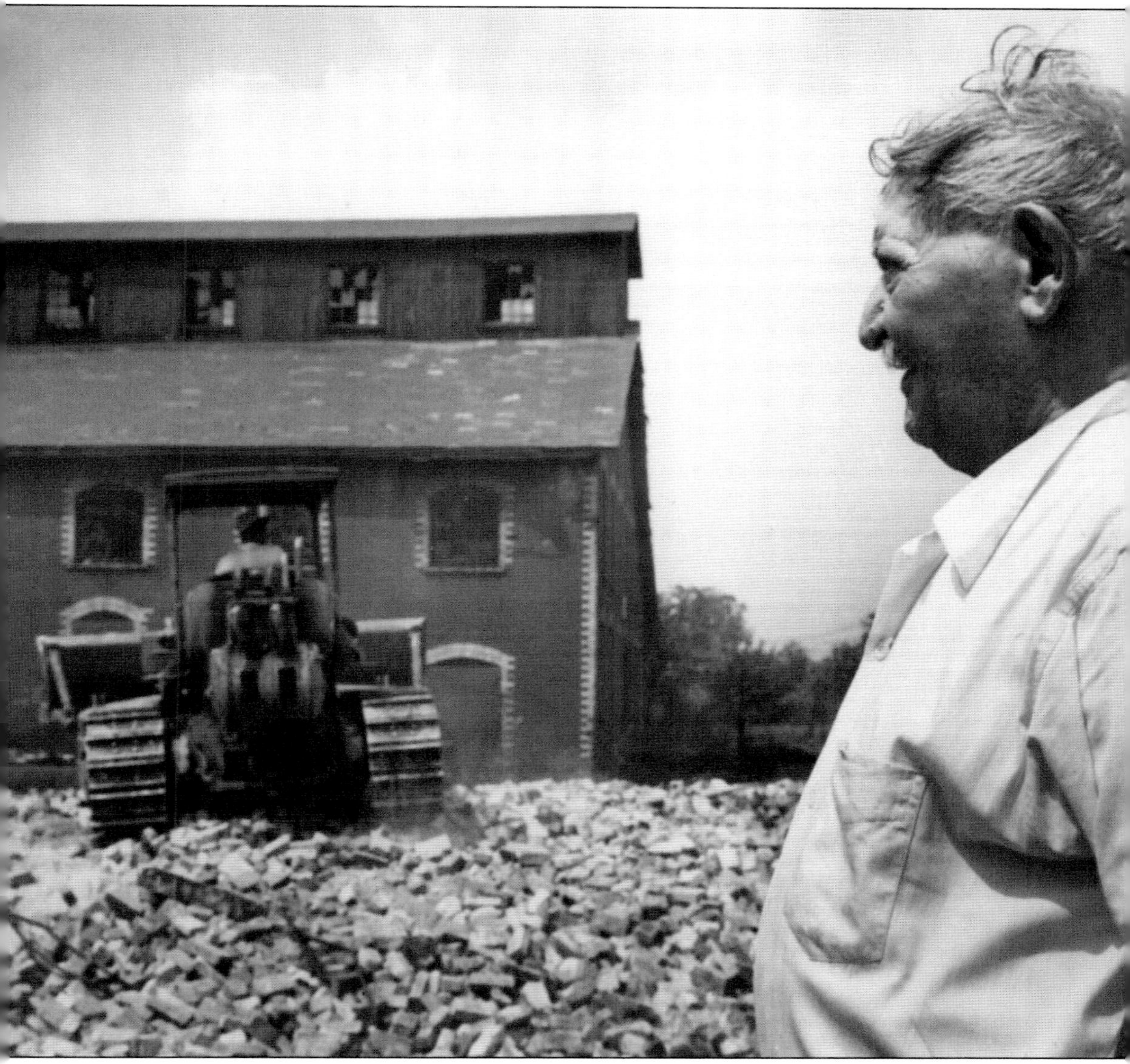

End of NFB. Louis Patrone, seen here, was recruited by Lorenzo Pallante in 1901, arriving in time to help rebuild the No. 1 plant after a fire. He worked there until 1961, when the last of his duties was to oversee the razing of the plant. In an interview, Patrone's son, Michael, described how his father came to work at the NFB: "He [Pallante] was one of the first ones that came over here [in 1890]. When he came over he brought the message back [to Bagnoli Irpino] that he had the job with the Niles Fire Brick and that they needed more men to help them around their plant . . . and my dad got word of it and he said, 'Well I'll go over there [to Niles] and see if I could get a job with them.'"

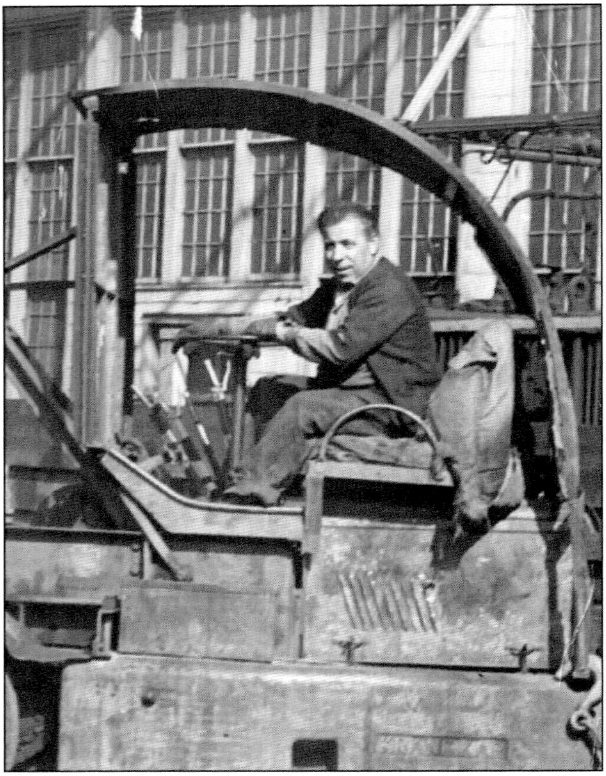

United Engineering & Foundry. One of the area's firms that provided equipment to the steel industry was United Engineering & Foundry. The company formed in 1849 under the name Parmalee & Sawyer and then became Ward & McKay, manufacturers of rolling-mill equipment. In 1900, following several mergers, it became United Engineering & Foundry. Under that name, it grew into one of the world's largest manufacturers of equipment for rolling mills and steel mills. Wean Industries acquired the company in 1971 and changed the name to Wean United. Attilio DiLallo, a resident of Smoky Hollow, worked at United in various capacities. He is seen operating machinery at work (left) and posing in his work clothing (below). (Both, courtesy of Anthony Worrellia.)

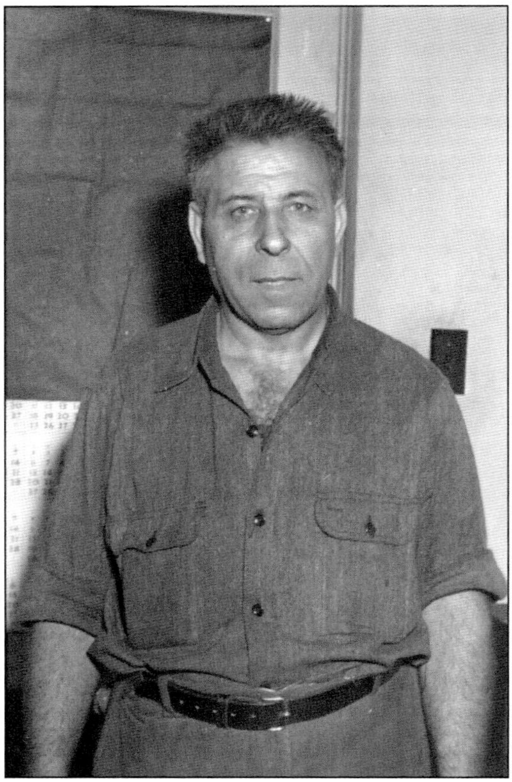

GENERAL FIREPROOFING COMPANY. An old Youngstown firm, General Fireproofing (GF) began operations in 1902, manufacturing fireproof building supplies. It quickly shifted to the manufacture of metal office furniture, including desks, chairs, filing cabinets, and related equipment. During World War II, the company made aircraft parts. At the time, the plant employed a number of women, including many Italian Americans. Seen here are two issues from *The GF News* company newsletter. At right, a cover from June 1944 shows the Army-Navy E flag, which the company received for excellence in war production. Shown below is a back cover from 1943, featuring GF police officers, including Italian Americans. (Both, courtesy of OHC-YHCIL.)

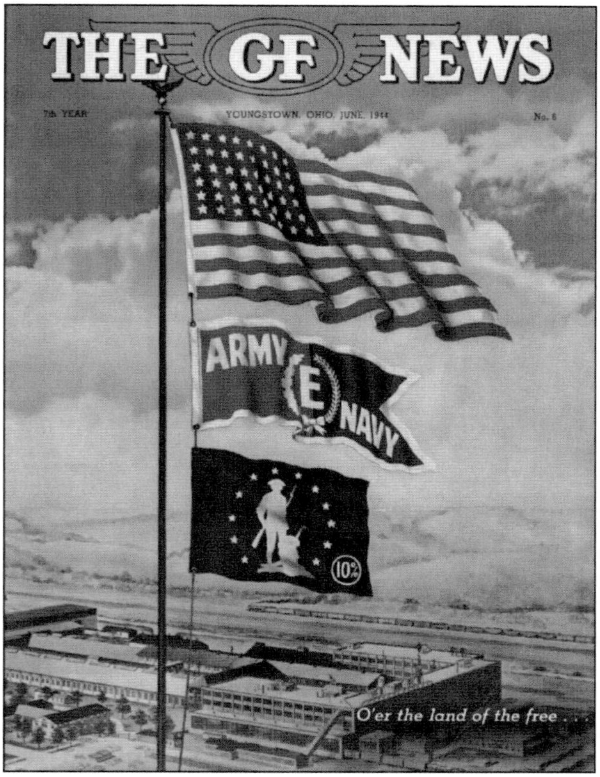

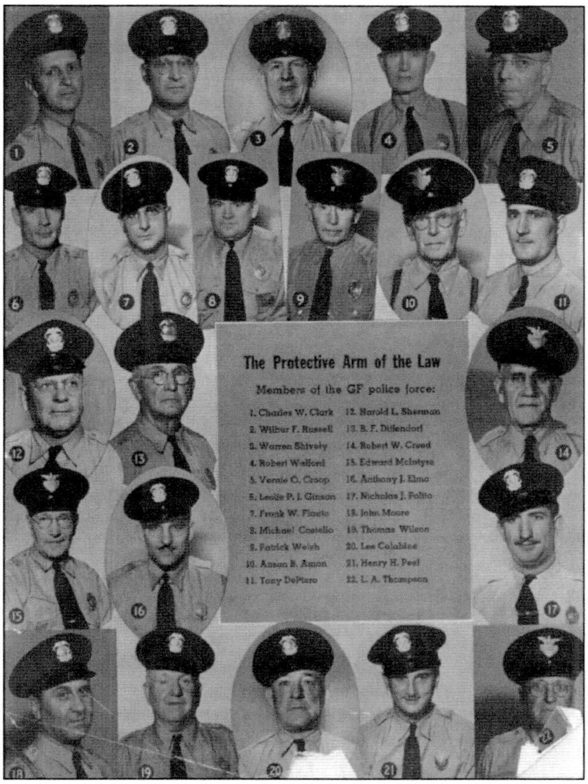

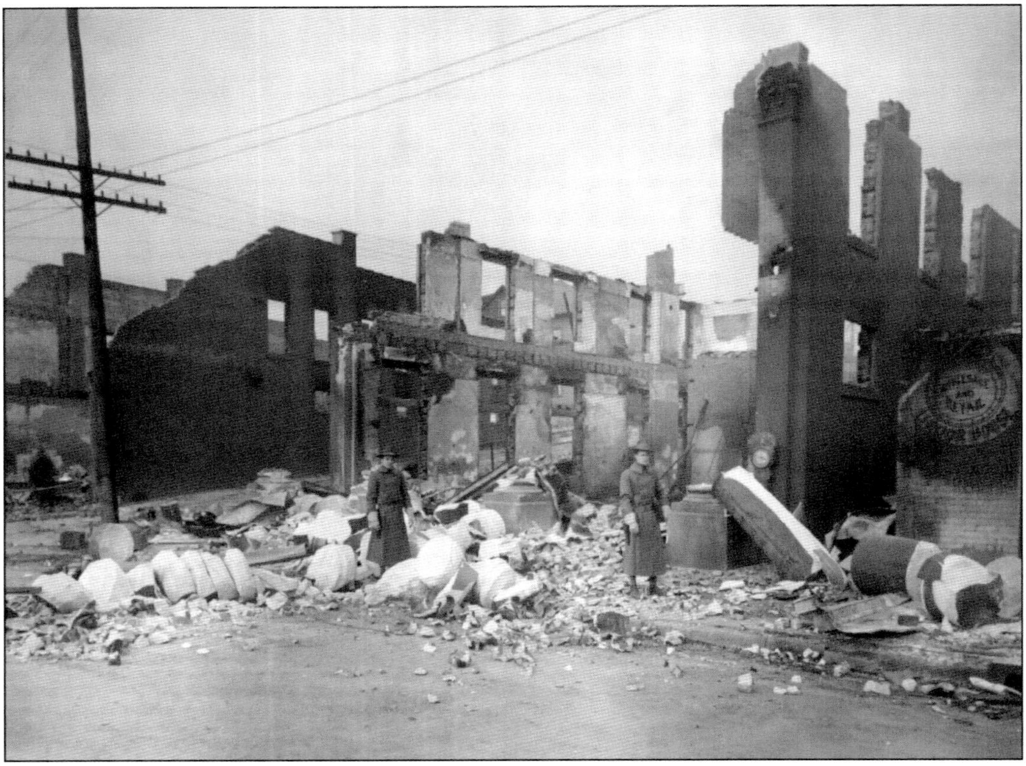

ON STRIKE. Labor disputes were common in the Mahoning Valley, especially in the steel industry. In 1916, workers at YS&T in East Youngstown walked off their jobs, protesting the low wages and long hours. On January 7, after company police fired into a crowd of picketers, a riot broke out. An ensuing fire destroyed half of the city's business district (above). The Ohio National Guard arrived the next day and ended the strike, in which most of the unskilled workers, including Italian Americans, participated. In 1937, another major strike occurred (below), known as "Little Steel," which got its name from companies like YS&T and Republic that were not part of US Steel (known as "Big Steel"). Italian American Dan Thomas was one of the local leaders of the Steelworkers Organizing Committee (SWOC), which led the strike. (Both, courtesy of OHC-YHCIL.)

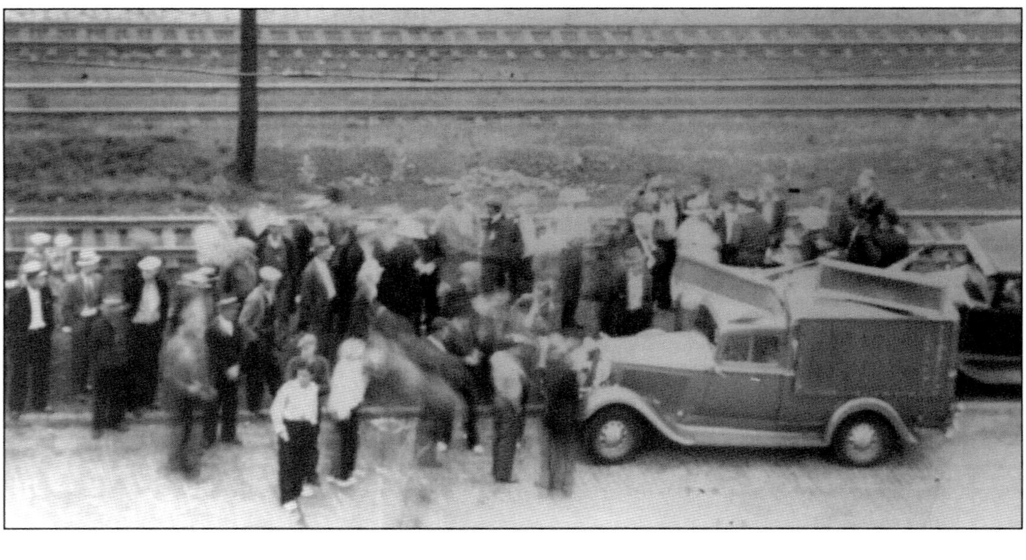

Five

Jacks of All Trades

Heavy industry was not the only source of employment in the Mahoning Valley. The steel industry was the biggest attraction for immigrants, given that the mills employed thousands of people, but the prosperity of the industry spawned economic opportunities in other areas. Many Italians worked in places not directly connected with heavy industry. The tremendous growth in population (in 1900, Youngstown had 45,000 people; by 1920, more than 120,000) meant a need for new construction. Not only residences, but new civic buildings graced the skyline. The Valley welcomed the services of skilled workers who came from Italy, like stonemasons and bricklayers. Italian Americans ran grocery stores and operated restaurants that originally served their own communities, but later expanded their customer base. Education was important among the Italian Americans in the Valley, and many were able to earn advanced degrees and enter the white-collar workforce. By the middle of the 20th century, they became respected members of the community; some entered into leadership positions throughout the Mahoning Valley. Women, besides working in the home tending to their families and boarders, also ran grocery stores and restaurants, taught school, and worked in offices and department stores. All kinds of work brought prosperity to the Italian American community and contributed to the vitality of the Mahoning Valley.

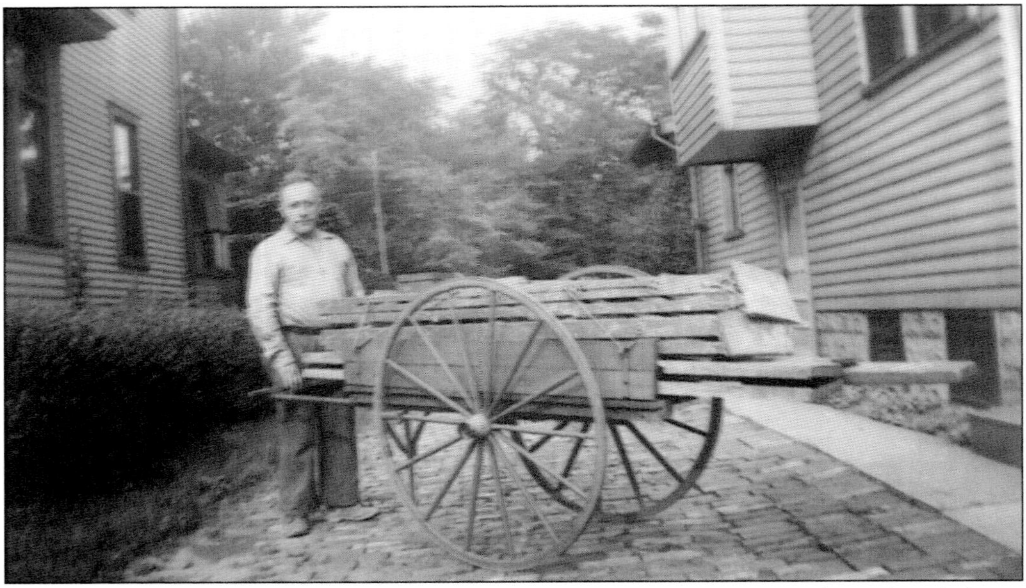

Skilled Work. Some Italians brought with them skills better suited to non-industrial workplaces. These occupations involved trade secrets that immigrants carried in their heads and their hands. In many cases, these occupations did not require brick and mortar. Such trades included wallpaper hanging and tailoring. Emidio D'Altorio, whose regular employment was at Trumbull Steel, later Republic Steel, in Warren, had a side job. When not on the factory floor, D'Altorio hung wallpaper for extra income. He is seen above with his cart of supplies and tools. The below photograph represents the culmination of two tailors' dreams—owning their own shop. Seen here around 1913, Solimando & Fusco Tailors was located in downtown Niles. (Above, courtesy of Carl and Edith Ritch; below, courtesy of NHS.)

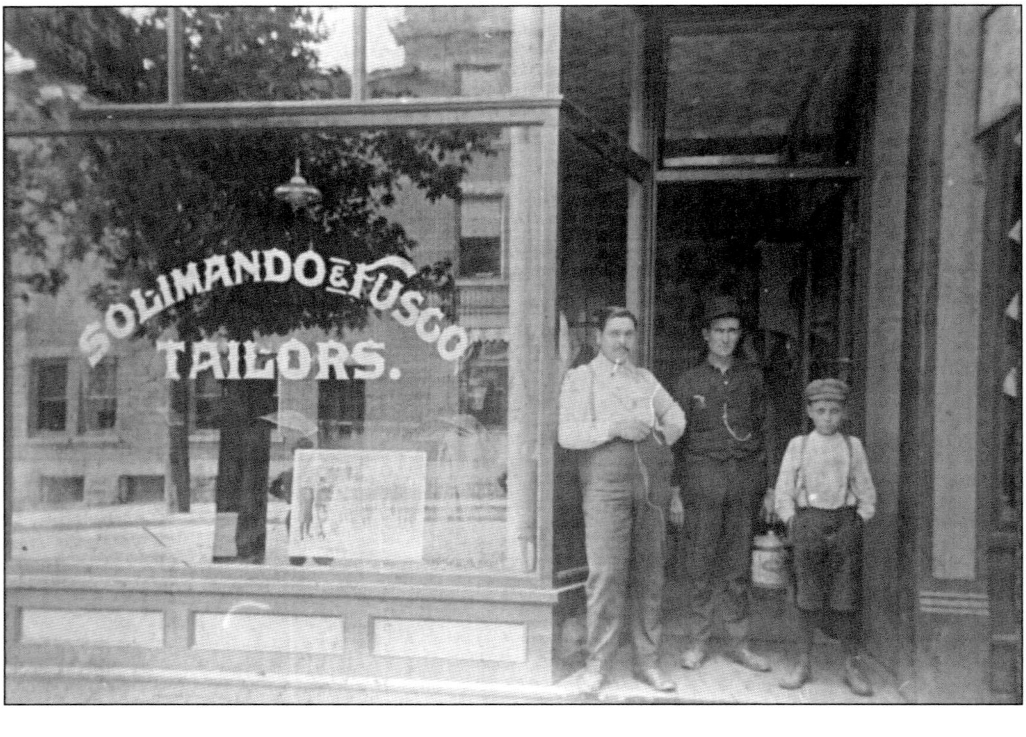

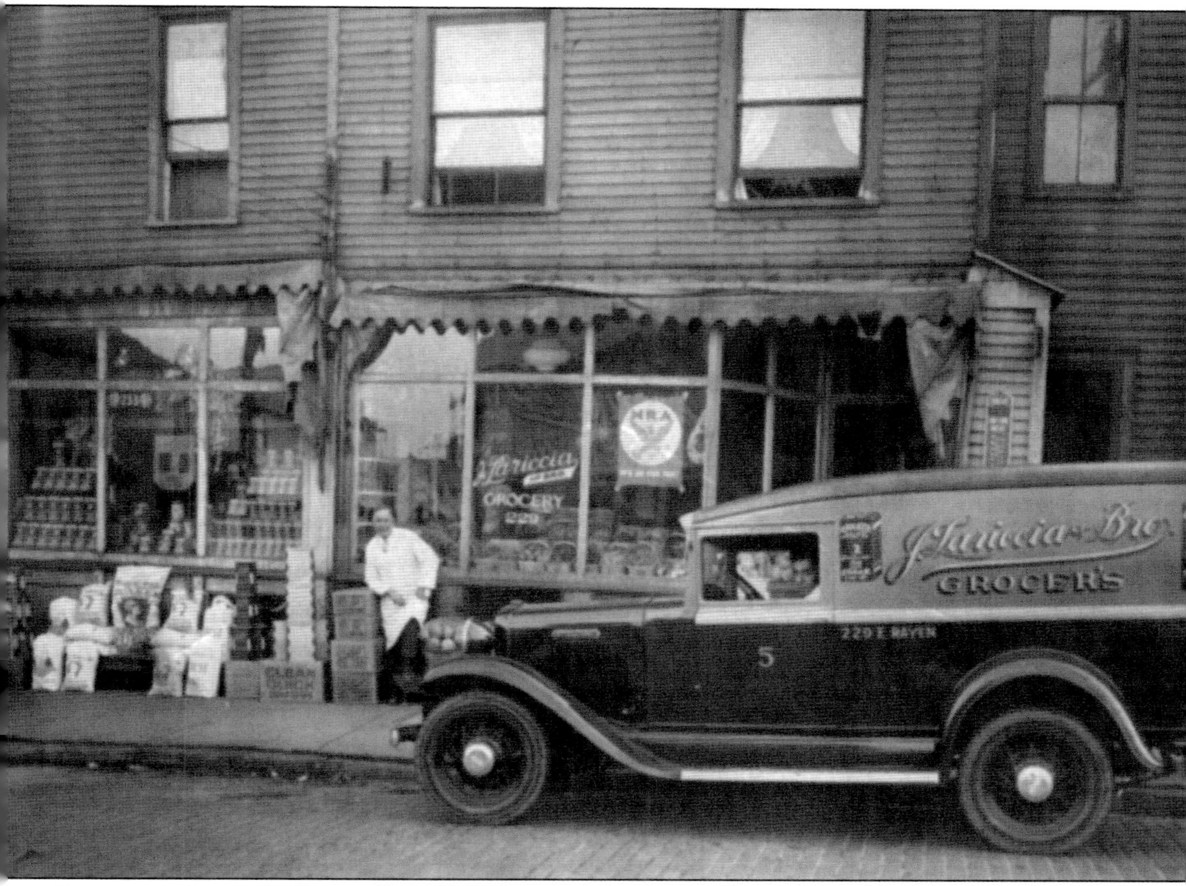

LARICCIA'S GROCERY STORE. One of the Mahoning Valley's oldest, still-operating grocery stores is Lariccia's Italian Market. Giuseppe (Joseph) and Gennaro Lariccia began their store in 1907 at 229 East Rayen Avenue, near Smoky Hollow. It was originally called J. Lariccia & Brother Grocery. Although they stocked all kinds of goods, they also provided specialty products for the many Italians in the neighborhood. In this photograph of the store and its truck, taken around 1933, note the poster in the window advertising that the business adhered to the regulations of the National Recovery Administration (NRA). Established as one of Franklin Roosevelt's New Deal agencies in 1933, the NRA sought to bring industry, business, and labor together by developing a series of codes that had to be followed. The symbol of the NRA was a blue eagle with the motto, "We Do Our Part." The US Supreme Court declared the NRA unconstitutional in 1935, but the labor provisions eventually became part of the National Labor Relations Act, or Wagner Act. (Courtesy of Ben Lariccia.)

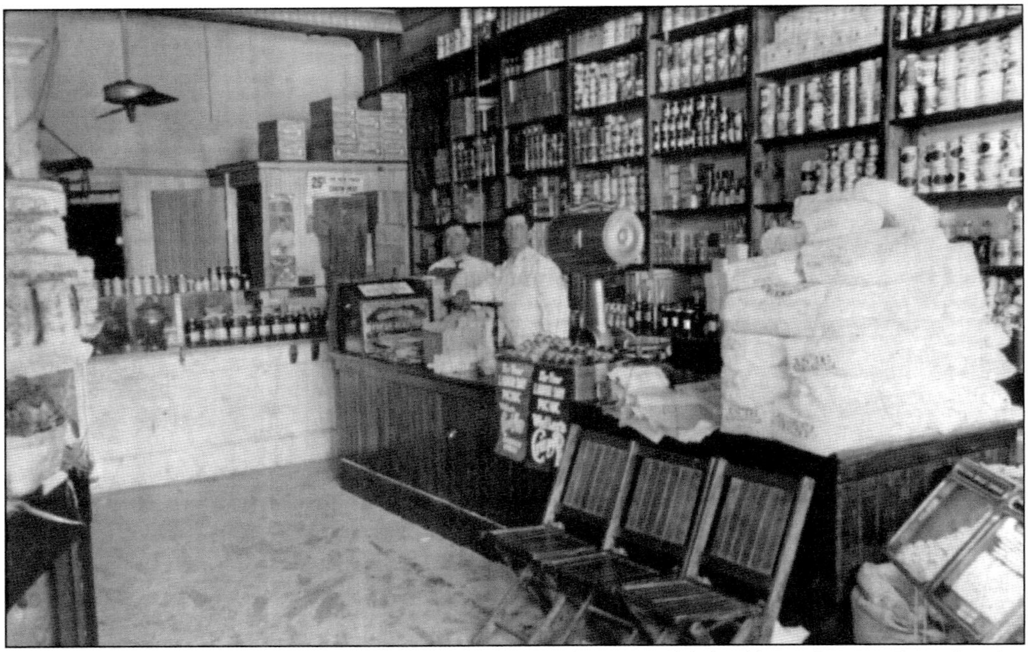

To Market, to Market. The Milano Market (above) was established by Salvatore Bartoli, who immigrated to Youngstown in 1900. The first store was located on the edge of Smoky Hollow, at 275 East Rayen Avenue. It specialized in Italian foods and meats. By the 1930s, Salvatore's son, Alfred, operated S. Bartoli & Son on Taft Avenue. By this time, the Milano Market manufactured sausage. The below photograph, taken in 1915, shows a peddler's wagon from Cicero's Store in Niles. From left to right, Pete Granada, Mariona Granada, and Nick Perna make door-to-door deliveries. (Above, courtesy of Adalea Marsch Moritz and Audrea Marsch Neri; below, courtesy of NHS.)

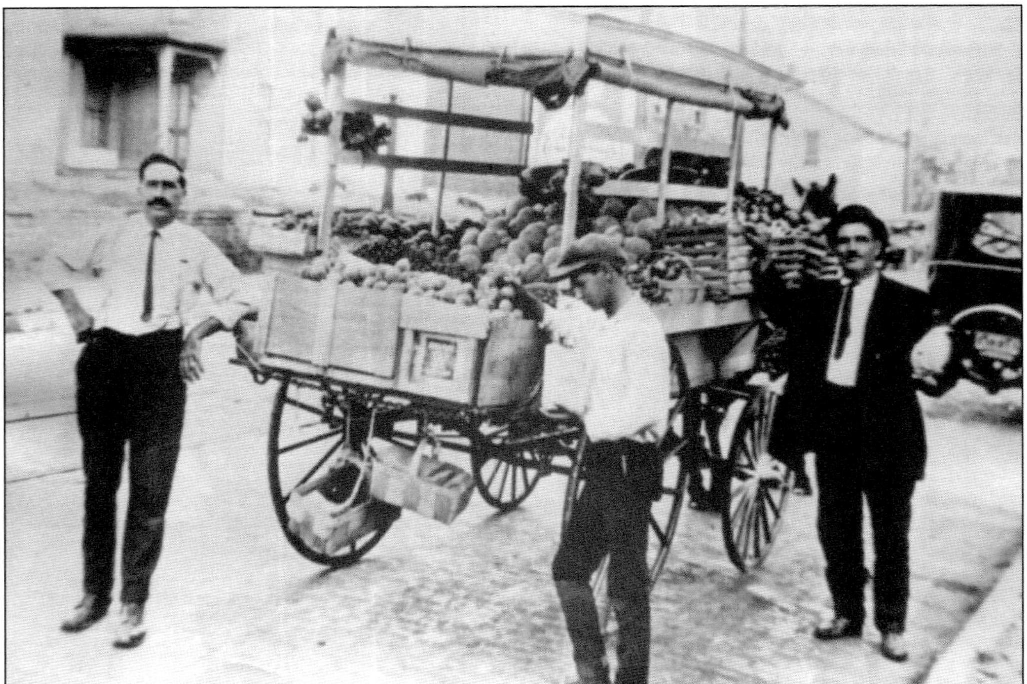

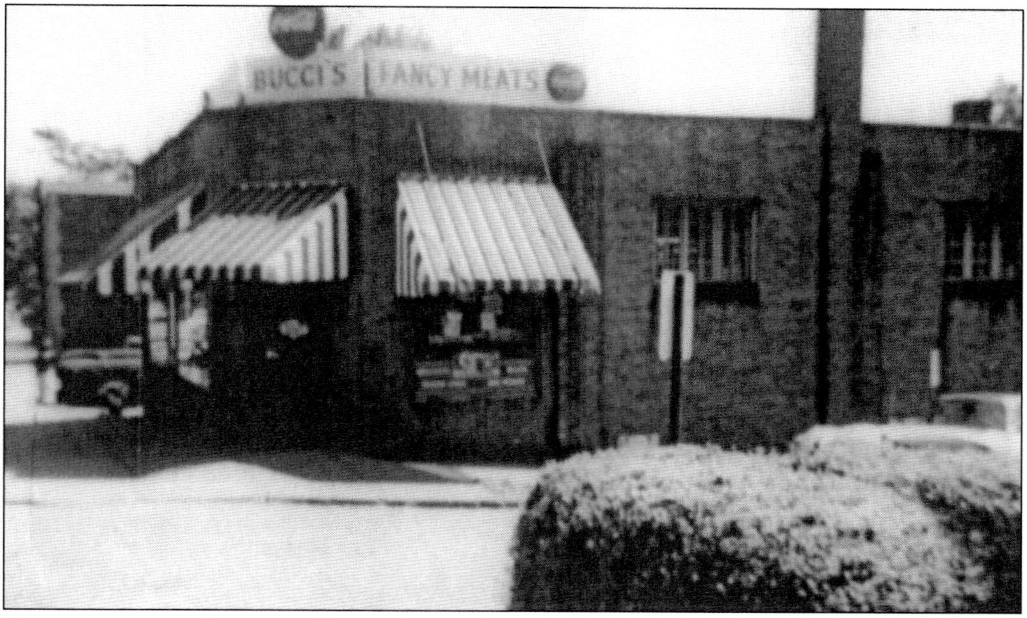

Marketing in the Hollow. With its large Italian population, Smoky Hollow supported numerous grocery stores catering to their needs. Some of them were operated out of people's residences to provide extra income. These enterprises were often run by the women of the house. As the population and the need for products grew, the stores expanded into standalone structures. Seen here are two later versions of the Italian grocery store. Shown above is Bucci's Market, which was on the corner of Court and North Walnut Streets. The Devito Dairy (below) was located on the corner of Emerald and Audubon Streets. (Both, courtesy of the Cassese family.)

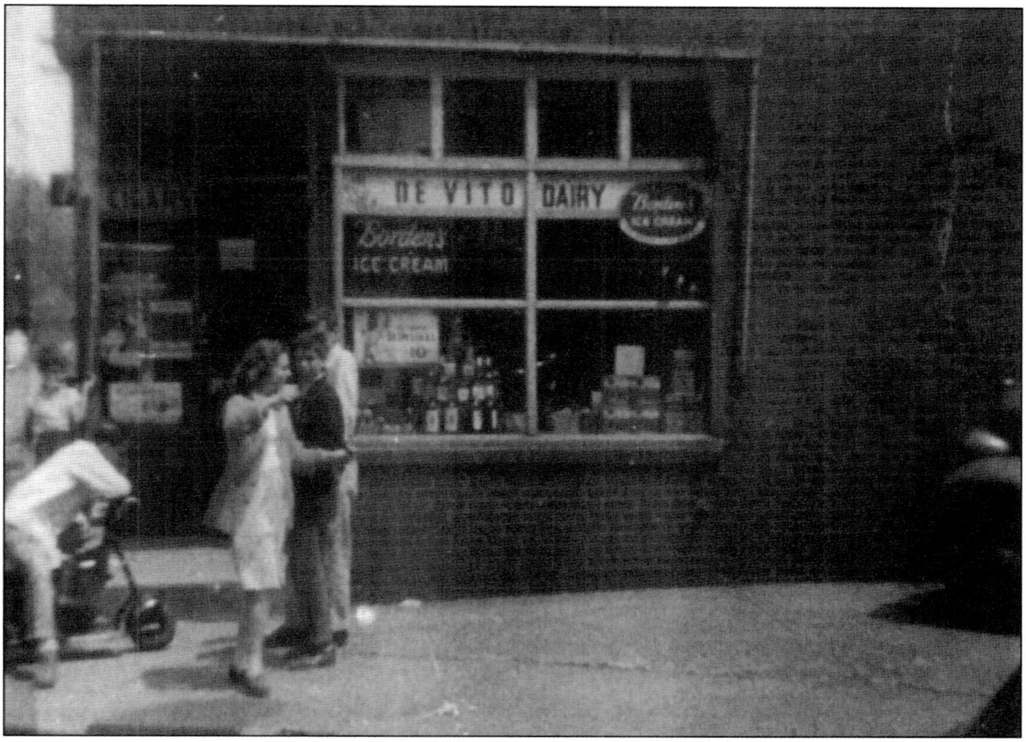

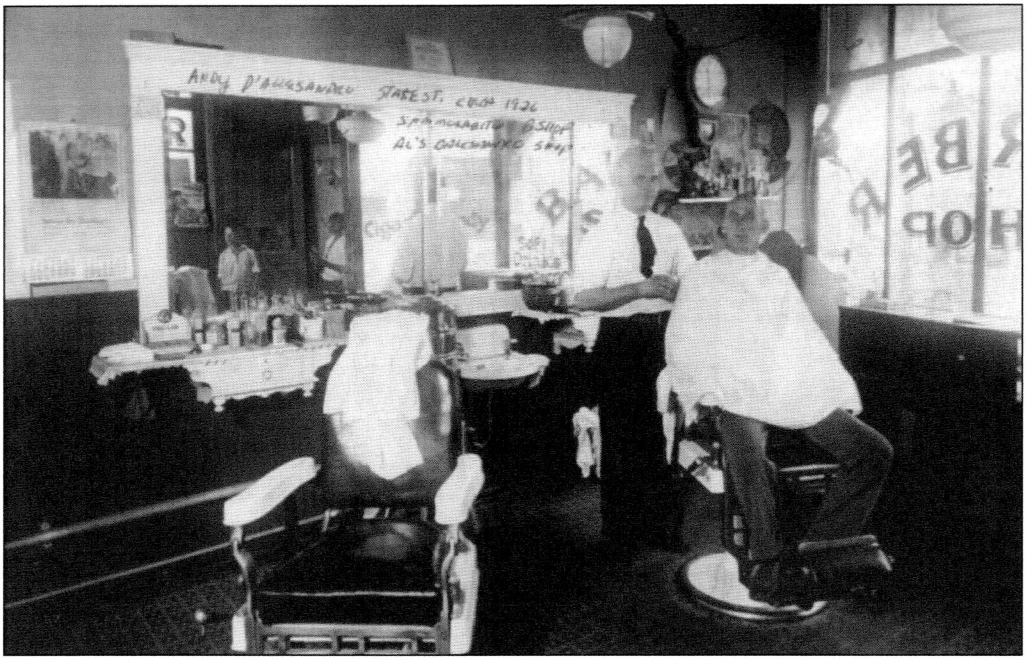

Downtown Niles. A number of Italian-owned businesses graced downtown Niles. Barbershops were important community gathering places, and many Italian Americans engaged in the art of barbering. Shown above is D'Allesandro's Barber Shop around 1926. Carmella's Confectionery Shop (below), on South Main Street, was remodeled in 1906. This interior view exhibits its newest attractions to tempt taste buds. Carmella's was a confectionery and an ice-cream parlor. Both of these enterprises evoke fond memories, especially since neither is still extant. (Above, courtesy of Joe Merlo; below, courtesy of NHS.)

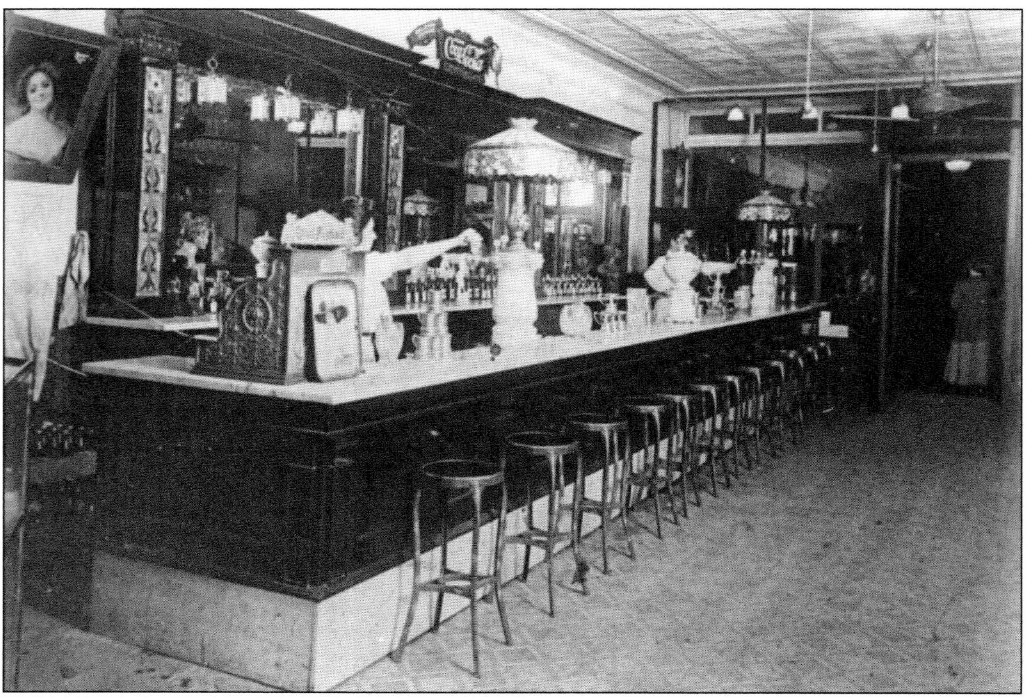

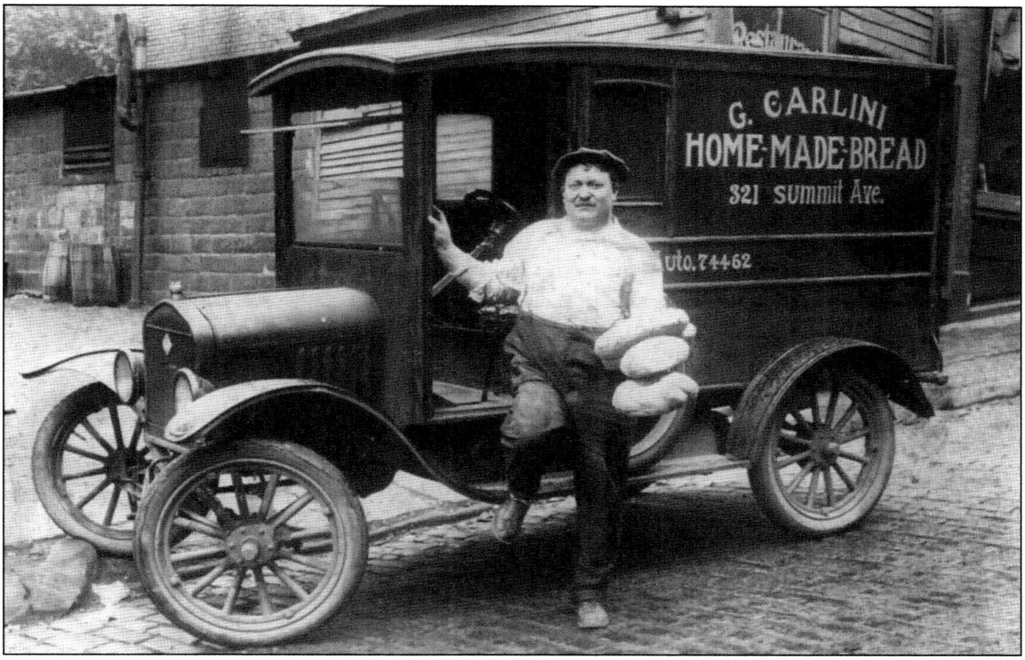

Baking Bread. Italian cuisine is known for its excellent baked goods, especially crusty, fresh-baked bread. In the Mahoning Valley, each community where Italians resided boasted its own bakery—sometimes more than one. A popular feature of bakeries was that they delivered to their largest customers. Shown above is the delivery truck of G. Carlini's Home Made Bread. The company was located on Summit Avenue, just south of Smoky Hollow. The truck is seen on Watt Street around 1922, making a delivery to a local restaurant. The Pasquale Scarnecchia Bread Company (below), located on Niles's east side, delivered throughout the area. Seen here is its delivery truck in front of the business. Scarnecchia's still exists as D'Urso's Bakery. (Above, courtesy of the Cassese family; below, courtesy of NHS.)

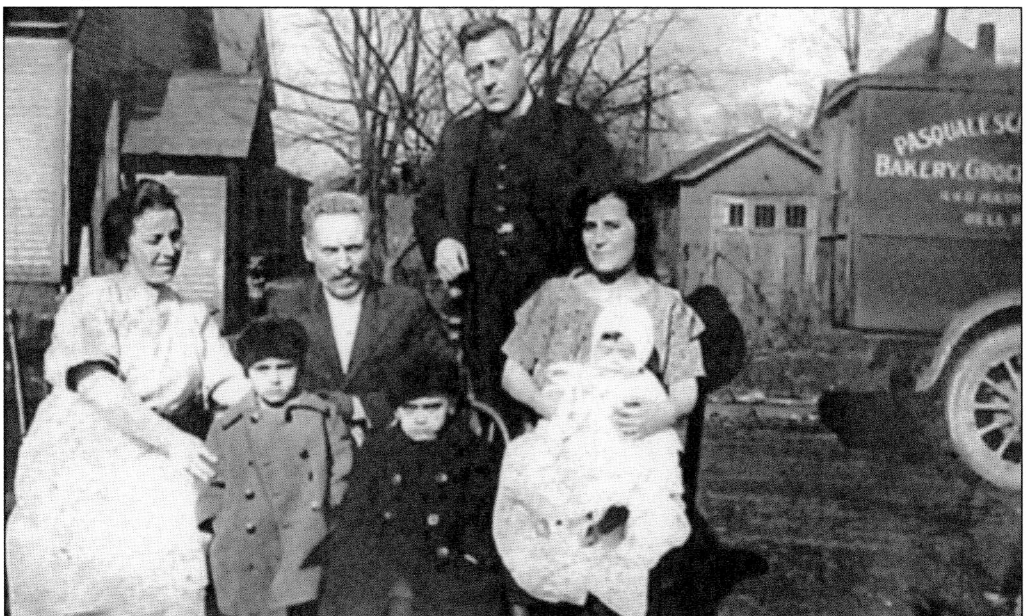

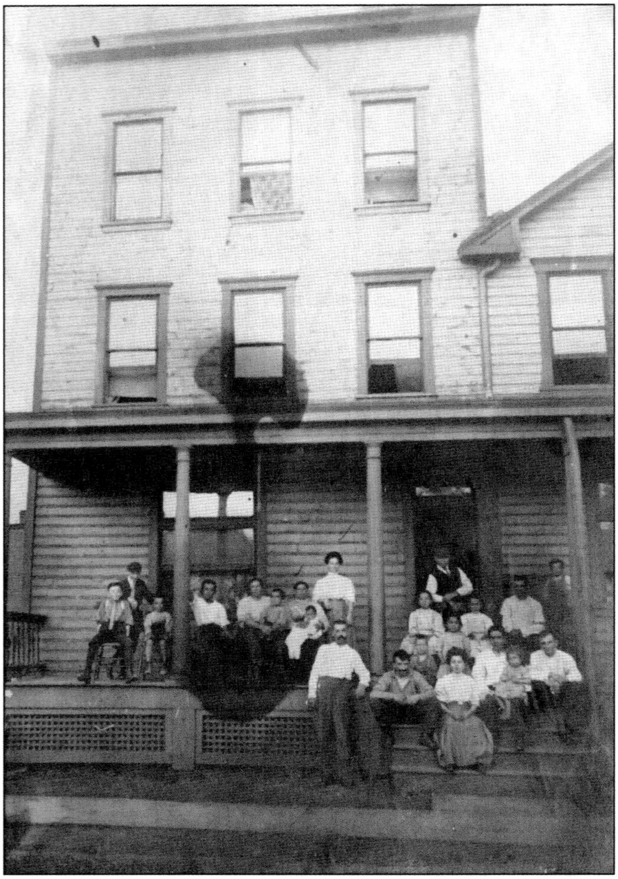

DINING OUT. Italian Americans established numerous restaurants throughout the Mahoning Valley, many of which are still in existence. The Steak House at 602 South Park Avenue in Warren, shown at left around 1910, was among the earliest in Trumbull County. In the early 20th century, several Italian Americans also lived above the facility; they are seen gathered on the front porch. The restaurant, renamed the Prime Steak House, became notorious when alleged mobster James Munsene was murdered in its barroom in 1941. The Mahoning Valley Restaurant (below), better known as the MVR, was established by Carmine Cassese in 1927. Still going strong over 80 years later, the restaurant is seen here in the 1940s, with Carmine Cassese seated near the entrance. (Left courtesy of Carl and Edith Ritch; below, courtesy of the Cassese family.)

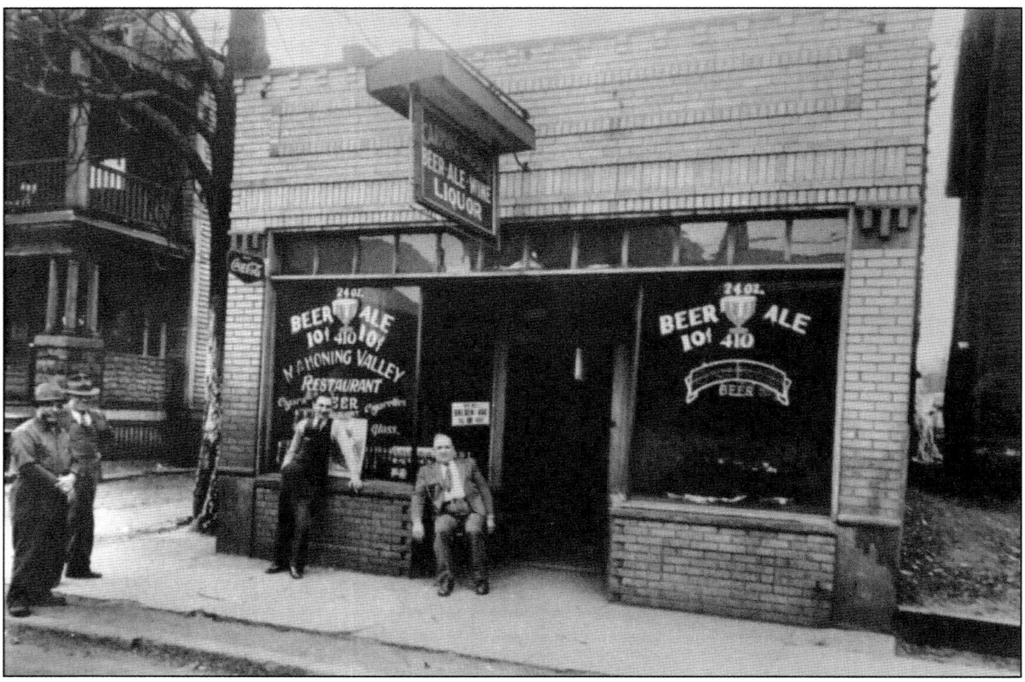

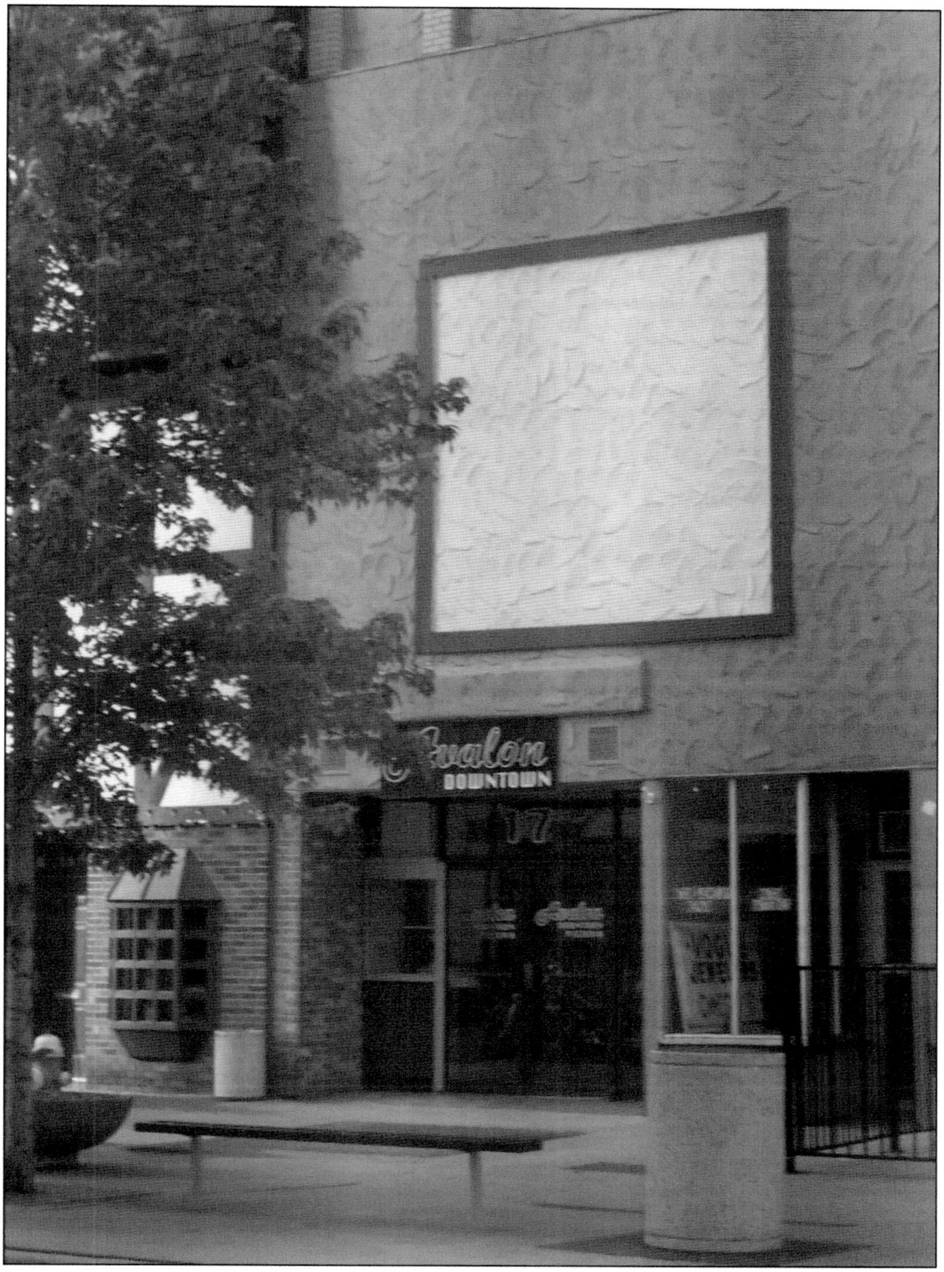

The Avalon. One of the area's favorite pizza places was the Avalon Gardens. Originally located on Belmont Avenue, "the Av" was the brainchild of Italian American immigrants James and Lena De Capita Massullo. James immigrated in 1912 and worked in several occupations, including as a barber and a steelworker. The family story is that Lena's sister, Irene, showed her photograph to James, and he sent for her to be his bride in 1920. The couple opened their establishment when Prohibition ended in 1933. The restaurant started life as a beer garden that also served food. The Av was known for its Brier Hill pizza and other Italian cuisine. Ownership of the Av changed hands several times until it finally closed in the 21st century. But that was not the end of the story. The Massullos' granddaughter Anne reopened the Av as a downtown Youngstown eatery—including the original pizza recipes.

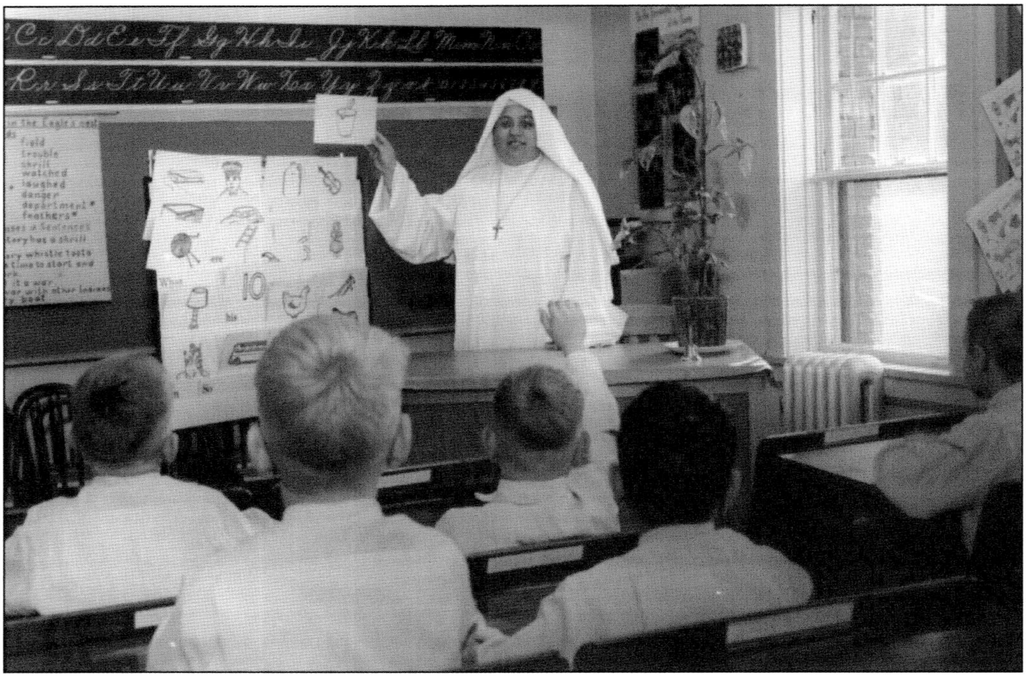

OBLATES AT WORK. The Oblate Sisters dedicated their lives to teaching and service. Sr. Mary Olimpia (above), a teacher at Our Lady of Perpetual Help School in McDonald, earned her teaching certificate at Youngstown University after her arrival in the United States from Italy in 1949. She is seen instructing the children in reading. Below, Sr. Mary Augustina (left) operates a mangle, and Sr. Mary Giuliva is sewing. The work was part of their daily tasks as they cared for the sisters in their community and their boarding students from nearby St. Anthony's parish. Part of their mission also includes caring for elderly, retired priests. (Both, courtesy of the Oblate Sisters.)

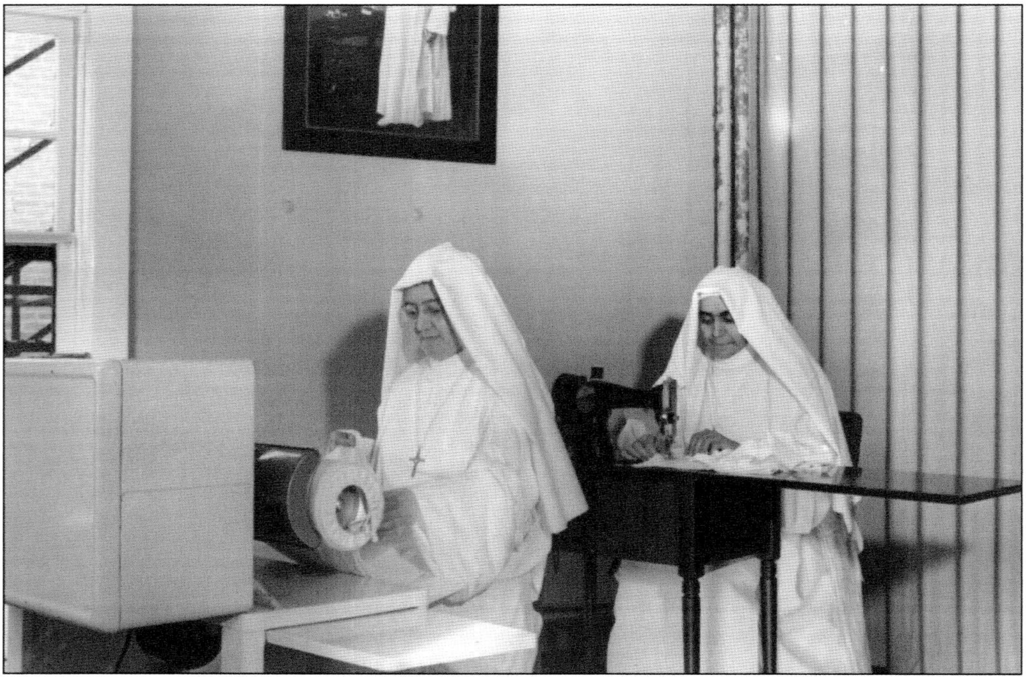

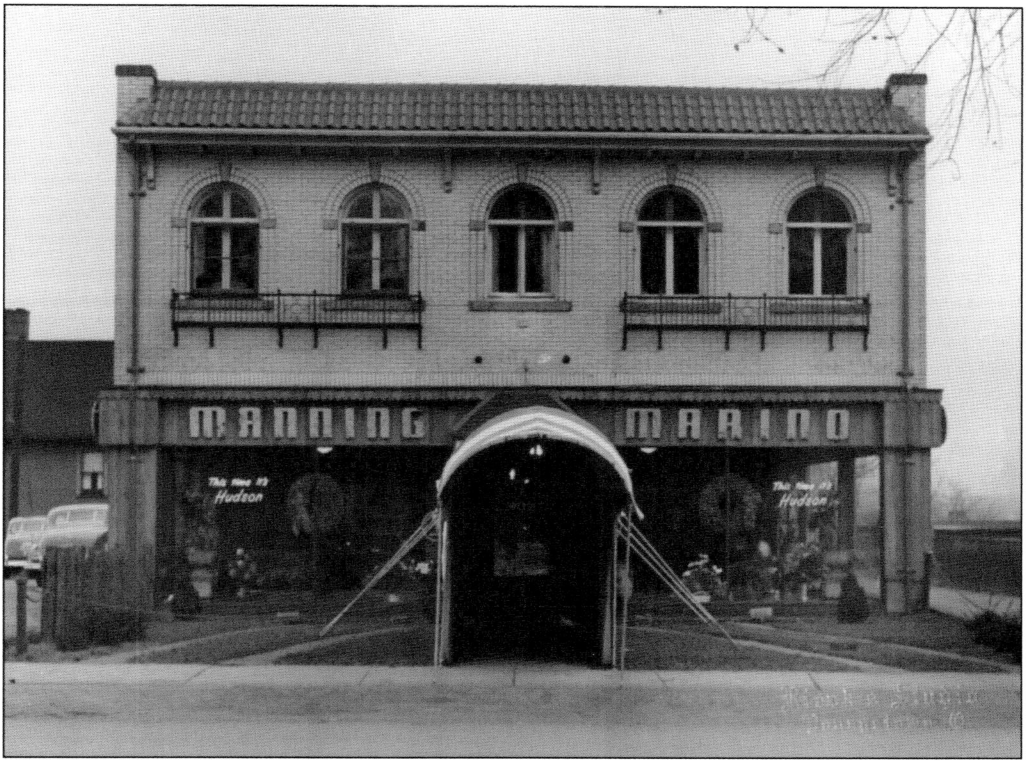

MARINO DEALERSHIP. Born in 1901 to Italian immigrants Mary and Fortunato Marino, Andrew J. Marino tried his hand at several occupations. From 1920 to 1930, he was a partner in Marino & Boggins Plumbing & Heating Company, located on West Federal Street in Youngstown. In 1924, he opened an automobile business, becoming one of the youngest Pontiac dealers in the nation at the newly formed Marino Motors. These two photographs were taken in the 1940s, when the business was known as Manning & Marino Motors, dealers in Hudson automobiles. Above, the dealership is seen at its home on Wick Avenue. At right, Marino's daughter Anna Mae is in one of the new Hudson automobiles. (Both, courtesy of the Marino and Massullo families.)

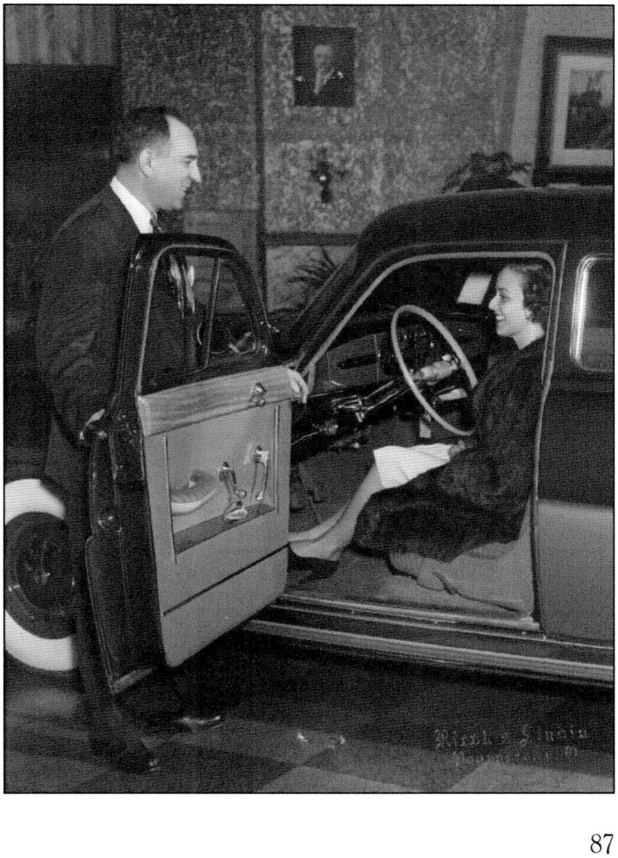

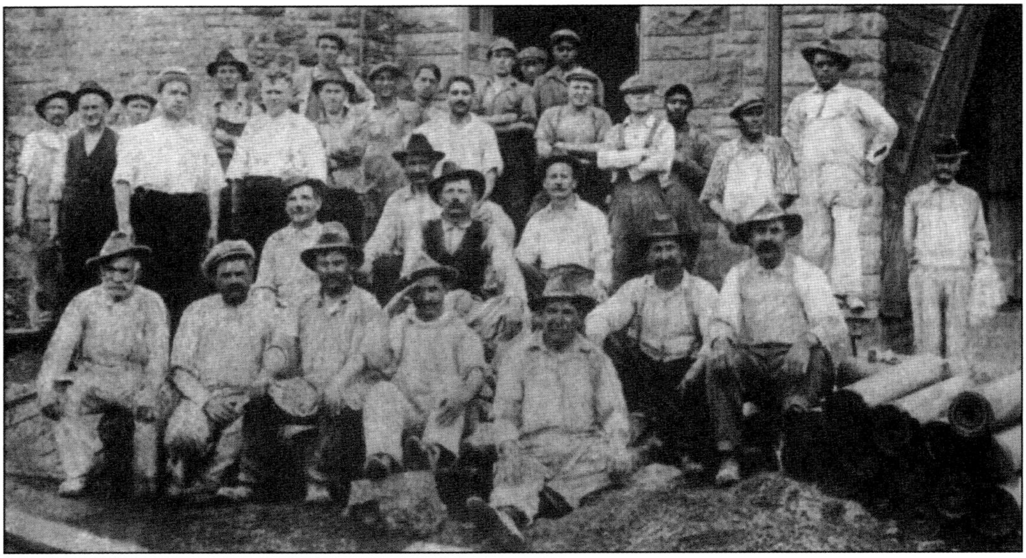

Stonemasons. While many Italian masons who worked with both brick and stone secured employment in local mills relining furnaces, others worked in the building trades. In the early 20th century, the Mahoning Valley was booming. More people meant more structures, and masons were in demand. Above, stonemasons pose in front of City Hospital, later Southside Hospital, on Oak Hill Avenue. The Italian American–owned firm of Pesa Construction often employed Italian masons; in the 1930s, the company built the chapel and gate at Forest Lawn Cemetery in Boardman. Italian stonemasons also worked on a large Depression-era project, the Main Building of the newly coined Youngstown College (below). Now called Jones Hall, the structure is seen in 1931, when it was completed. (Above, courtesy of OHC-YHCIL; below, courtesy of YSU.)

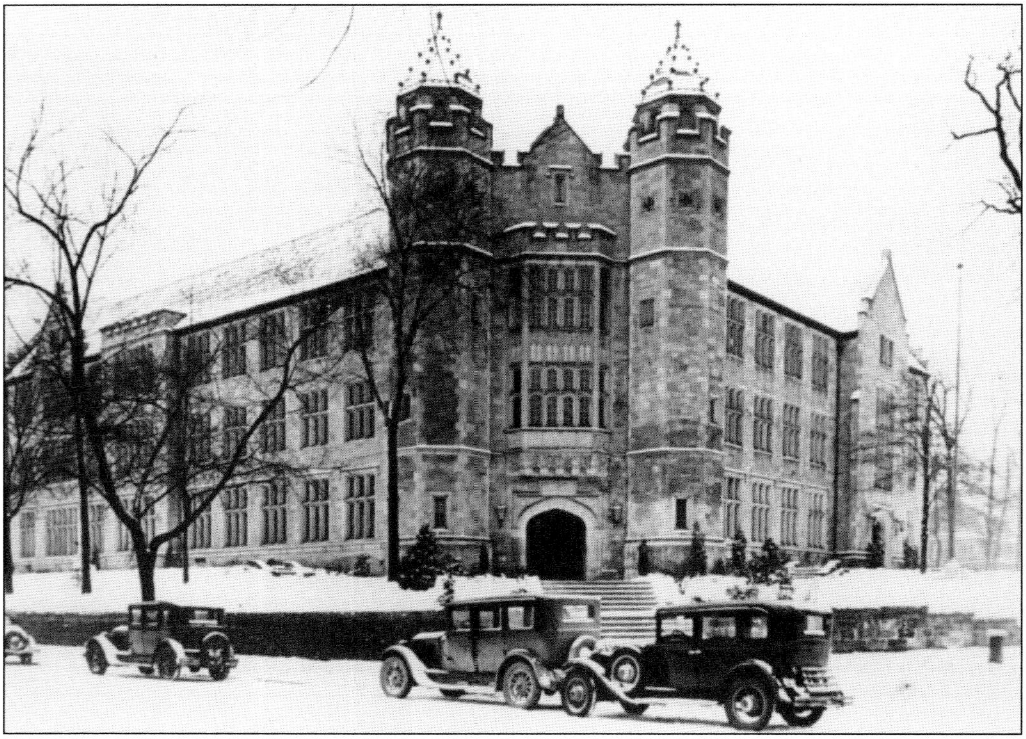

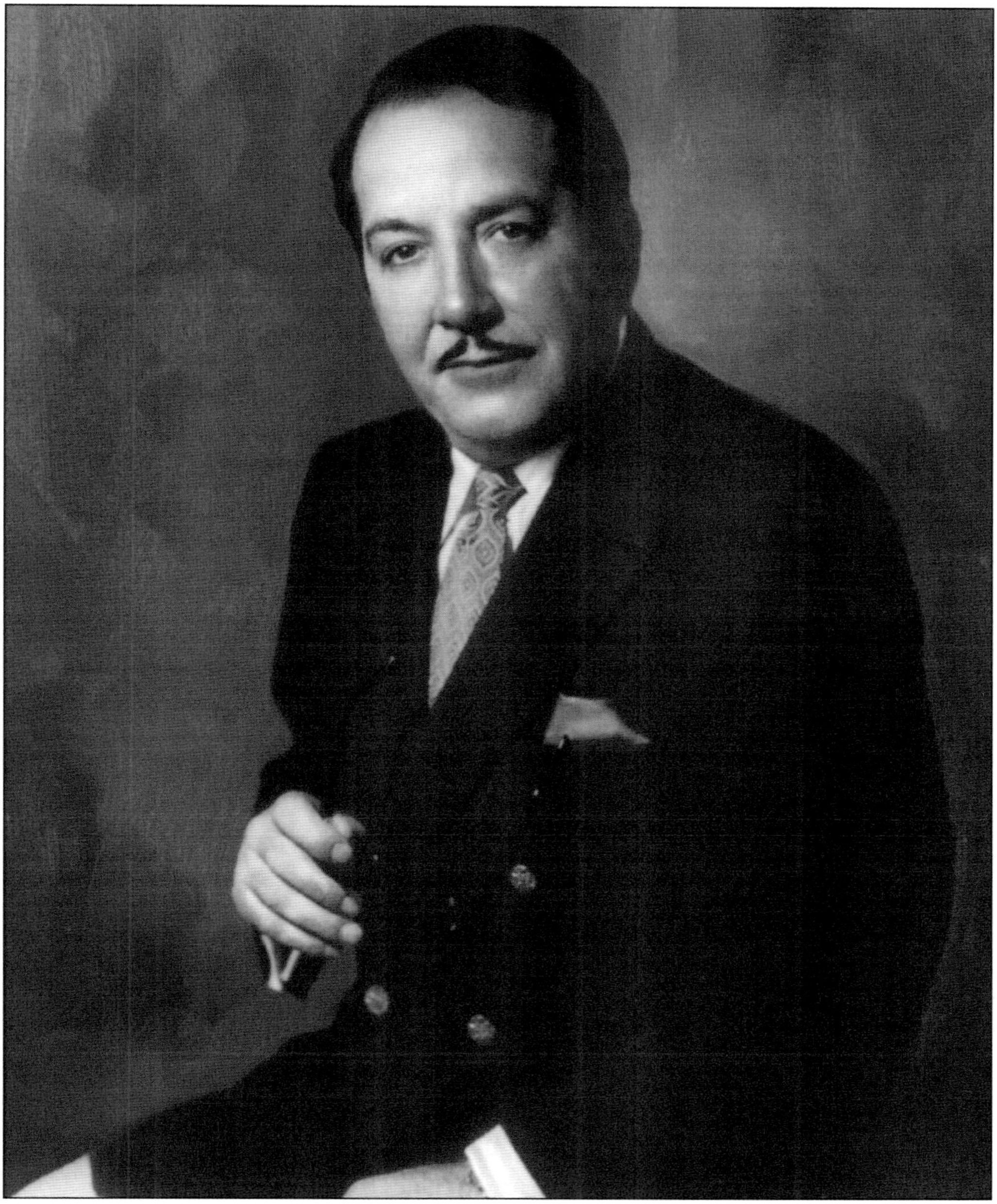

MODERN RETAIL. The Mahoning Valley boasts the presence of two of the largest retail developers in the United States: Italian Americans William Cafaro and Edward J. DeBartolo Sr. Both hailed from Youngstown—Cafaro from the east side and DeBartolo from Smoky Hollow. William Cafaro (pictured) was born in 1913, the son of Anthony and Flora Diana Cafaro. He grew up in the Hazelton district in the shadow of the Republic Iron & Steel plant and was a graduate of East High School. Cafaro worked his way up at Republic, becoming a foreman. At the same time, he and his brother Joey operated a restaurant, the Ritz Bar and Grille, on the city's east side. Cafaro began buying up real estate in the 1940s. By the 1950s, he developed retail outlets, including grocery stores and strip plazas. His crowning achievement was the opening in 1969 of Eastwood Mall in Niles, one of the first "super regional" malls. Cafaro became a philanthropist and was especially generous to Youngstown State University. (Courtesy of Anthony Cafaro Sr.)

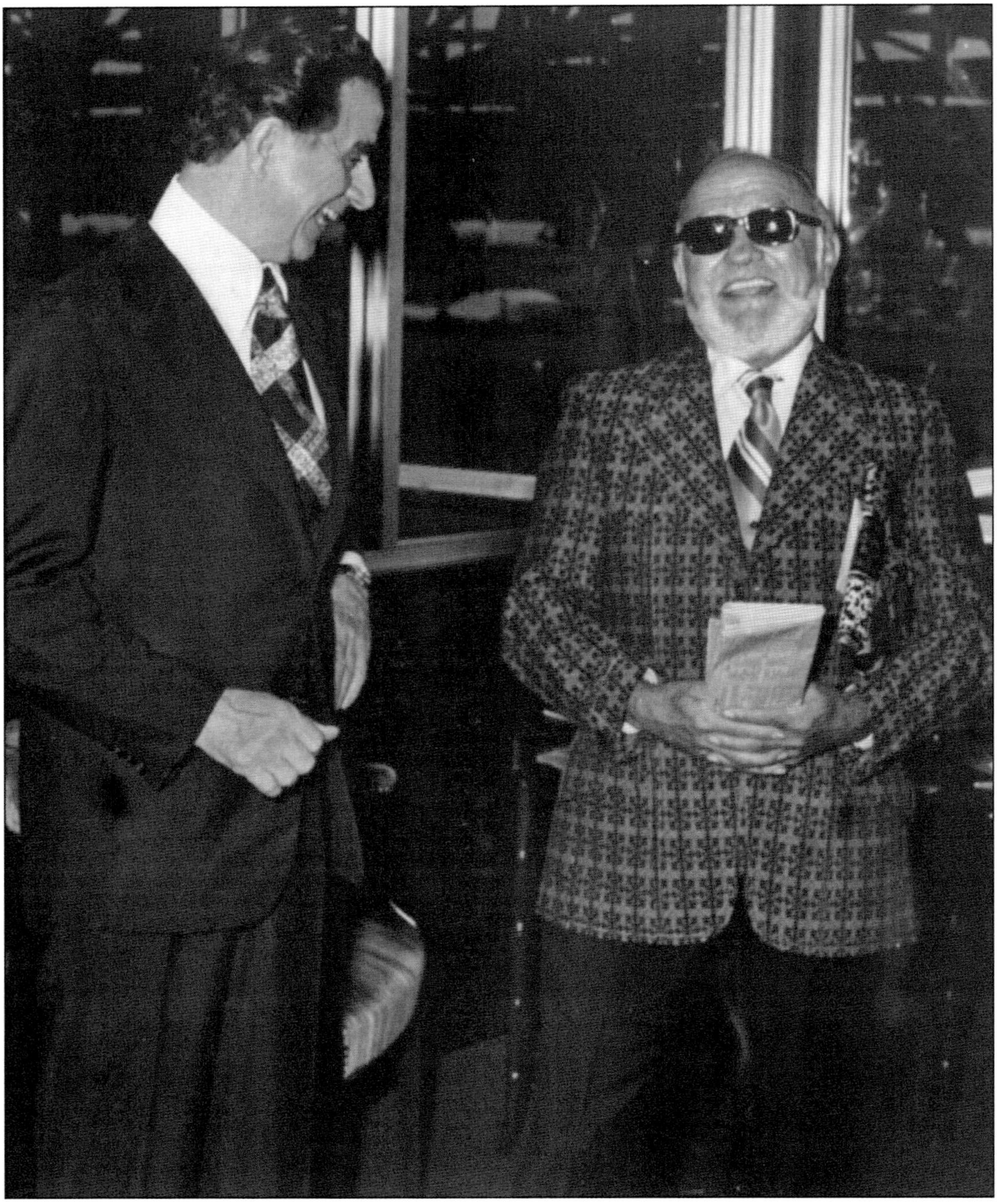

Mall King. Edward J. DeBartolo was born in 1909; his biological father, Anthony Paonessa, died two months before Edward's birth. His mother, Rose Villani, remarried Michael DeBartolo in 1911. From an early age, Edward DeBartolo worked in construction. He earned an engineering degree from the University of Notre Dame. During World War II, he served in the US Army Corps of Engineers, putting his education and experience to good use. DeBartolo took advantage of the postwar trend to suburbia; his was one of the first major construction companies to build primarily retail stores. He started with plazas and then began building enclosed malls. At one point, he was the industry's leader, owning about 10 percent of the mall space in the nation. DeBartolo gave generously to numerous charities; buildings at both Notre Dame and Youngstown State University bear his name. He is seen here at left with his brother Frank, who was also his chief architect. (Courtesy of YSU.)

Six

Daily Life and Leisure

As Italian Americans settled into their new homes in the Mahoning Valley, their daily life was colored by the old traditions and adaptations to a new living situation. Many first-generation immigrants came from rural areas. Upon arriving in the Valley, they had to adapt to living in an urban environment. For those who were wage earners, their work was now attuned to the clock, as opposed to the rhythms of nature. In their new neighborhoods, they were not farmers—but nearly everyone cultivated a garden. Most women who did not work outside the home had to maintain the house for their family and their boarders. Despite the hard work, there was time for leisure activities. Children found time to play; many of them learned American games, like baseball and kick the can. Adults spent time visiting over food and drink; they also gathered to play cards, including *tre e sette*, as well as bocce, which they brought with them from their native land. Italian Americans also gathered at local entertainment venues, including movie theaters, bowling alleys, dance halls, and, of course, Idora Park. The amusement park hosted an Italian Day nearly every season beginning in the 1930s. As the community grew more prosperous, many Italian Americans took vacations away from town. One of the most popular venues to escape the summer heat was Geneva-on-the-Lake in Ashtabula County, Ohio. By midcentury, Florida became a popular destination as well. In the second half of the 20th century, many Italian Americans opted to journey to the old country, to revisit or discover their roots.

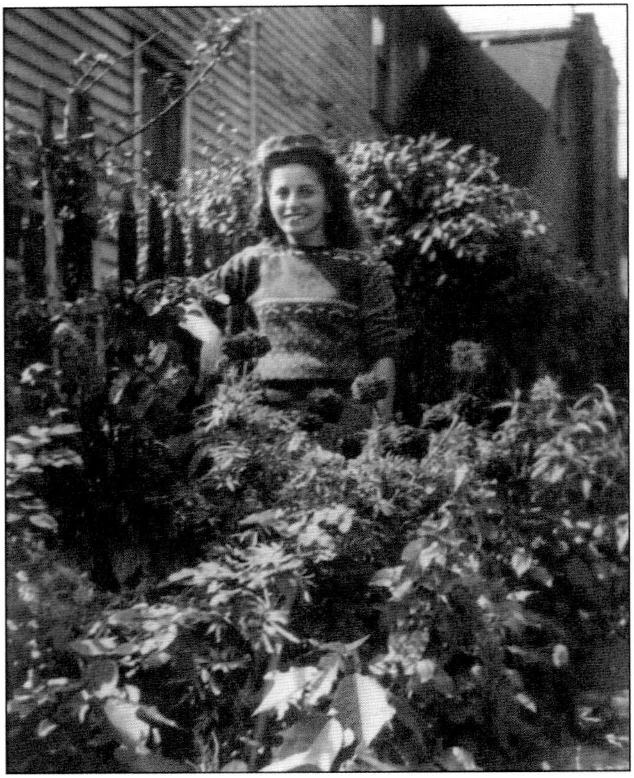

Fruit of the Vine. Many of the Italians who settled in the Mahoning Valley hailed from southern Italy's largely rural areas. When they resettled in an urban area, they turned to creating gardens in their backyards. They grew all kinds of crops, including tomatoes, peppers, and beans. They also cultivated pear, peach, and apple trees. Despite the colder temperatures, many gardens boasted a fig tree, which either had to be wrapped in tarps, or, more likely, buried to withstand the harsh Ohio winters. Shown at left is a garden in Smoky Hollow. Italian Americans also brought with them their tradition of winemaking. Below, a DiLallo family baby is posed against the boxes of grapes that would be used to make that season's wine in the early 1950s. (Both, courtesy of Anthony Worrellia.)

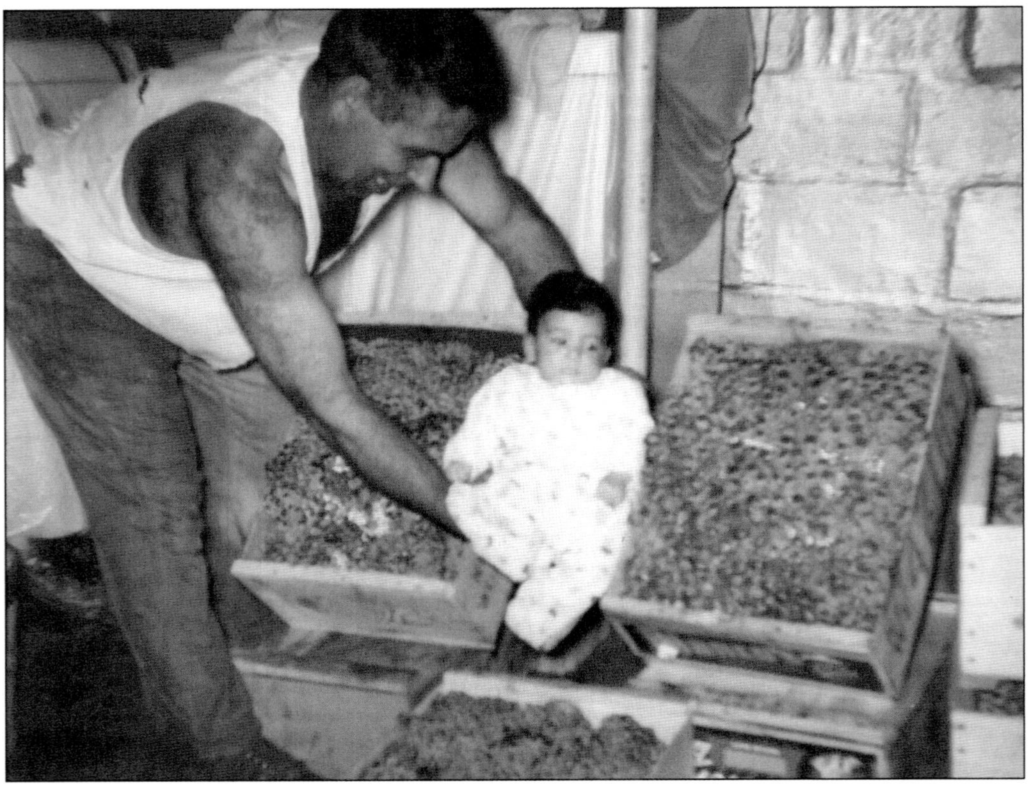

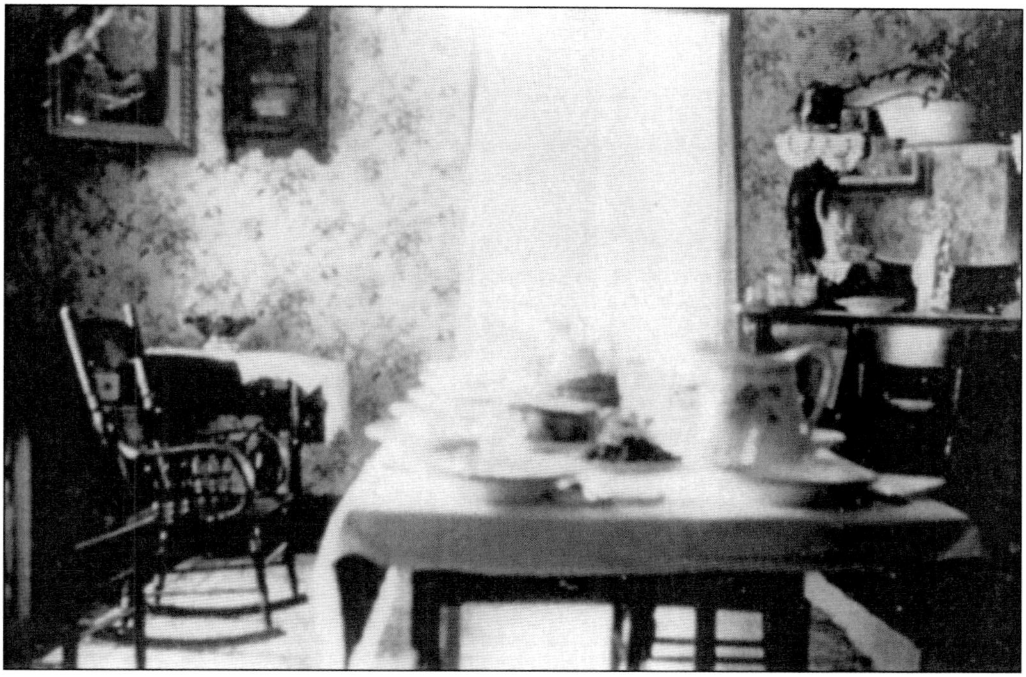

Eating at Home. Italian Americans are known for their generosity and hospitality. Meals were meant to be shared around the dining room or kitchen table. Sunday and holiday meals were especially important; the food and drink were plentiful, and the best china, crystal, and silverware were used. Shown above is the dining room at 807 Highland Avenue in Warren, where the D'Altorio and Ricciuti family lived. At right is the dining room of the Worrellia house in Smoky Hollow in the 1950s, ready for Christmas dinner. (Above, courtesy of Carl and Edith Ritch; right, courtesy of Anthony Worrellia.)

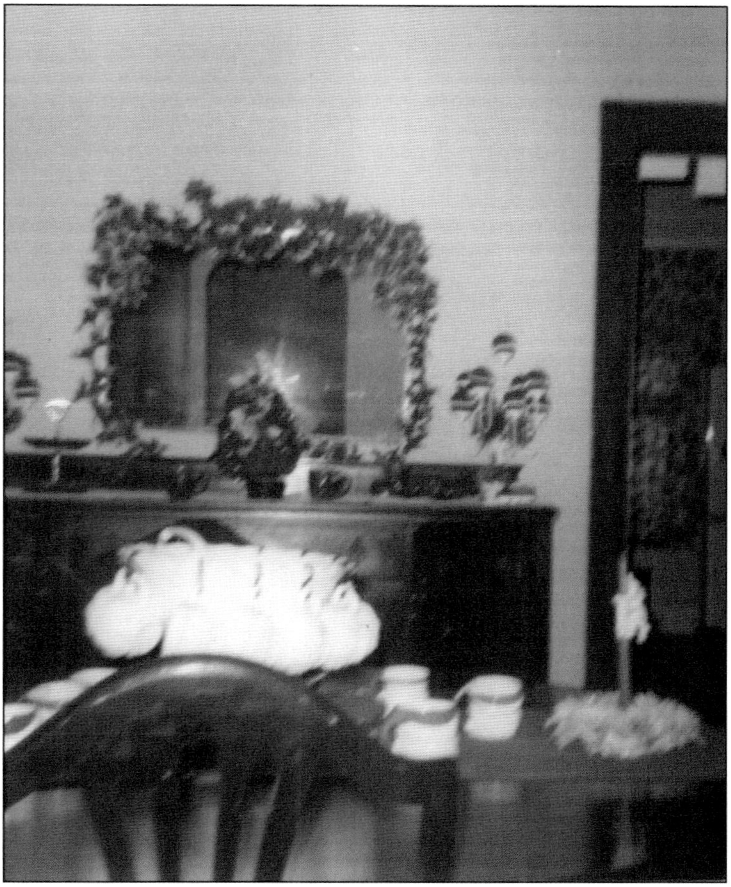

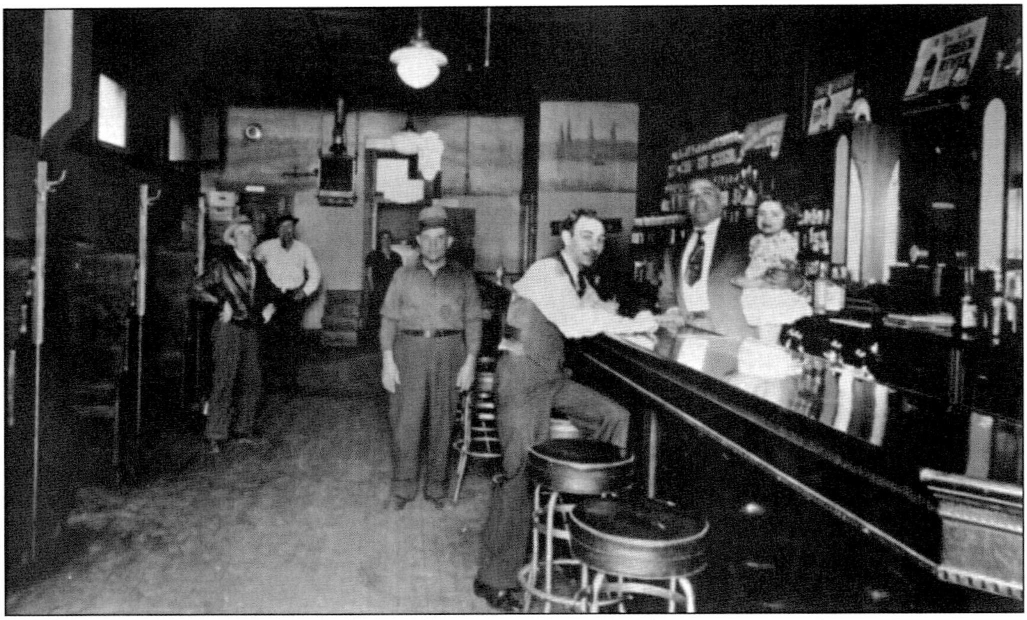

Gather at the Bar. At the beginning of the 20th century, the American saloon was important as a place where working-class men, including Italian Americans, could gather after a hard day on the job. It was not just about the shot and the beer; it was about socializing with friends. Progressive-era reformers distrusted the saloons, seeing them as places where the unruly masses could only get into trouble. These reformers eventually succeeded in legislating that grand failure known as Prohibition, which was directed at the immigrant working class. Once people could again drink legally, places like the MVR (above) flourished. A well-stocked home bar was also important. Below, Frank Listorti serves his friends and family in the mid-1950s. (Above, courtesy of the Cassese family; below, courtesy of Frank Pape.)

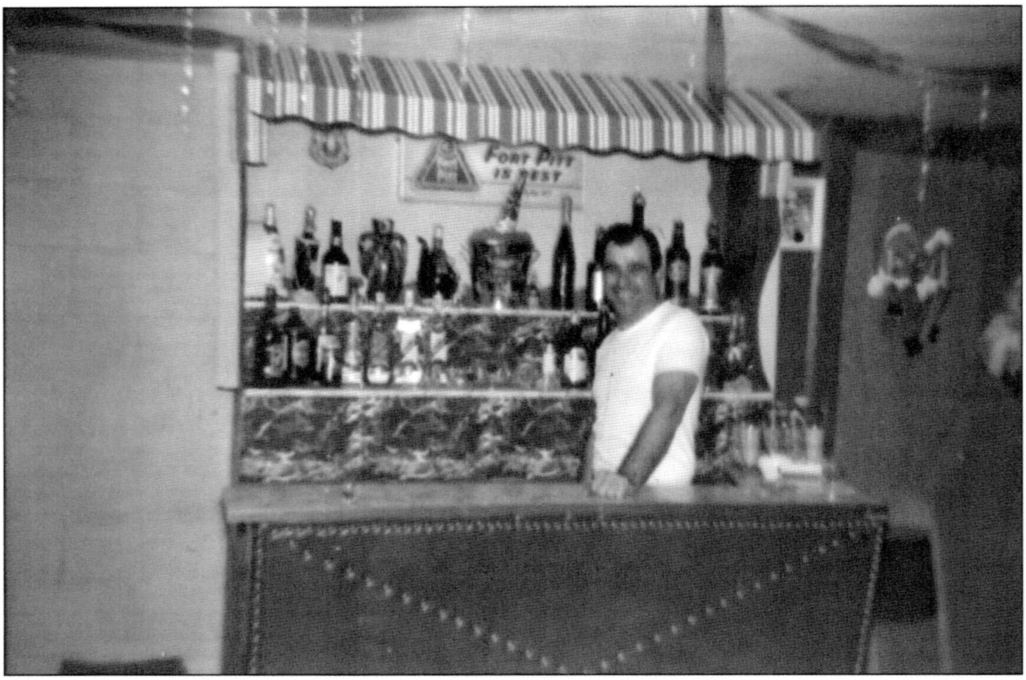

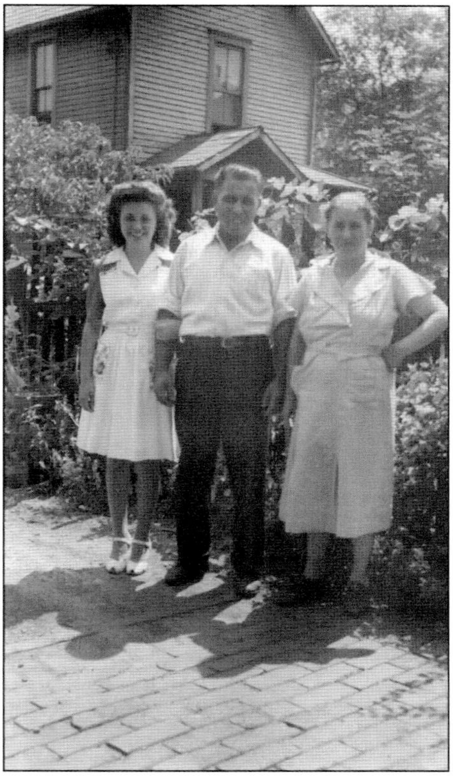

Relaxing at Home. For many Italian Americans, especially until the middle of the 20th century, home was usually where one relaxed. Going out cost money, so it was reserved for special occasions. Families found all kinds of ways to spend their leisure time. Sometimes, it might be taking pictures by the house in beautiful weather, like the members of the DiLallo family at right. From left to right, Rose, Attilio, and Philomena DiLallo stand by their garden in Smoky Hollow. Below, children have a ball in an inflatable pool in their backyard on Helena Street on Youngstown's south side. From left to right are Angela Pasquinelli, Mary Pasquinelli (holding Paul Pasquinelli), and Rosanne Pasquinelli. (Right, courtesy of Anthony Worrellia; below, courtesy of Rosanne Pasquinelli Dando.)

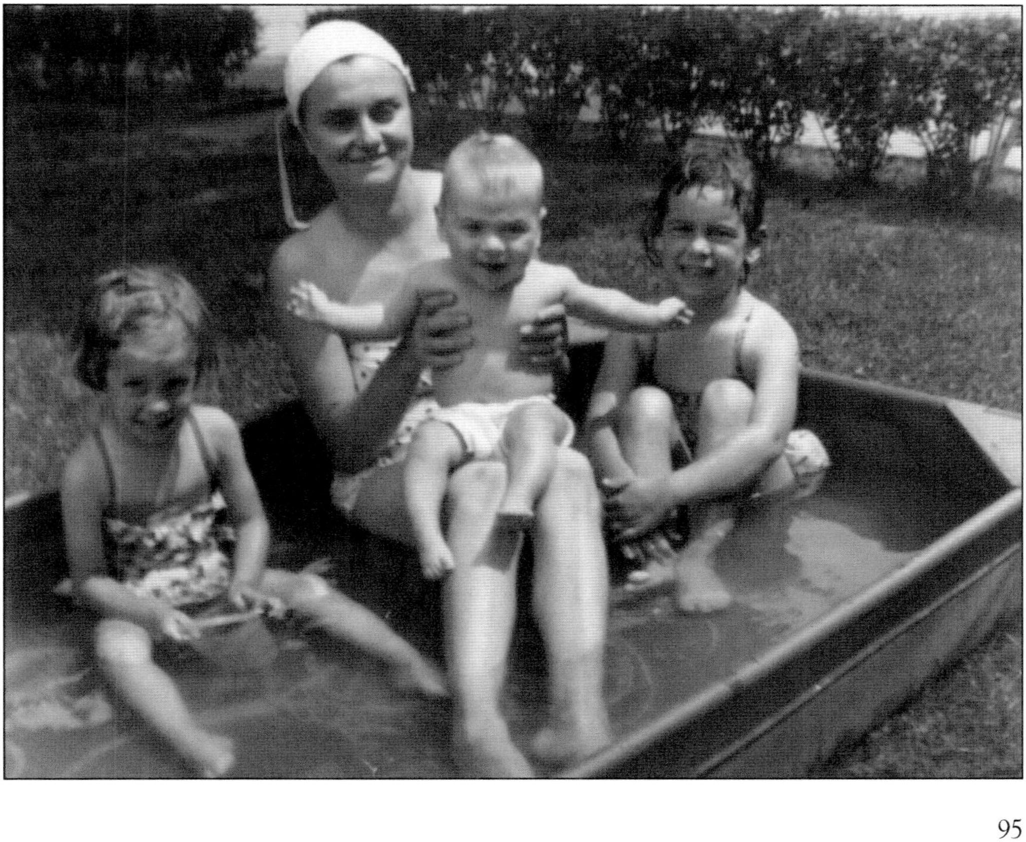

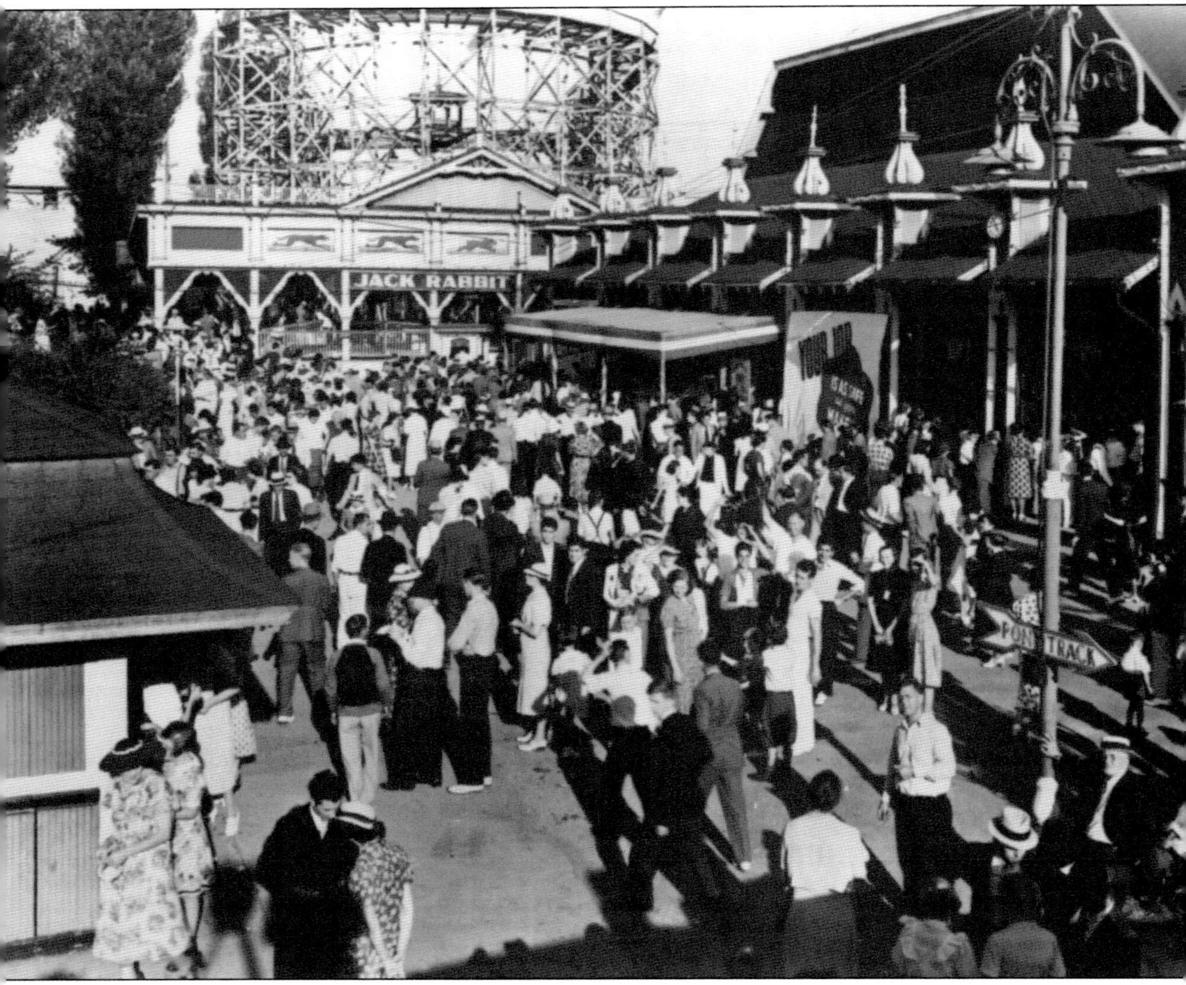

Labor Day at Idora. One of the special places where Italian Americans joined in the fun was Idora Park. Located on Youngstown's south side, Idora Park started life as a trolley park. Opening on Decoration Day in 1899, Terminal Park was the brainchild of the management of the Park & Falls Street Railway Company. In the early 20th century, hundreds of these trolley parks dotted the American landscape and were used to lure customers to their line during off-peak hours, such as evenings and weekends. Renamed Idora Park in 1900, the site became an important regional attraction. Groups from as far away as Detroit held picnics at the park. Most of the local steel firms, and later the unions, held annual company picnics at Idora. Italian Americans were present at the park from its earliest years. A reporter for the *Youngstown Vindicator* commented in 1920 about the "polyglot nature" of the park, where myriad languages were heard. Idora Park is seen here on Labor Day 1939, sponsored by the YS&T Company. The people are milling around in front of the ballroom (right) and the Jack Rabbit roller coaster (rear). (Courtesy of OHC-YHCIL.)

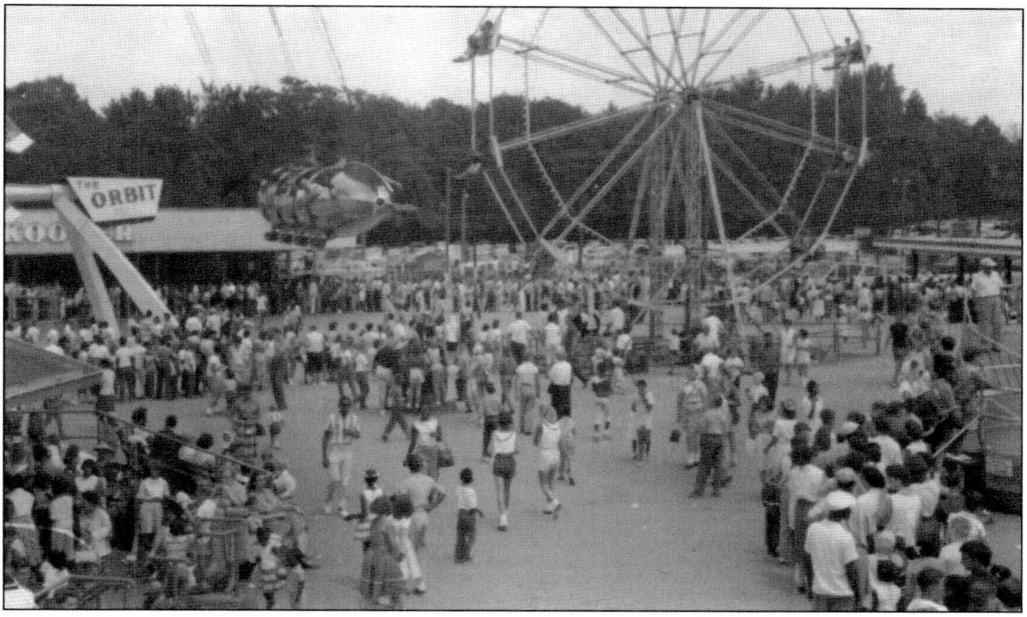

CELEBRATING ETHNIC HERITAGE. By the 1930s, Idora Park set days aside for the Mahoning Valley's various ethnic groups. Italian Americans had their day every summer at Idora, and they brought their own food to the park's picnic grounds—usually pasta and all the trimmings for lunch and American fare of hamburgers and hot dogs for dinner. Ethnic music and dancing were also featured on these days. Idora Park is seen in these 1950s photographs. The above photograph, facing north, shows the midway, with the Ferris wheel in the center and the rocket ships on the left. The below photograph, facing north on the midway, shows games of chance and concession stands. The peaks of the world-class roller coaster the Wildcat rise over the other structures. (Both, courtesy of OHC-YHCIL.)

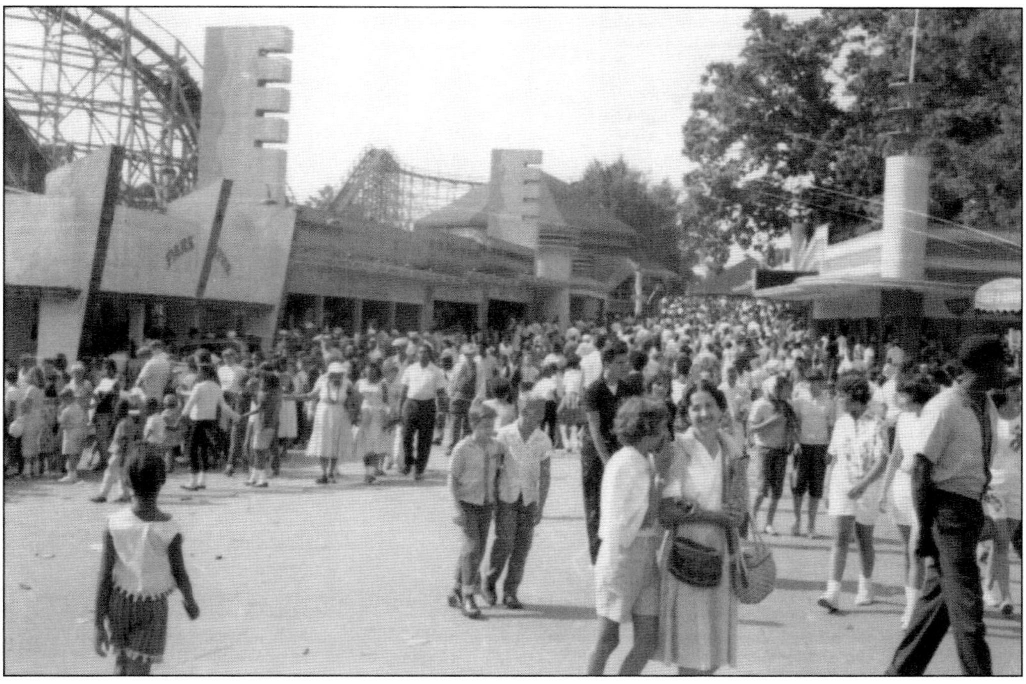

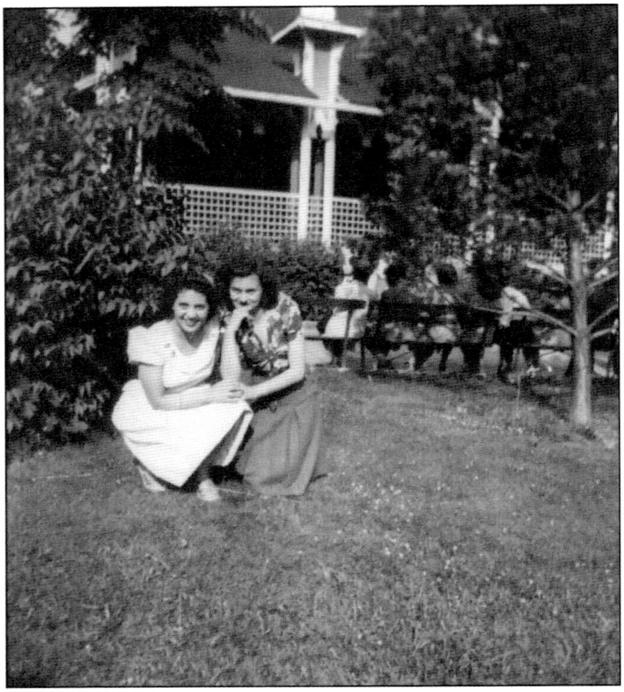

Ladies Go to Idora. By the 1940s, young women ventured to Idora with their friends. The exciting rides were not the only attraction. At left, two young women, Mary Pasquinelli (left) and a friend, relax on the lawn in front of the Idora Park Ballroom. This venue boasted one of the largest dance floors in the region and hosted the very best in big bands, including Duke Ellington and the Jimmy Dorsey Orchestra. During World War II, soldiers who were in boot camp near New Castle, Pennsylvania, were brought to the park to dance with the area's young women. Below, Clotilda DiLullo (left) and her friends Helen (center) and Lucy pose in the Idora Park photo booth in 1942. (Left, courtesy of Rosanne Pasquinelli Dando.)

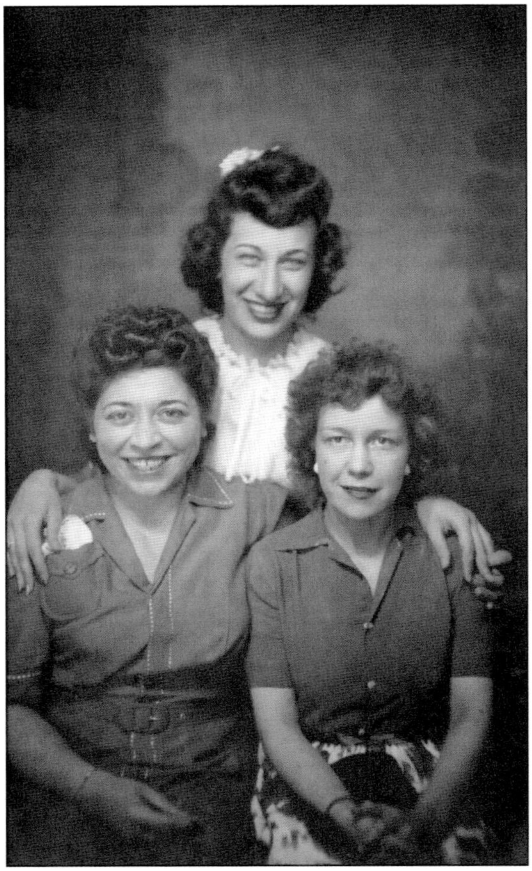

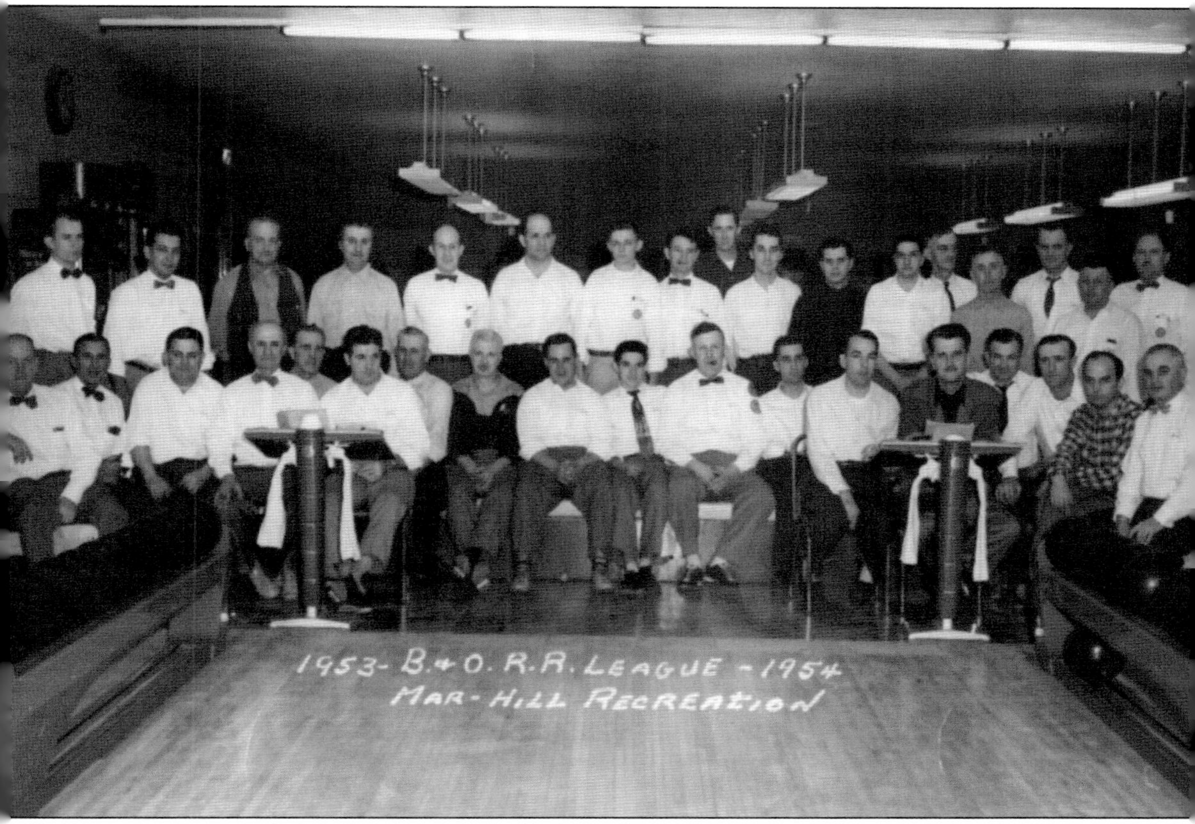

Bowling. Games of all kinds were popular in the Italian American community. On many a lazy afternoon, groups of adults and children could be found playing bocce, the Italian version of lawn bowling. Even today, there are a number of bocce leagues in the community. Bocce, however, is an outdoor sport and can only be played in good weather. In the colder months, indoor bowling became popular throughout the Mahoning Valley, especially among working-class people. Many workplaces sponsored all kinds of sports teams for baseball, basketball, and bowling. Shown here is the B&O Railroad bowling league of 1953–1954 at the Mar-Hill Lanes, located on Market Street in Youngstown. Seated at center, to the right of the only woman in the photograph, is Geno Pasquinelli, one of the stars of the league. (Courtesy of Rosanne Pasquinelli Dando.)

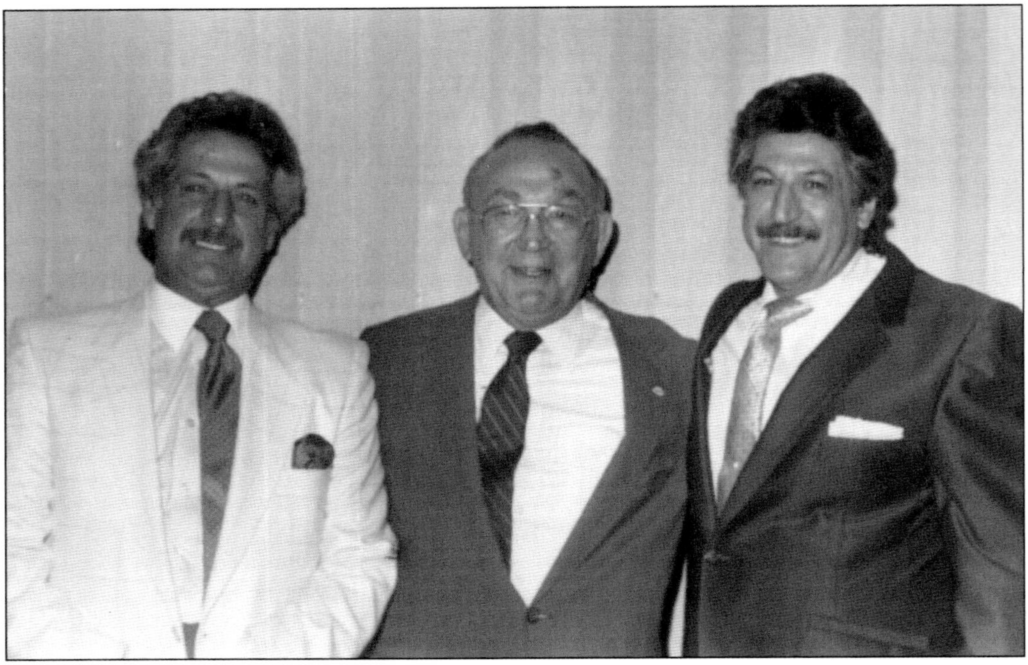

Boxing. The Mahoning Valley's Italian Americans have a long association with professional and semiprofessional boxing. The tradition is so strong that there is a proliferation of boxing groups at all levels, professional and amateur, including Golden Gloves. One of the staunchest supporters of the sport was Sal Marino. He was the sports editor and writer for several area newspapers, including the *Review*, the *Newton Falls Herald*, the *Niles Times*, and the *Vindicator*. In the above photograph, Marino (right) poses with Leo Marino (left) and Carmen Basilio. The Marino brothers, with Bill Ruman, founded the Legends of Leather Boxing Hall of Fame in the 1980s. At right, Marino speaks to a group of boxing enthusiasts. (Both, courtesy of the Marino family.)

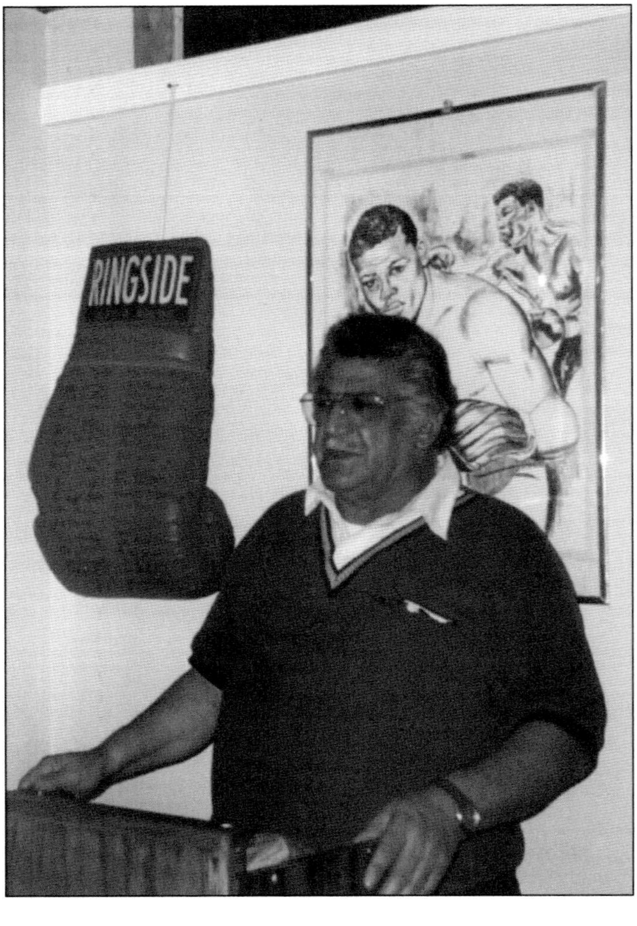

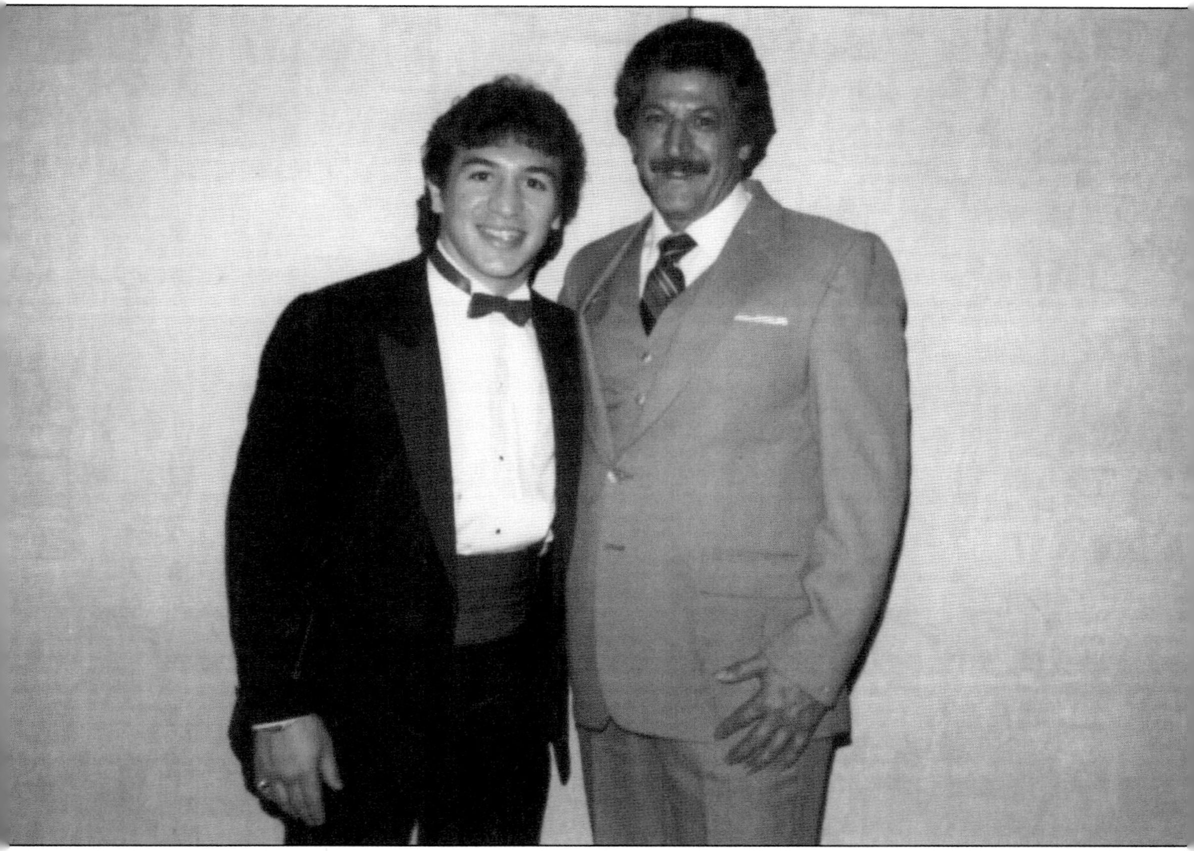

Boom Boom. One of the best-known professional prizefighters to emerge from the Mahoning Valley was Italian American Ray "Boom Boom" Mancini. He was born in Youngstown in 1961. Ray's father, Leonard, the original "Boom Boom," was also a boxer. Ray began fighting as an amateur lightweight in 1977, compiling a stellar 43 wins in Golden Gloves competition. He won his first World Boxing Association title in 1982, defeating reigning champion Arturo Frias in the first round. Since his last fight in 1992, Mancini turned to film, producing several documentaries, including *Youngstown Still Standing* in 2010. In the 1980s, Mancini was inducted into the Italian American Sports Hall of Fame. Here, Mancini (left) poses with sportswriter Sal Marino at the induction ceremony. (Courtesy of the Marino family.)

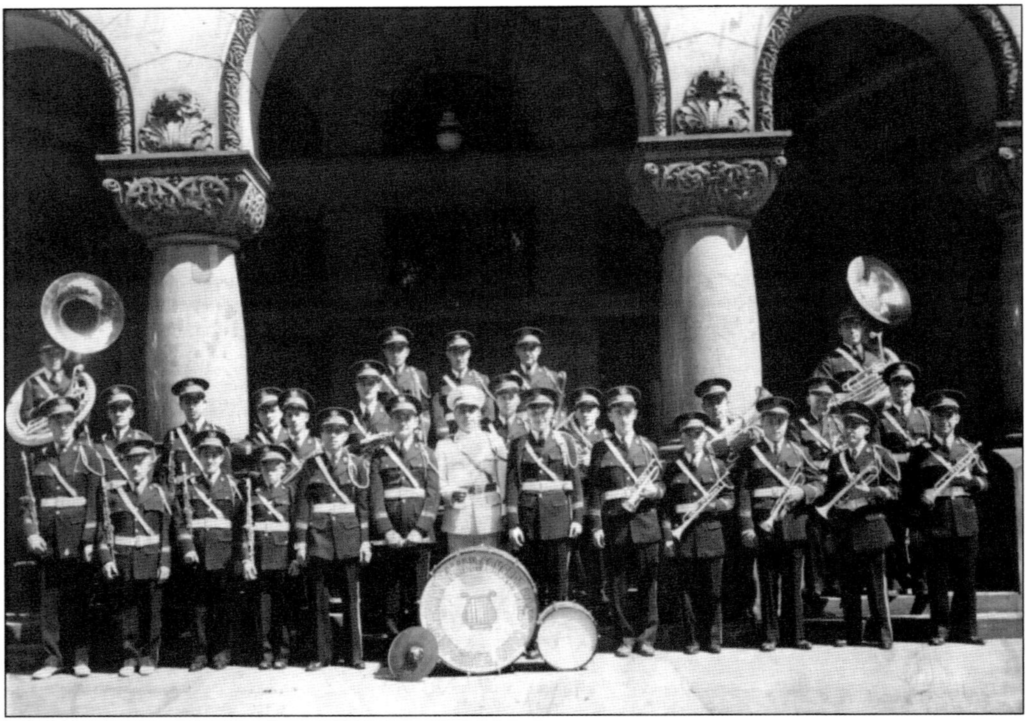

BOYS IN THE BAND. Music has always played an important role in the Italian American community. Above, members of the Warren Italian Band pose in front of the Trumbull County Courthouse in 1936. Below, the Niles Concert Band, many of whose members were Italian American, gathered in front of the Niles Municipal Pool on Independence Day 1946. (Above, courtesy of the Warren Italian American Heritage Festival Committee; below, courtesy of Joe Merlo.)

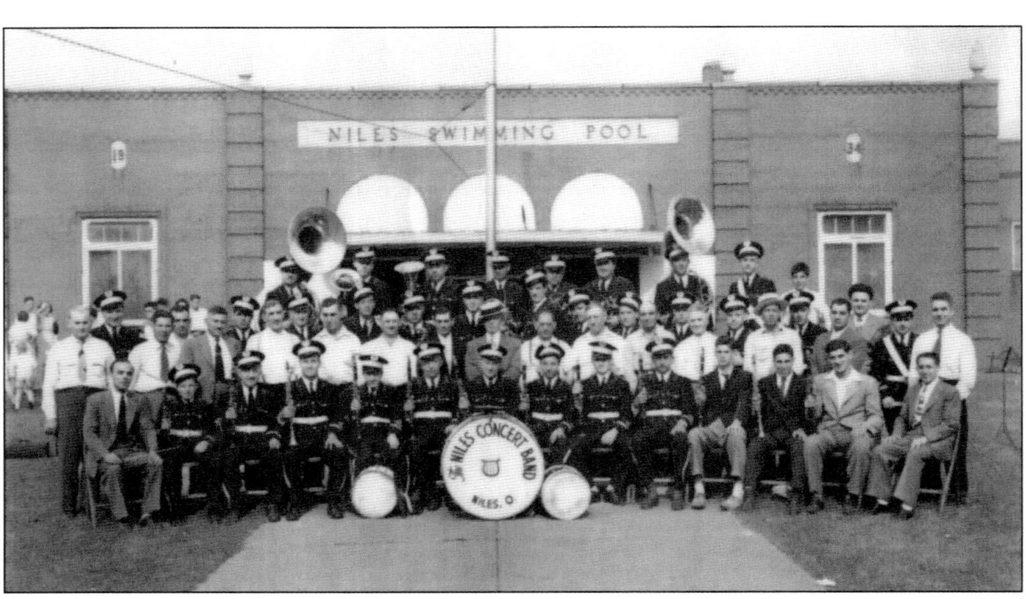

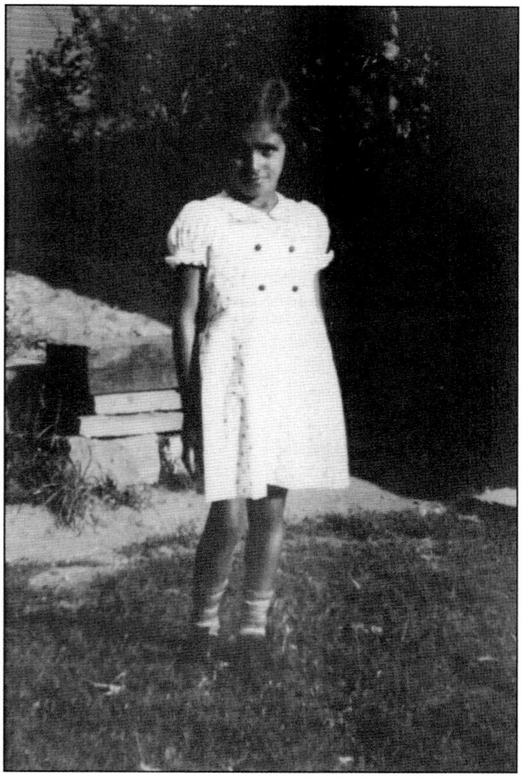

Going on Vacation. In the 20th century, as Americans in general became more prosperous, and as paid vacations became a benefit in the workplace, more people took time off for vacations. Like their fellow Americans, Italian Americans took advantage of this leave time and planned a vacation away from home. In some cases, they did not go far. The D'Altorio family of Warren had relatives in nearby Ravenna, Ohio. Edith D'Altorio's parents sent her on summer vacation to Ravenna. At right, Edith poses by herself. Below, she is with her aunt Mary Bevilaqua in July 1938. (Both, courtesy of Carl and Edith Ritch.)

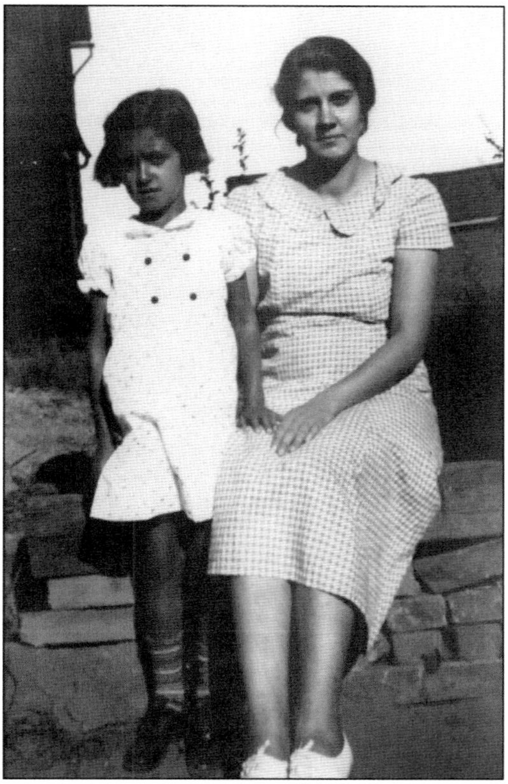

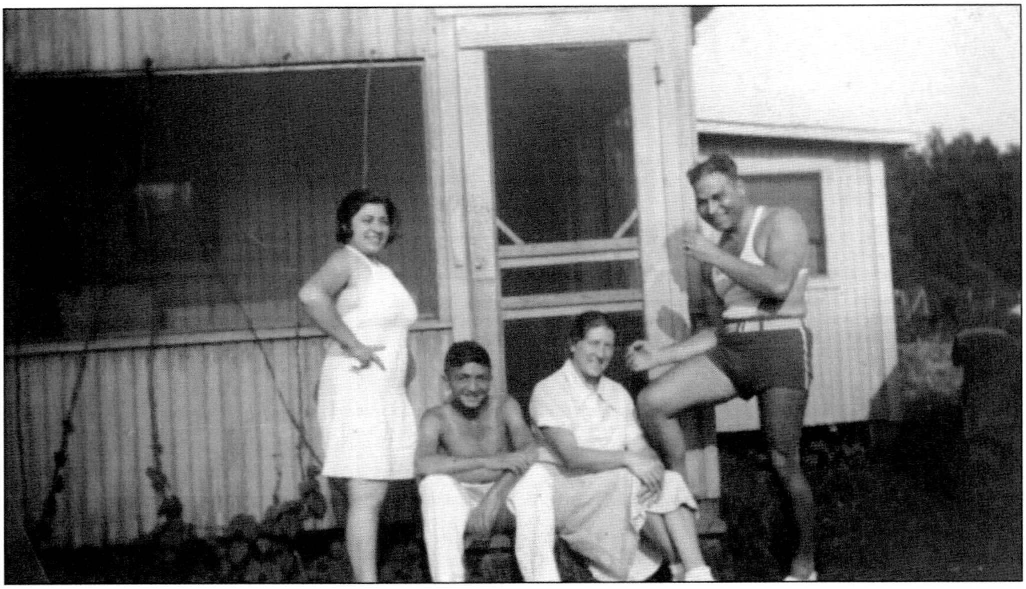

GENEVA-ON-THE-LAKE. Some Italian American families ventured a little farther from home for their summer vacations. One of the most popular places to beat the heat was Geneva-on-the-Lake, a resort town on Lake Erie in Ashtabula County. Families could rent cabins on or near the lake and spend lazy days relaxing in the water, picnicking, and strolling on the beach. In 1931, the DeSantis family rented a cabin at Geneva-on-the-Lake. While Venturina and John DeSantis had no children of their own, they shared their vacation with the children of the DiLullo family, who lived next door to them. Above, posing in front of their cabin are, from left to right, Clotilda DiLullo, Joe DiLullo, Venturina DeSantis, and John DeSantis. Below, from left to right, Clotilda, Joe, and John frolic in Lake Erie.

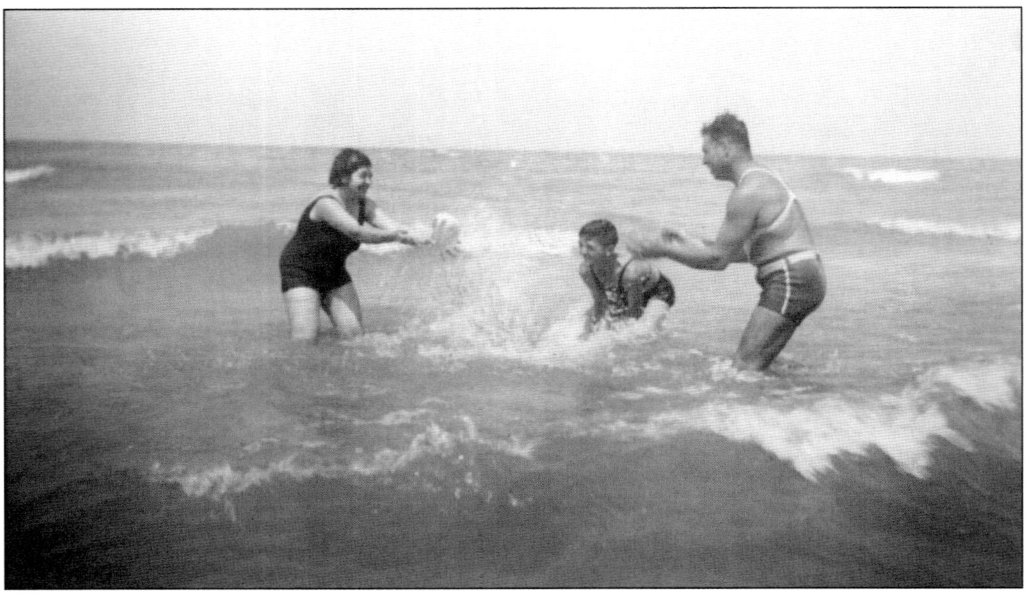

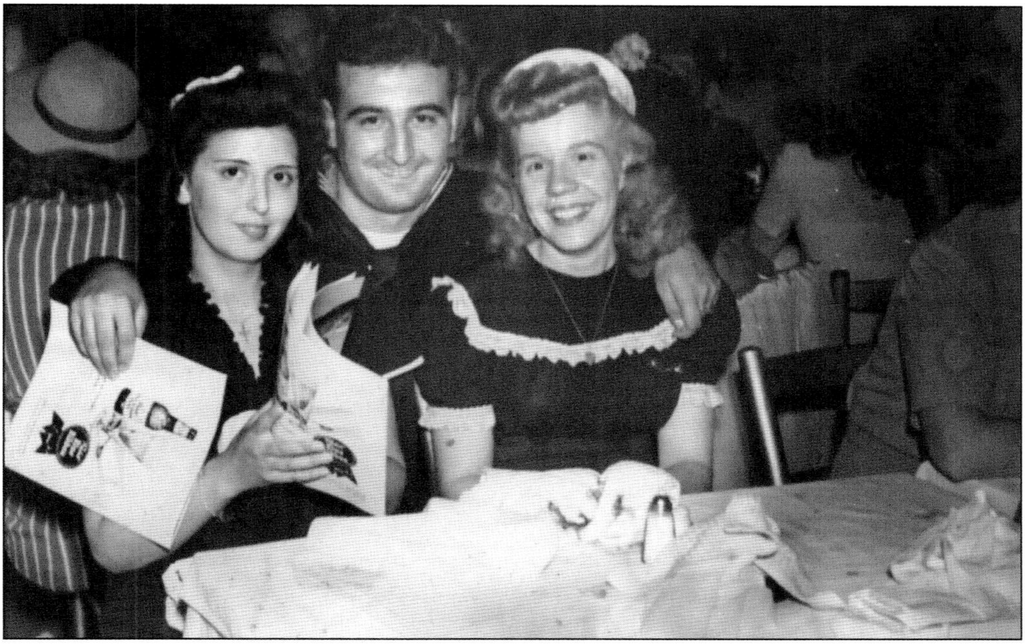

The Big Apple. New York City was a popular location for a getaway. Youngstown provided convenient train service to New York and other cities at reasonable prices. With the end of the Great Depression and the arrival of wartime prosperity, the train was a popular and affordable option for those seeking a brief respite from war work. Since it is a major port, New York City was also a great meeting place for families whose loved ones had a short leave from the service. As seen in the above photograph, Margaret Pallante of Niles (left) went to New York in 1942 to visit with her brother Donald (center), who was on leave from the US Navy. Accompanying Margaret was her friend Mary Jane Knott, as she was not permitted to travel so far by herself. Shown below is the photograph's cover, noting that it was taken at Billy Rose's Diamond Horseshoe at the Paramount Hotel.

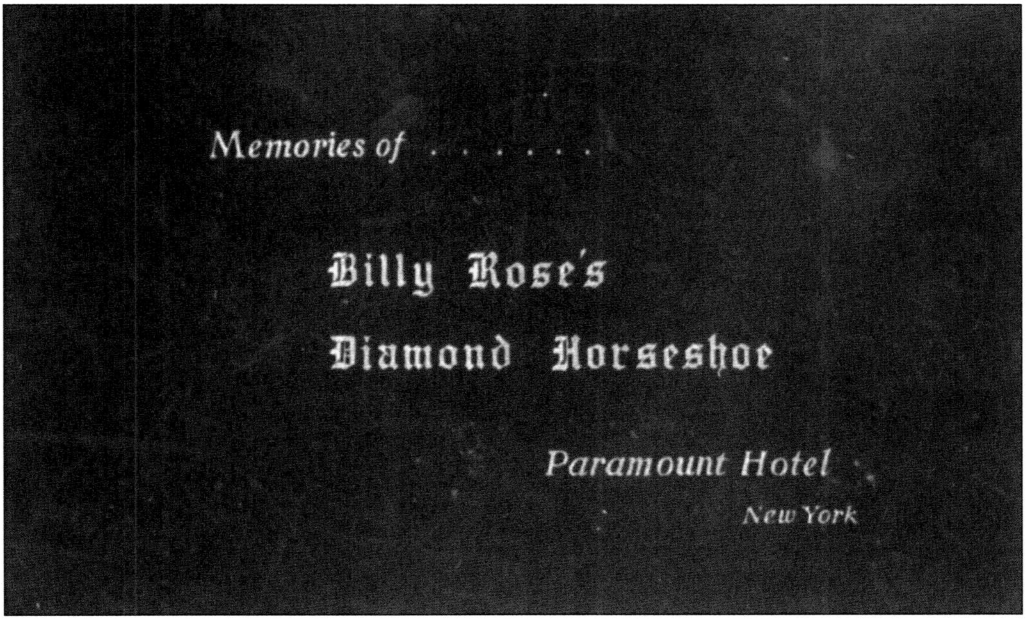

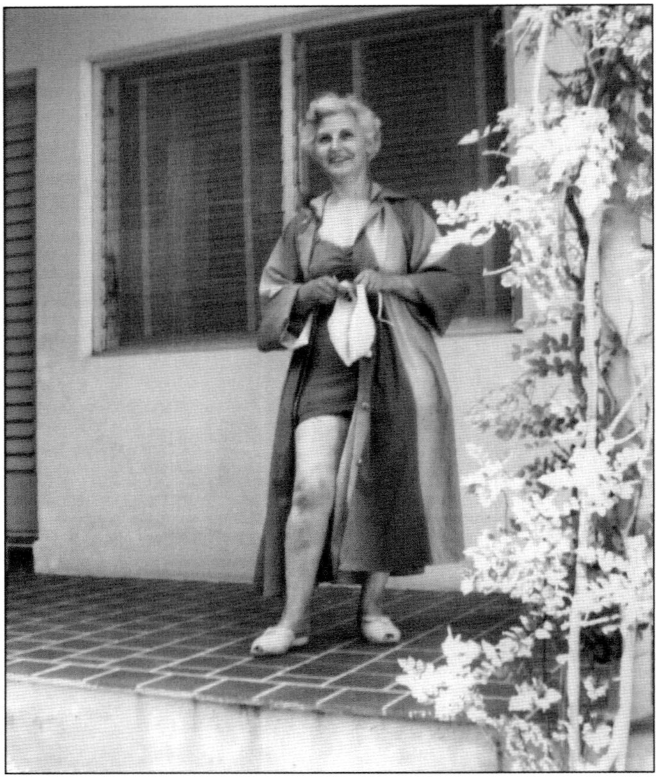

Florida Bound. The prosperity that arose following World War II meant more money and more leisure time. Italian Americans shared in the affluence, as many entered the middle class. The family vacation, in which everyone piles in the car and heads off to a distant locale, became commonplace by the 1950s. One of the destinations of choice was Florida. The widespread use of air-conditioning made the Sunshine State an attractive place, even in the summer. At left, Mary Bernard poses on the balcony of her hotel in Fort Lauderdale around 1950. Below, Andrew Marino shows off his brand-new Hudson automobile while in Miami Beach in the 1940s. (Below, courtesy of the Marino and Massullo families.)

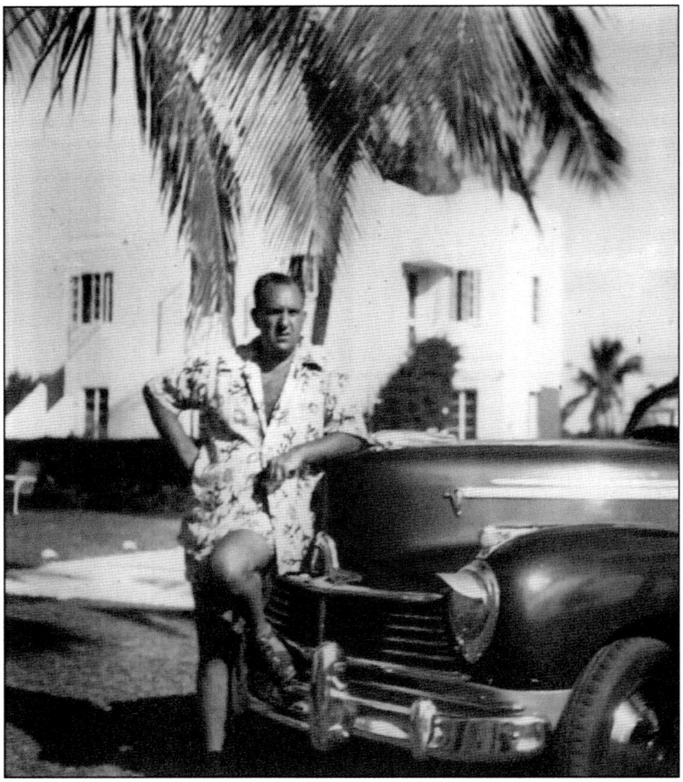

Seven

Celebrations and Commemorations

Holidays, weddings, First Communions—all of these events were times of celebration in the Italian American community. These were rites of passage and were often connected with the Roman Catholic Church, which was the faith of the great majority of Italian Americans. Celebrations brought families and friends together, usually over plentiful food and drink. In the early days, many of these festivities were held in homes. As the community became more prosperous, transportation improved, and families grew; events like wedding receptions moved to larger facilities. Even First Communion, Confirmation, and graduation parties left the confines of the family home for other facilities. Holiday festivities, especially Christmas and Easter, remained within the home for the most part. At all of these events, the old traditions were respected and followed, but over time, they gained American flair. Thanksgiving, an American holiday, usually had the traditional turkey and trimmings. But an Italian family Thanksgiving dinner might also include wedding soup or pasta. Funerals were occasions for family and friends to gather to mourn the passing of a loved one. For many years, the wake ("viewing," or calling hours) took place in the home. Later, funeral homes handled the arrangements. Following the wake, there was the funeral mass, followed by the mercy lunch. The support from family and friends was important in times of trial and an integral part of the mourning ritual. These traditions still play a vital role in the community, as evidenced by the many festivals held throughout the summers celebrating Italian American history and culture.

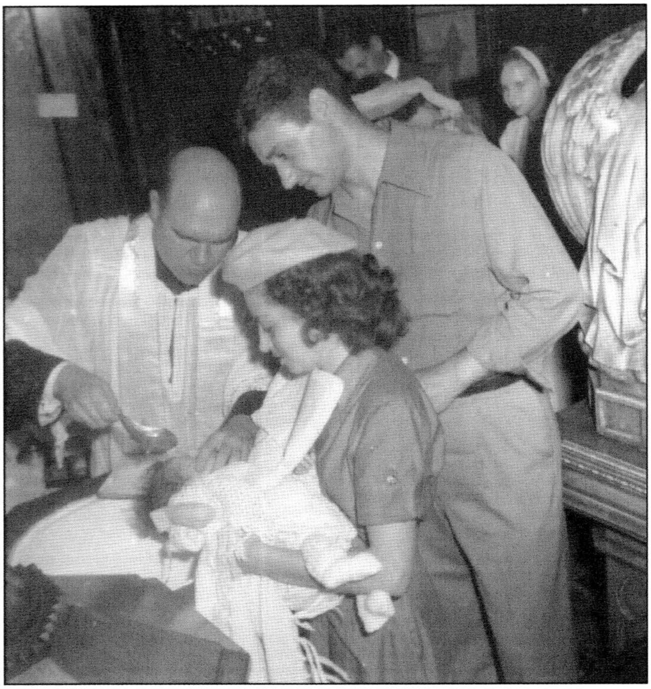

Baptism. The rites of the Roman Catholic Church were very important in the lives of the majority of Italian Americans. Traditionally, babies born into Catholic families were baptized promptly following their births. Until recently, Catholics believed that if an unbaptized infant passed away, their soul went to a place called limbo and could not enter heaven, hence the urgency for Baptism. Baptism, one of the seven sacraments, welcomes another soul into the faith. Here are two photographs of a DiLallo family Baptism from the 1950s held at Our Lady of Mount Carmel Church in Youngstown. (Both, courtesy of Anthony Worrelia.)

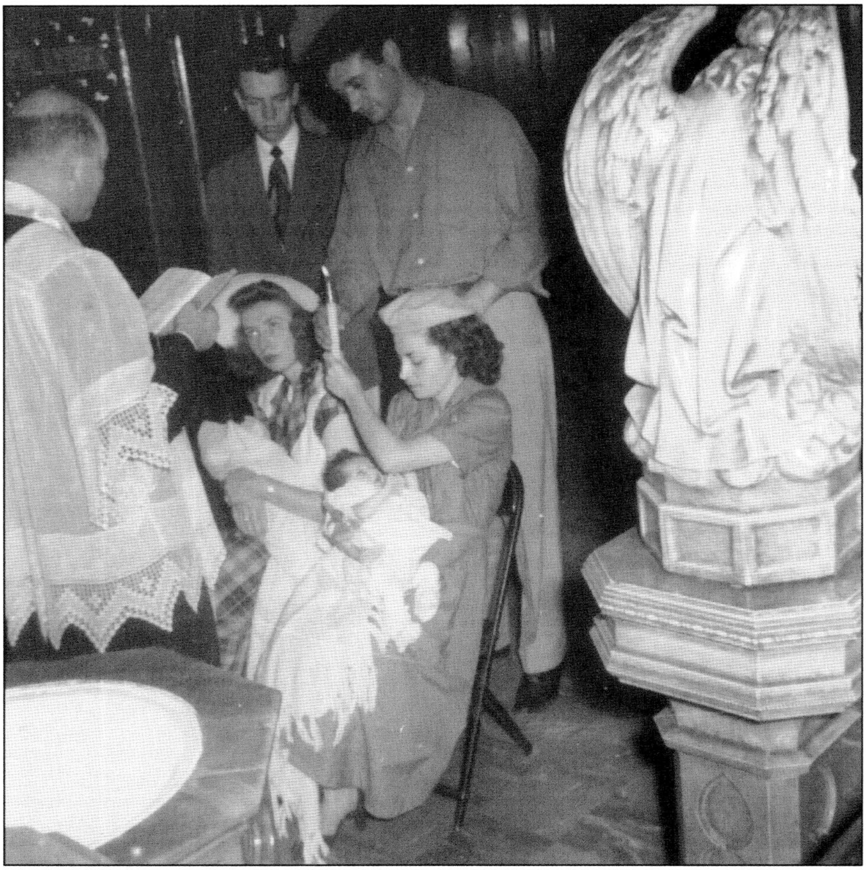

FIRST COMMUNION. After Baptism, one of the first important rites for most Catholics was First Communion, another of the seven sacraments. This ceremony is considered of great importance, because it is tied to one of the chief beliefs of Catholicism: transubstantiation. Catholics believe that, during the celebration of the mass, the bread and wine are transformed into the body and blood of Jesus Christ. Prior to receiving First Communion, communicants receive training in the faith. They must also make their First Confession, another of the seven sacraments, to ensure the purity of their souls, before taking Communion. At right, Venturina Porfirio, who made her First Communion around 1905, is dressed in white as a symbol of purity. Below, from left to right, Bob McClosky, Bob Bartoli, and Tom Gerst pose in their First Communion suits around 1955. (Below, courtesy of Robert Bartoli.)

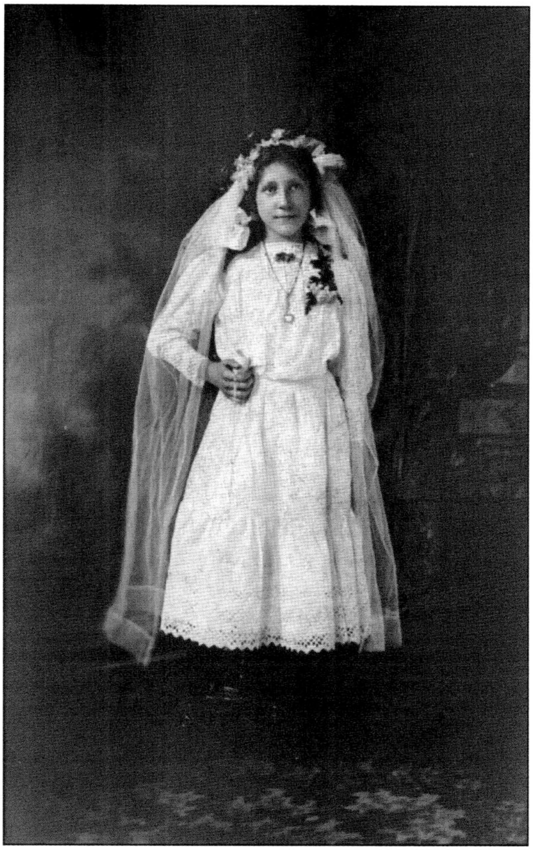

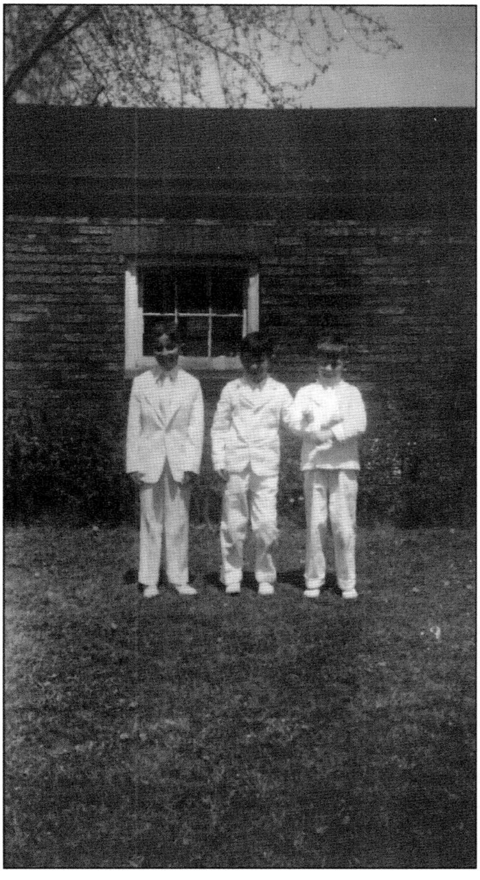

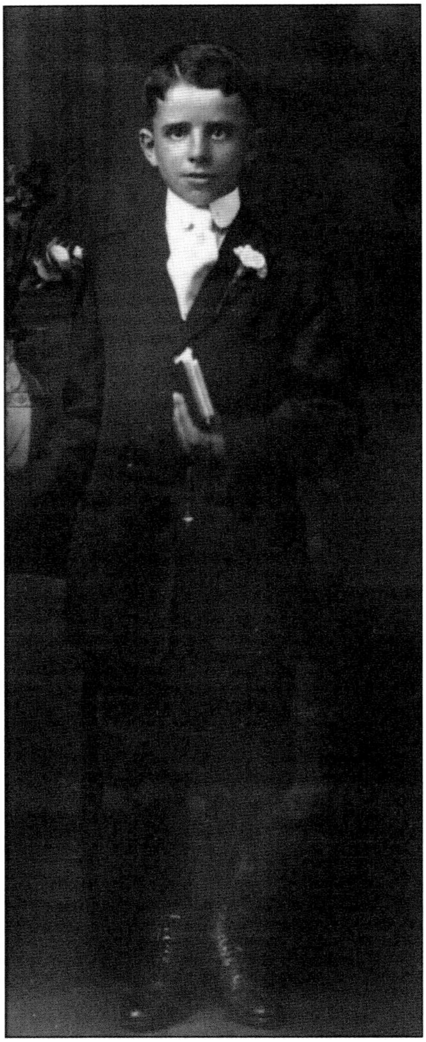

Confirmation. The sacraments of the Roman Catholic Church mark various events in the circle of life. Confirmation, according to the catechism of the Catholic Church, is the sacrament in which the baptized "are more perfectly bound to the Church and are enriched with a special strength of the Holy Spirit. Hence, they are, as true witnesses of Christ, more strictly obliged to spread and defend the faith by word and deed." At the time of Confirmation, those receiving the sacrament adopt a new name, usually a saint's, who will be another guardian. At left, Edward J. DeBartolo Sr. poses in his Confirmation suit around 1922. Below, Audrea Marsch (left) is garbed in the robe traditionally worn during the ceremony. She is with her godmother, Sylvia Mariani, in 1953. (Left, courtesy of YSU; below, courtesy of Rosanne Pasquinelli Dando and Audrea Marsch Neri.)

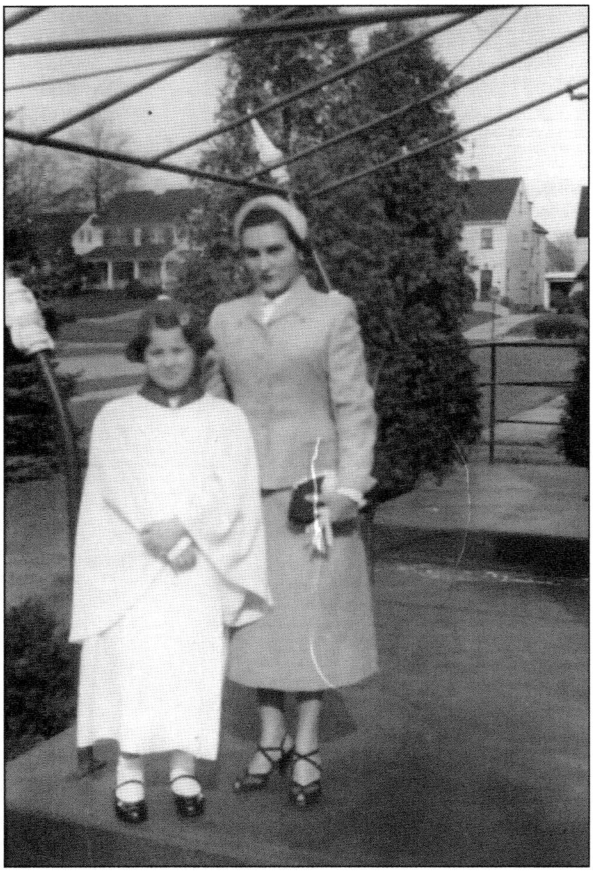

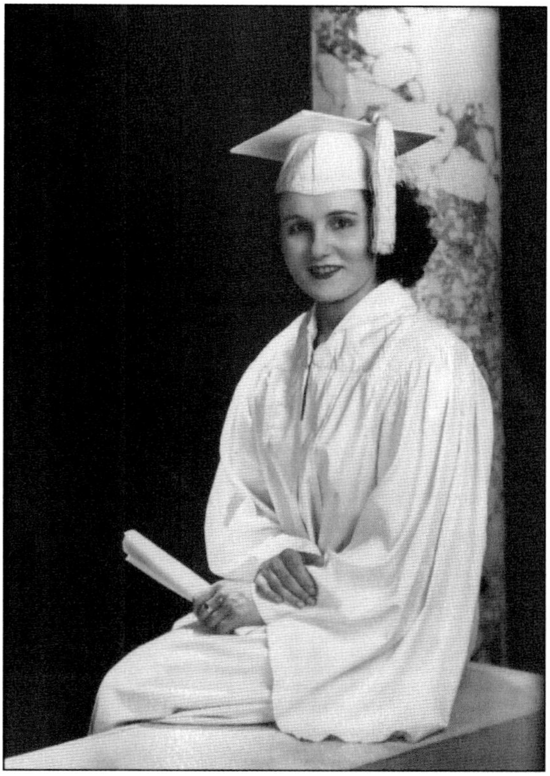

Graduation. For Italian Americans in the Mahoning Valley, educating their children was a priority, defying trends seen in larger communities, like New York City and Buffalo. Unlike other Catholic immigrants, especially prior to World War II, they frequently sent their children to public rather than Catholic schools, even if the parochial school was located within walking distance. Unlike their parents, baby boomer Italian Americans did attend Catholic school. Sylvia Mariani (right) was a 1947 graduate of Wilson High School, on Youngstown's south side. Rose DiLallo (below) also graduated in the mid-1940s, from Rayen High School on the north side of Youngstown. (Right, courtesy of Rosanne Pasquinelli Dando; below, courtesy of Anthony Worrelia.)

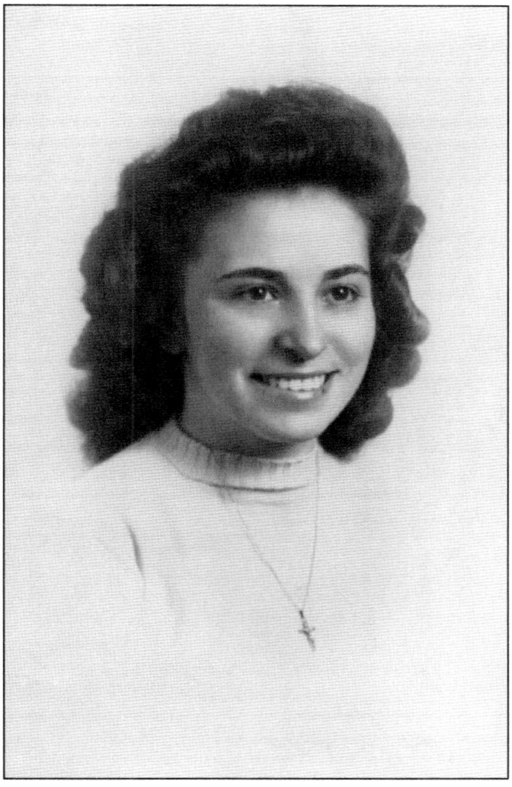

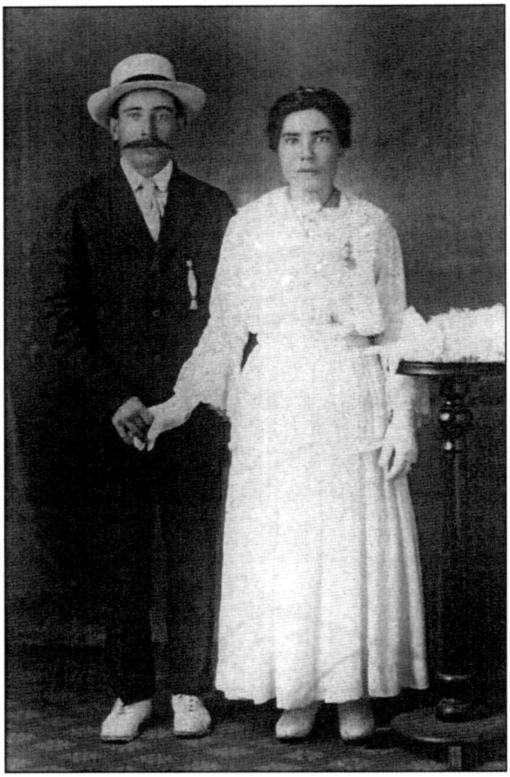

WITH THIS RING. One of the most important life events in any family is marriage. Italian American weddings are very important days, celebrated with much pomp and ceremony. Even in the early 20th century, the white wedding gown was integral to the event. Antonio Torella married Giovana DiDomenco (left) on August 26, 1915, in Wilburton, Oklahoma. Antonio immigrated to Lowellville, Ohio, in 1905, but left, fearing the influence of the Black Hand. He went to work in the mines in Wilburton, where there was a large Italian presence, and met his future bride. As mining was a very dangerous occupation, the Torellas moved back to Lowellville in 1924, where Antonio found work at Sharon Steel. Below, Venturina Porfiro and John DeSantis of Youngstown pose in their wedding finery in 1920. (Left, courtesy of Roslyn Torella.)

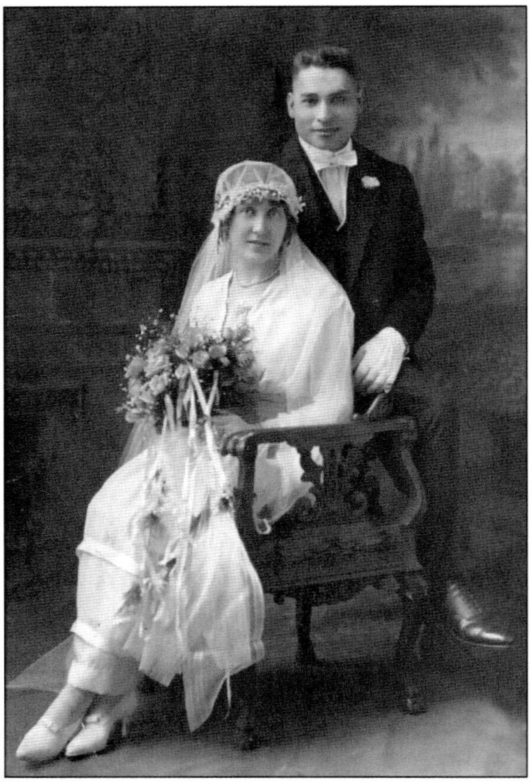

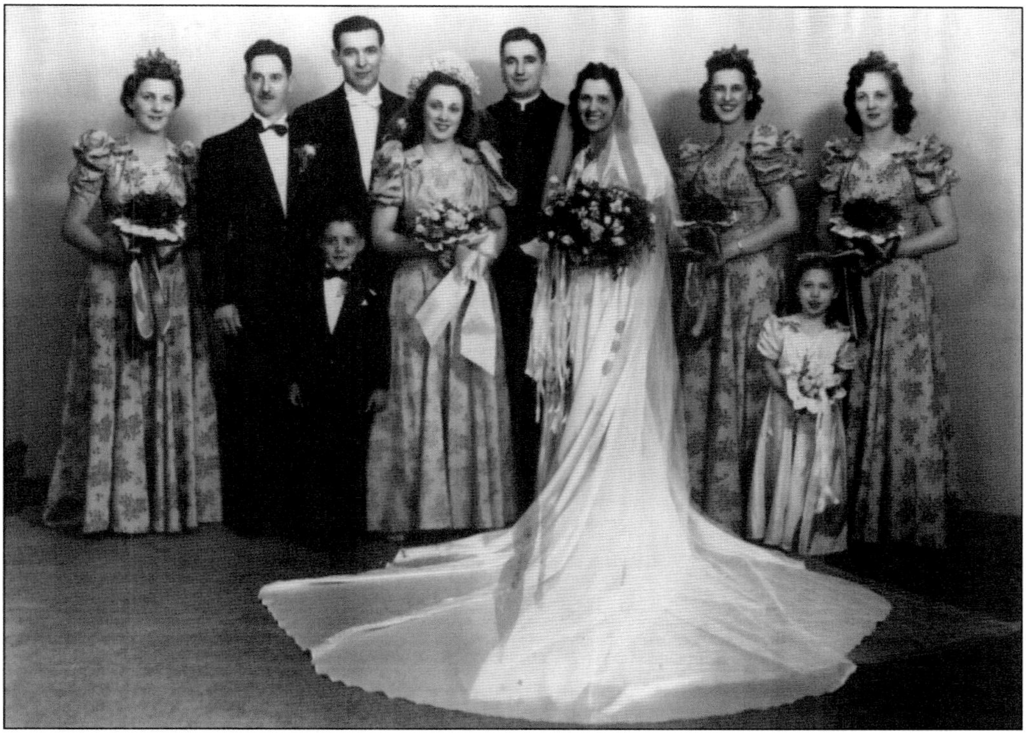

Weddings in Hard Times. Even when times are difficult, families find ways to celebrate weddings. The onset of the Great Depression was one such era. By the end of the 1930s, as prosperity slowly returned, more elaborate weddings occurred, like the Bartoli-Marsch union (above) on September 26, 1940, at Our Lady of Mount Carmel in Youngstown. Members of the bridal party are, from left to right, unidentified bridesmaid, Angelo Bartoli, Richard Cagna, Albert Marsch, Stella Pasquinelli, unidentified clergy, Edith Bartoli, Minnie Marsch, Linda Lupp, and Joanne Priori. At right, soldier Edward J. DeBartolo Sr. weds his bride, Maria Montini, while on leave on December 18, 1943. (Above, courtesy of Rosanne Pasquinelli Dando; right, courtesy of YSU.)

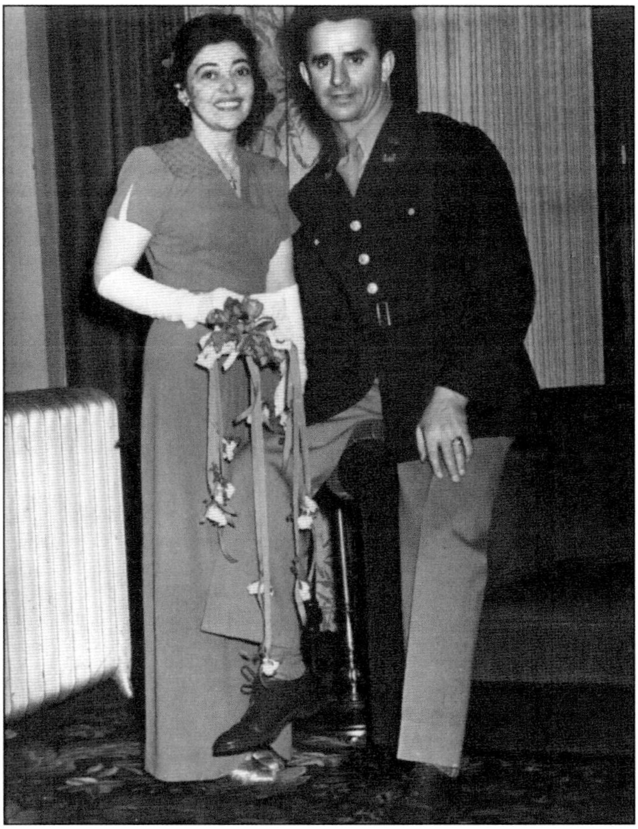

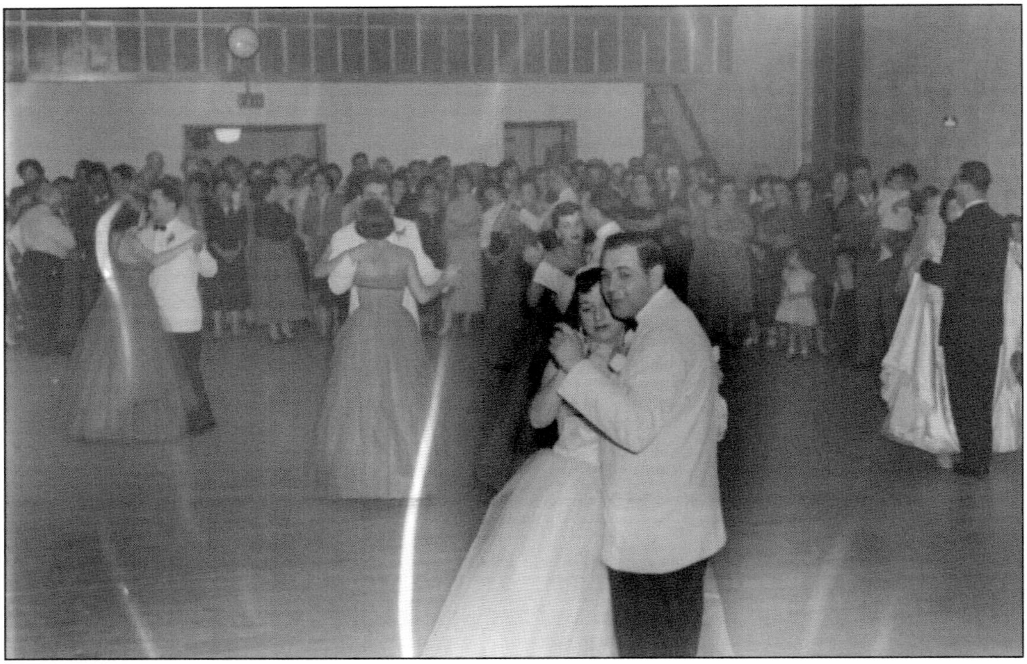

Reception. By the mid-1950s, Italian American weddings were elaborate affairs, beginning in the morning with breakfast, followed by the church ceremony, lunch, and a reception in the evening. Above, the wedding party at the DeBlasio-DiLullo nuptials dances at the Elms Ballroom on Youngstown's north side. The Pallante-Markle wedding reception (below) was at a different venue. Instead of going indoors on a beautiful summer's day, this family chose to hold their event outdoors in a lovely garden in Niles. Both weddings took place in 1952.

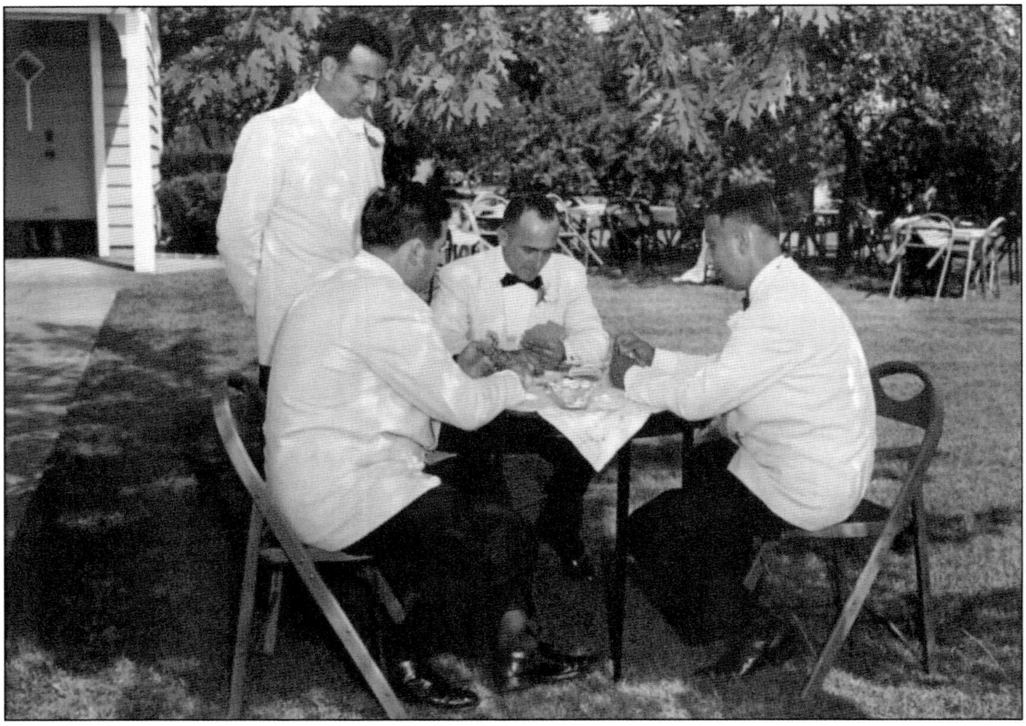

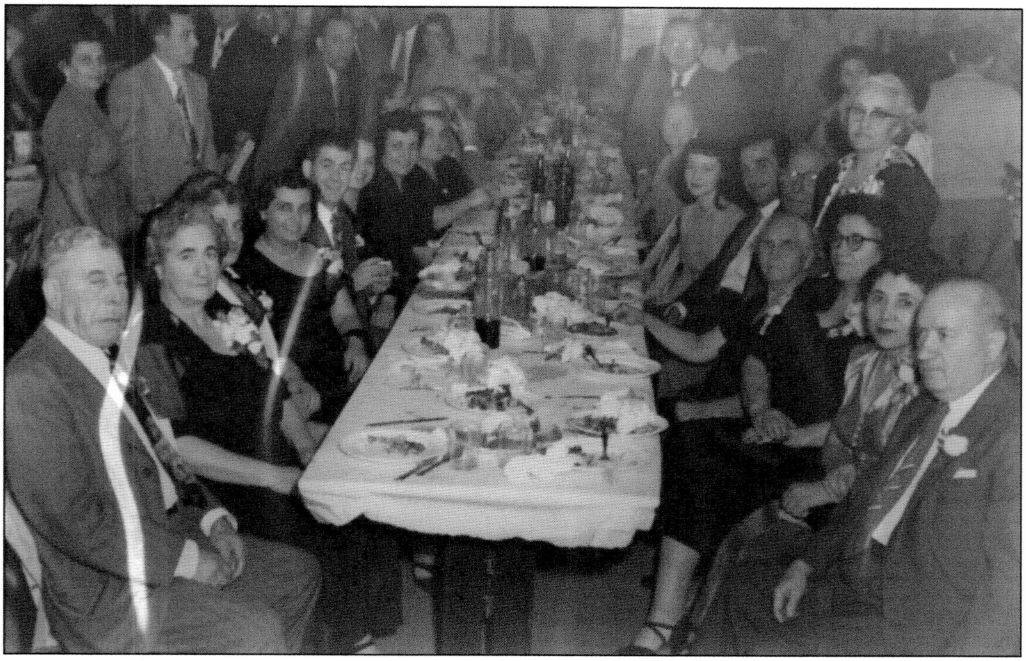

Wedding Lunch. For Italian Americans, food was an important part of every occasion—none more so than at wedding feasts. Well into the early 1960s, an elaborate lunch prepared by friends and family was standard at Italian American weddings. The evening reception featured the cake and a light meal. These two photographs from the DeBlasio-DiLullo wedding on September 20, 1952, depict the lunch meal. Above, members of both families enjoy the food; below, the men and women who cooked and served the delicious meal pose for a photograph.

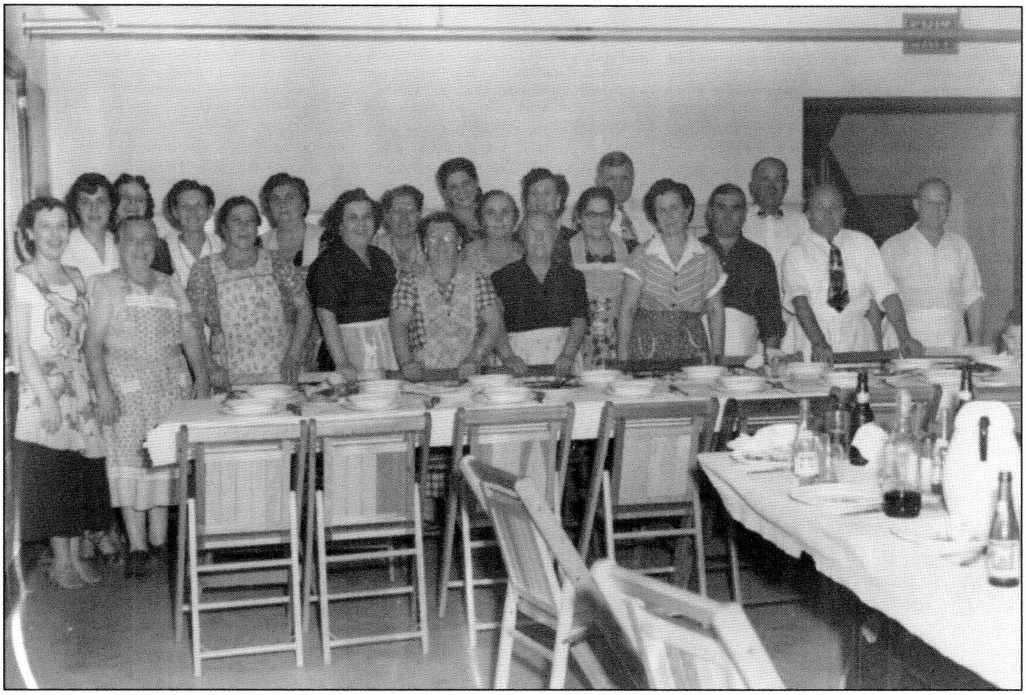

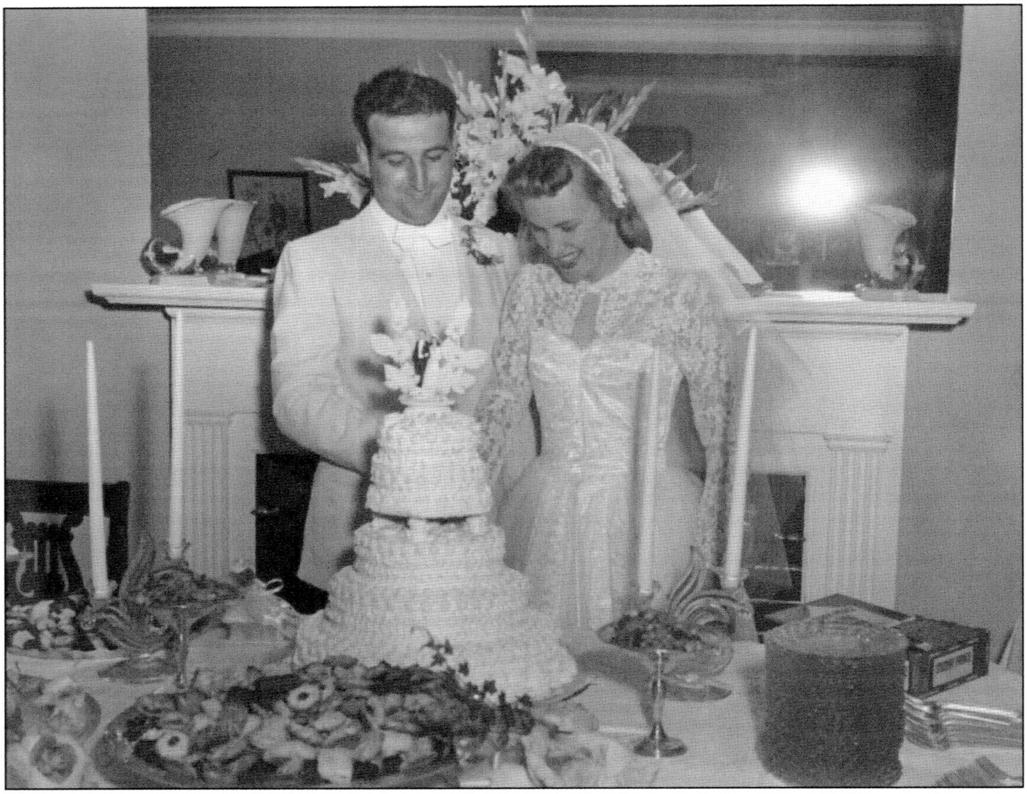

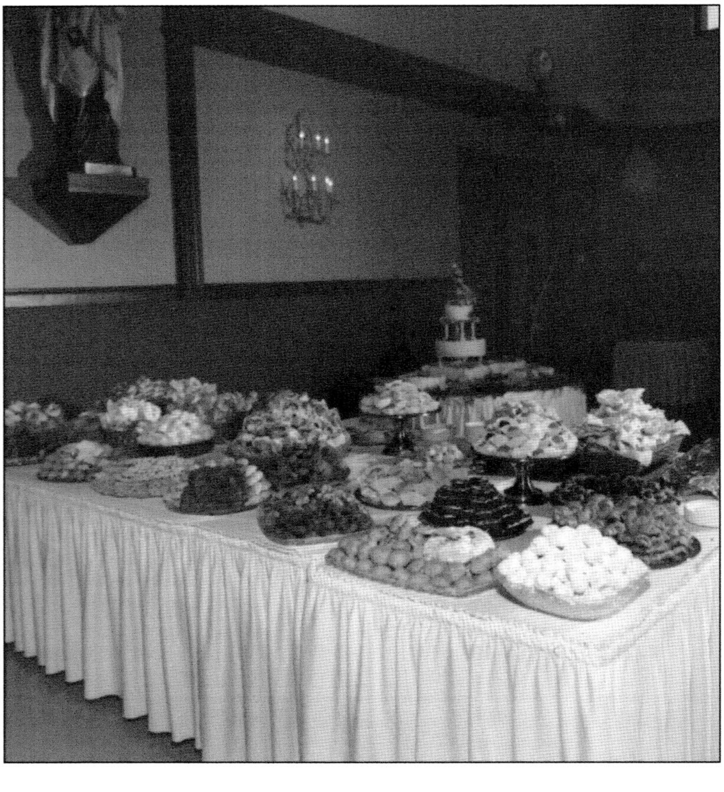

Cookie Table. One of the most iconic features of Italian American weddings in the Valley is the cookie table. Begun in the early days of settlement, the sharing of sweets on special occasions became a measure of the community's prosperity. Particularly for women, the ability to ask others to provide and to reciprocate was a measure of her acceptance in the community. Seen here are cookie tables from two eras, 1952 (above) and 1992 (left). Note how elaborate the cookie table has grown over time. People vie with each other for the "best" one.

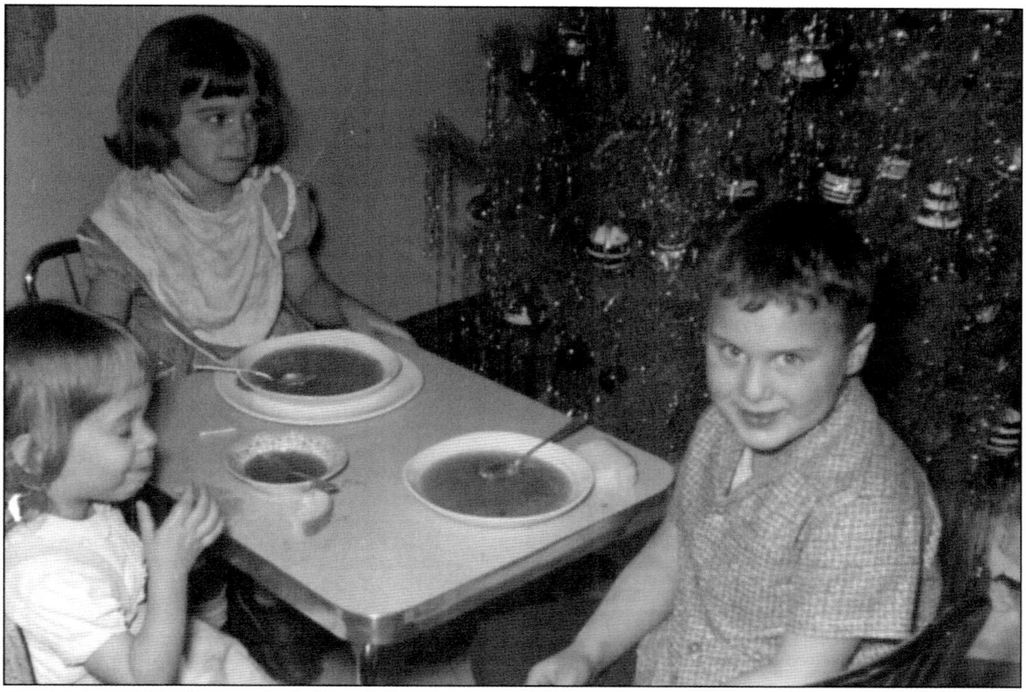

Christmas. The biggest holiday of the year was Christmas. All of the trappings—food, presents, family, and friends—were integral to the holiday celebration. For Italian Americans, Christmas Eve was as important as the holiday itself. Keeping with Italian tradition, Valley residents served the Feast of the Seven Fish for Christmas Eve dinner. The Christmas meal blended Italian foods, like wedding soup and pasta, with more American victuals, like ham or turkey. Above, from left to right, Angela Pasquinelli, Rosanne Pasquinelli, and Eugene Robison dine at the children's table on Christmas 1956. Shown below is the 1938 Christmas card of the Cagnlia family, which included family photographs. (Above, courtesy of Rosanne Pasquinelli Dando; below, courtesy of Carl and Edith Ritch.)

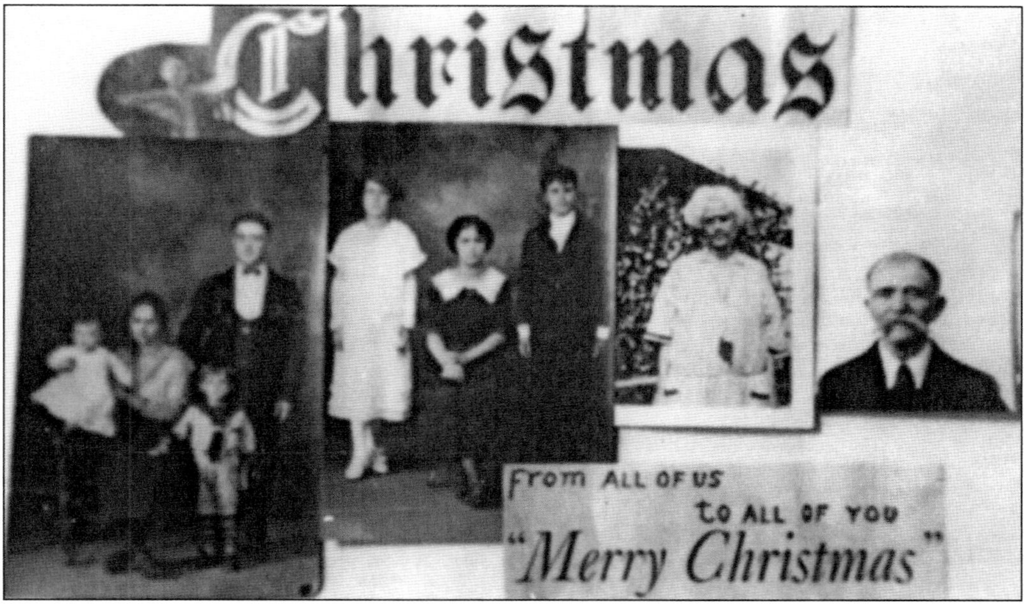

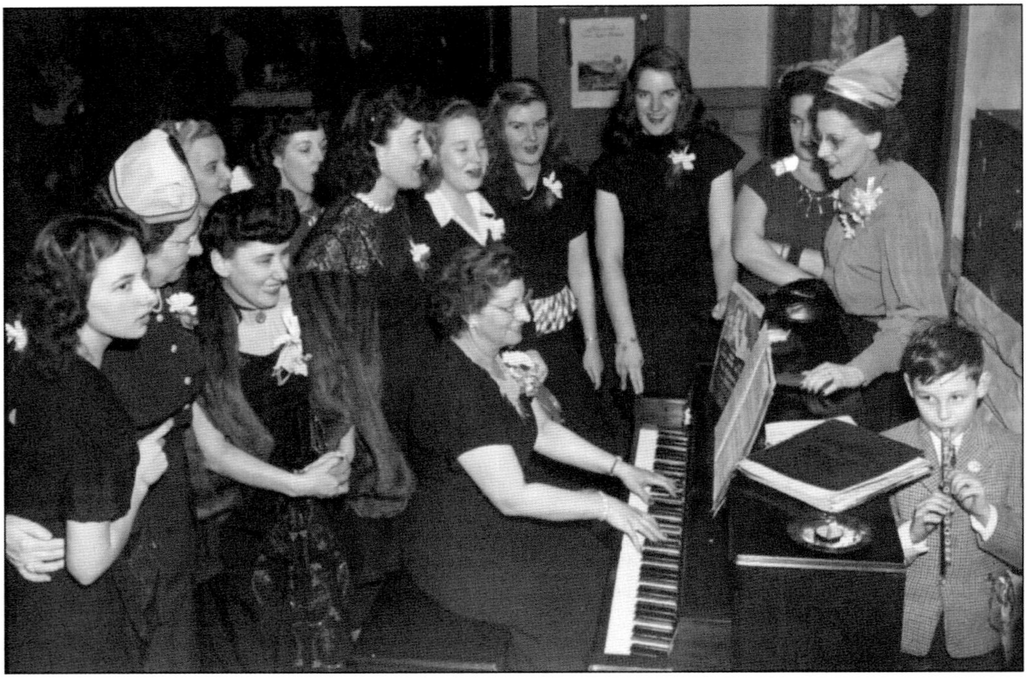

NEW YEAR'S EVE. One holiday celebrated in many nations is New Year's Eve. American traditions include the dropping of the ball at Times Square in New York City, fireworks, and champagne. Italian Americans eagerly adopted such American festivities as well. On New Year's Eve 1947, Manning-Marino Motors threw a party for its employees and their families, including the children. Food and drink were plentiful, and everyone enjoyed the holiday spirit, as seen in these photographs. The event was held at the dealership, located on Wick Avenue in Youngstown. (Both, courtesy of the Marino and Massullo families.)

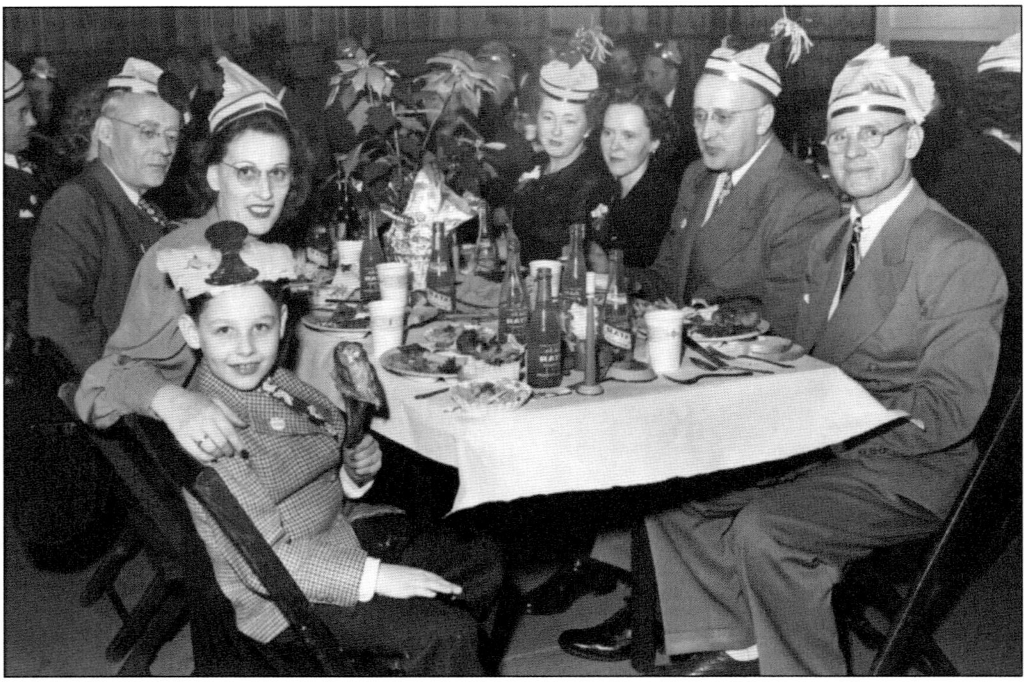

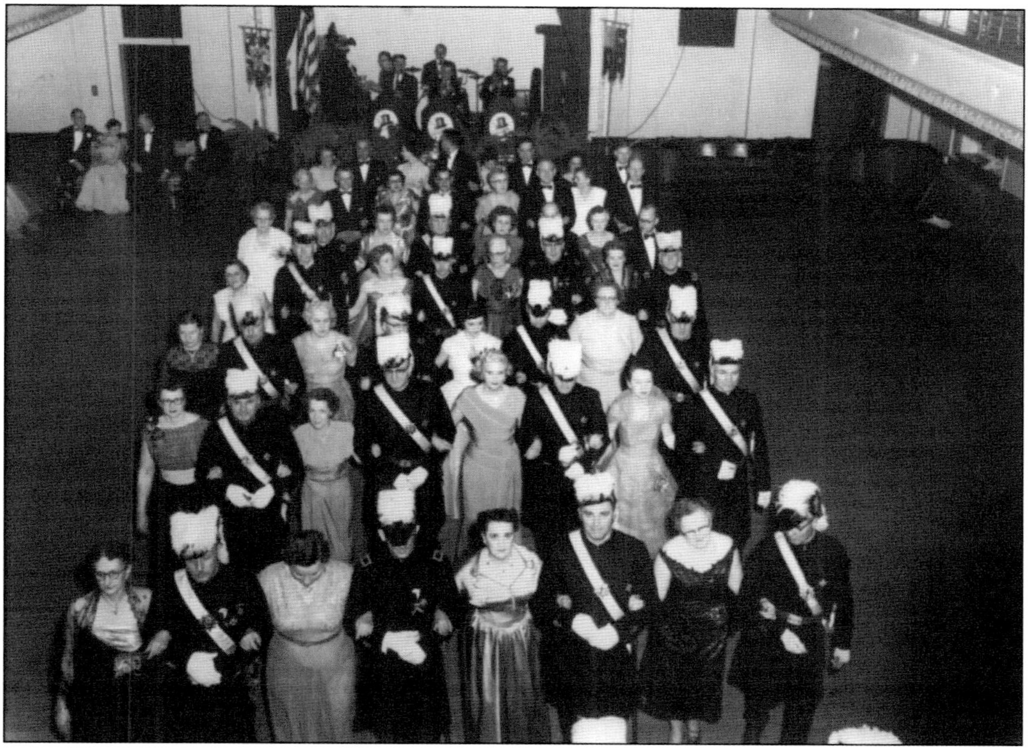

K of C. The Knights of Columbus is the world's largest Catholic fraternal organization. Founded in 1882 by Fr. Michael J. McGivney in New Haven, Connecticut, it originally served as a mutual benefit society for low-income Catholic immigrants. The K of C emerged at a time when Catholics were barred from joining other fraternal groups, like the Freemasons. When the Ku Klux Klan re-emerged in the 1920s, the K of C was one of its targets. Since that time, the organization has focused on charitable acts and evangelization. Its motto is "Charity, Unity, Fraternity, and Patriotism." These photographs depict a K of C social event in the 1950s. (Both, courtesy of OHC-YHCIL.)

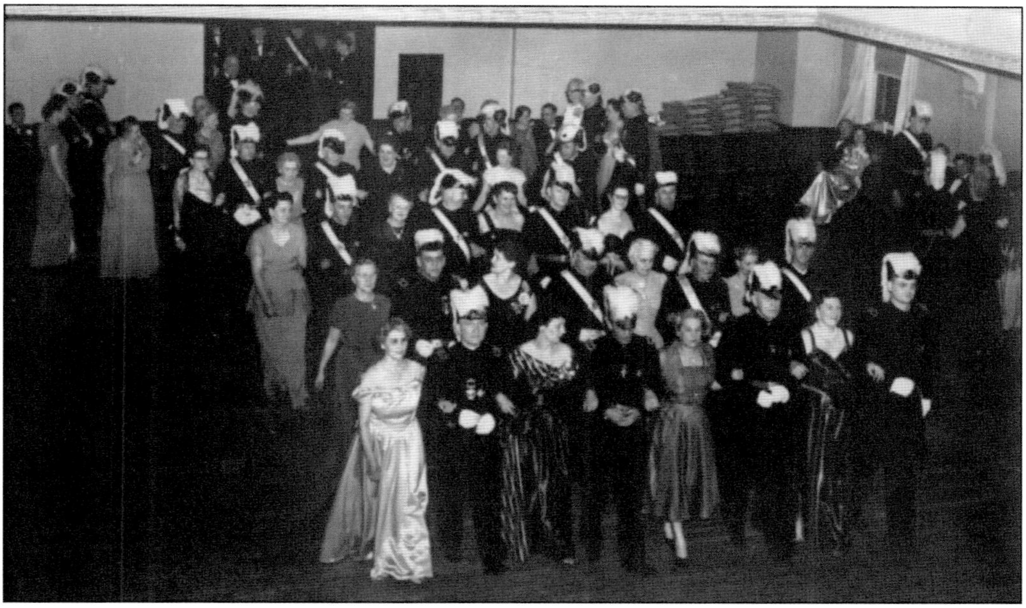

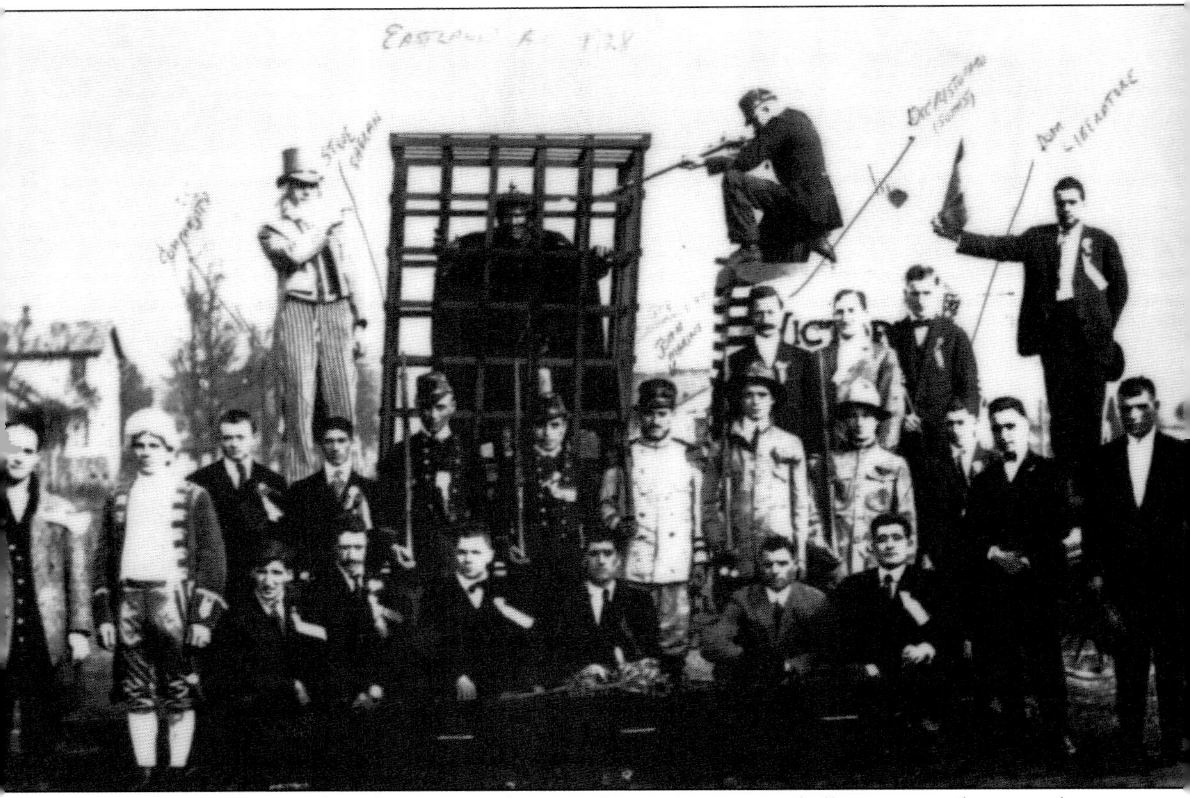

FOURTH OF JULY. Italian Americans, showing their patriotism and allegiance to their new home, celebrated Independence Day. Here, a group of Warren Italian Americans commemorate the holiday in 1928 by staging a patriotic "Kill the Kaiser" event in honor of the United States. The kaiser (represented in the center) was the leader of Germany at the start of World War I. After the war's end in 1918, the tenets of the Treaty of Versailles stipulated that the kaiser be replaced by a more democratic form of government, known as the Weimar Republic. In this reenactment by Italian Americans, men portray American personages such as Uncle Sam and soldiers from all of the American wars, starting with the Revolutionary War. A man dressed as a Civil War soldier is seen "killing" the kaiser. (Courtesy of Joe Merlo.)

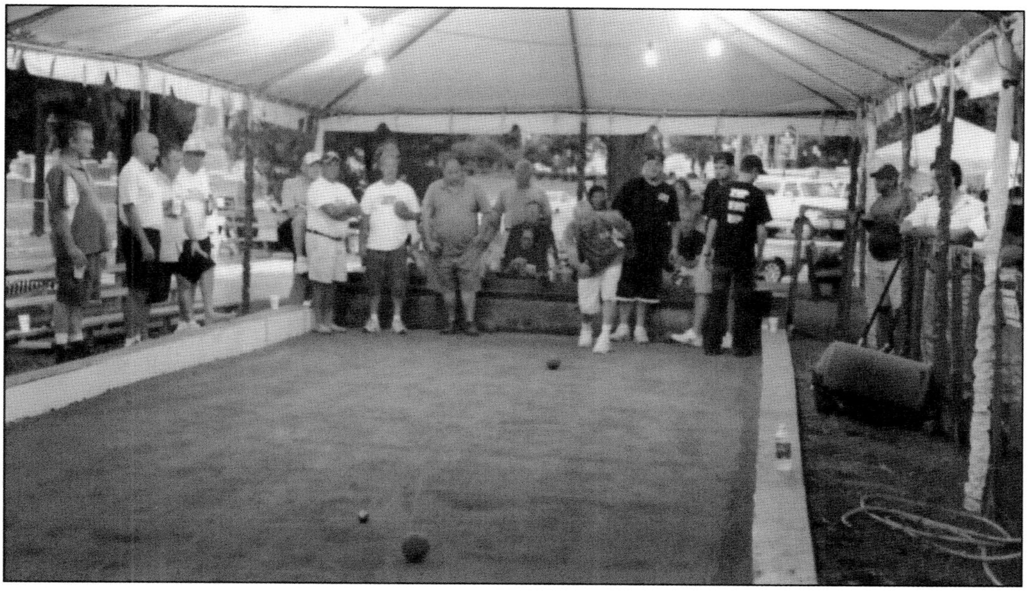

Keeping Italian Games Alive. One of the things that Italians brought with them from the Old World was their love of games. Several of these have withstood the test of time; some have even become a part of the larger culture, like bocce. Others, like *morra* and *tre e sette*, a card game, are still played, but mostly by Italian Americans. Above, people compete in a bocce tournament at the Warren Italian Heritage Festival. Below, at the same event, several men are engaged in the game of morra, which is related to rock-paper-scissors. (Both, courtesy of the Warren Italian American Heritage Festival.)

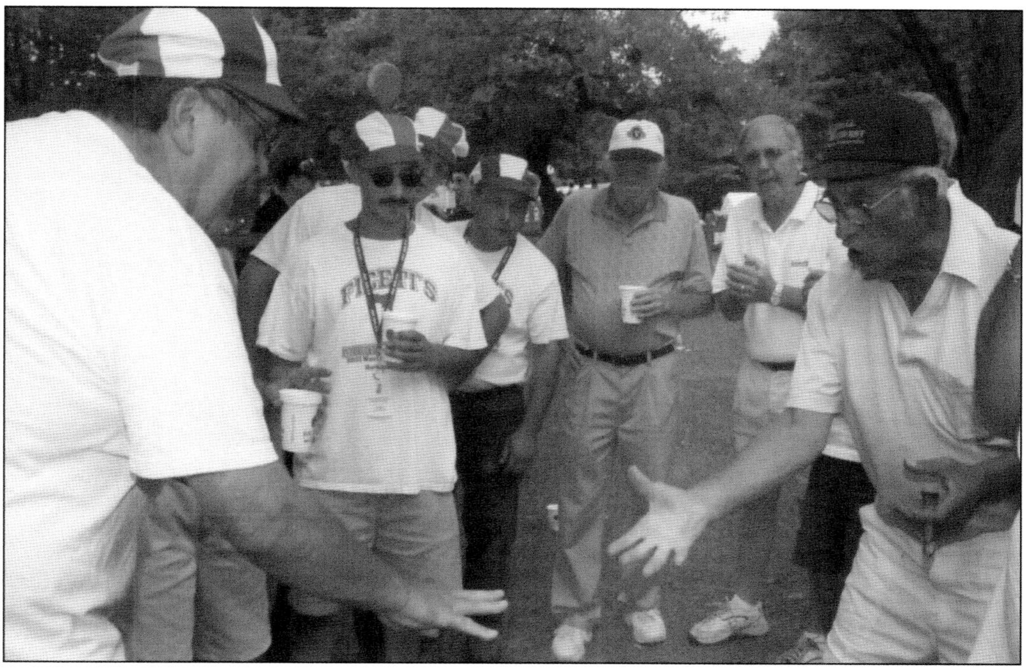

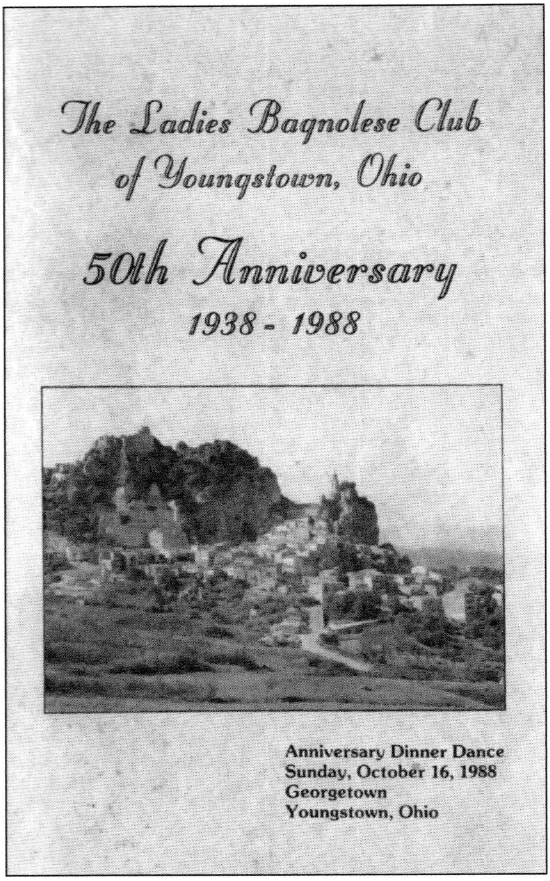

CELEBRATING ITALIAN HERITAGE. While Italian Americans adapted to their new home in the United States, they also maintained ties with their heritage. Often, men and women from the same hometown formed social clubs, where they gathered over food and drink to enjoy each other's company. Shown at left is the program book for the 50th anniversary of the Bangolese Ladies Club in 1988. Founded in 1938, the club, which is still in existence, gathers women from Bagnoli del Trignio in the Abruzzi region (now Molise) and their descendants. Shown below is a picnic of the Rivisondoli Club, the Rivisondale, in the 1930s. (Below, courtesy of Carl and Edith Ritch.)

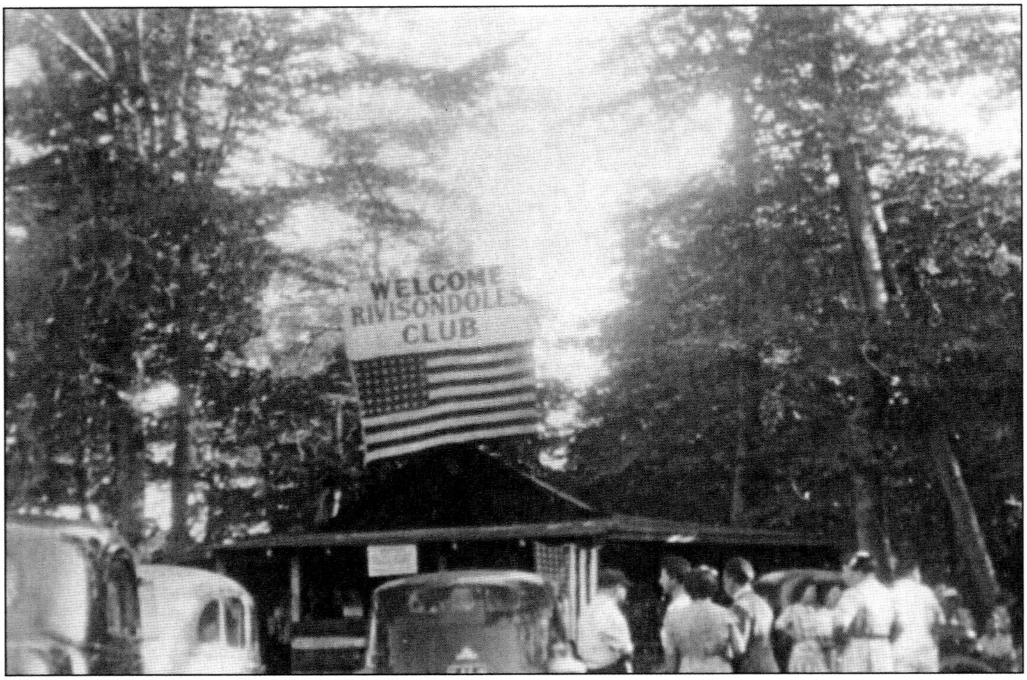

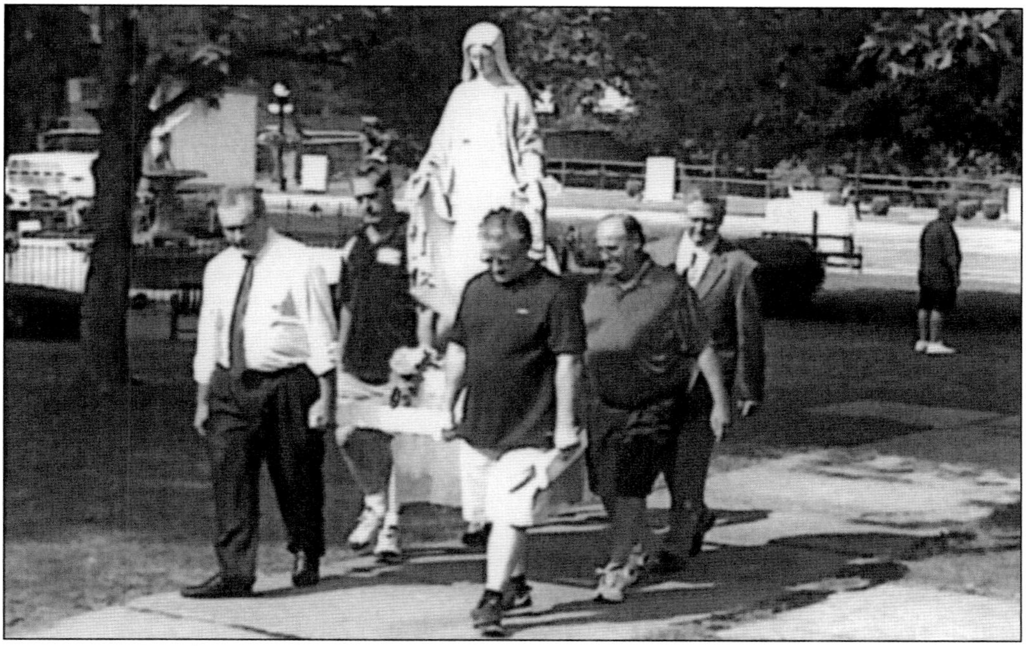

ITALIAN FESTS. The Mahoning Valley is home to many Italian festivals throughout the summer. Several of the churches that are ethnically Italian Catholic honor various feast days or the neighborhood where they are located. The two largest cities in the Valley, Youngstown and Warren, each hold separate Italian festivals, honoring connections to Italy and contributions to the United States. Both of these major festivals feature not only the ubiquitous food, but also Italian music, speakers, cultural exhibits, and honors like the Italian Man and Woman of the Year. Above, men carry a statue of the Virgin Mary in a procession in Warren. Shown at right is the program for Youngstown's 25th anniversary festival in 2010. (Above, courtesy of the Warren Italian American Heritage Festival.)

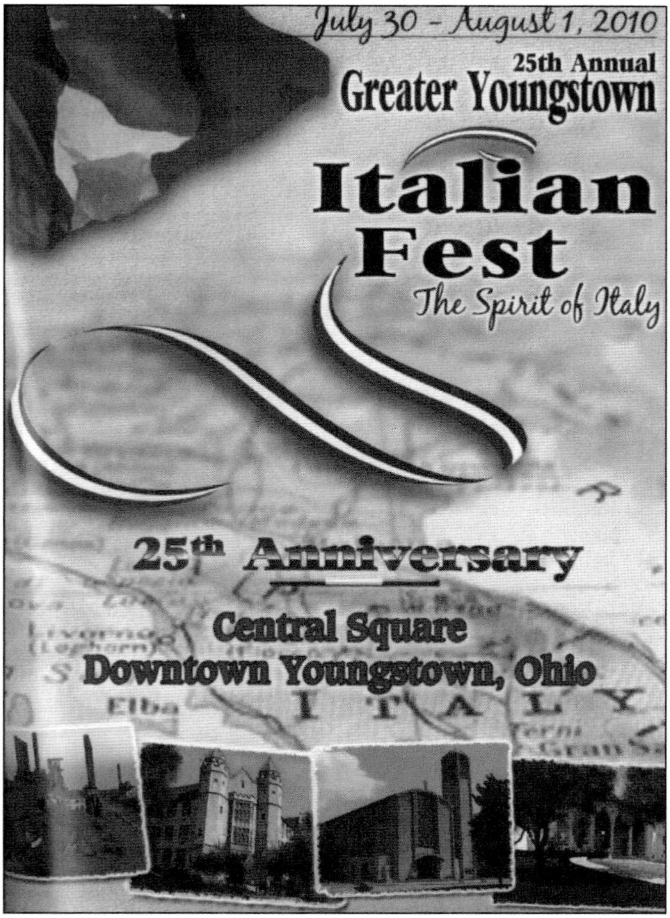

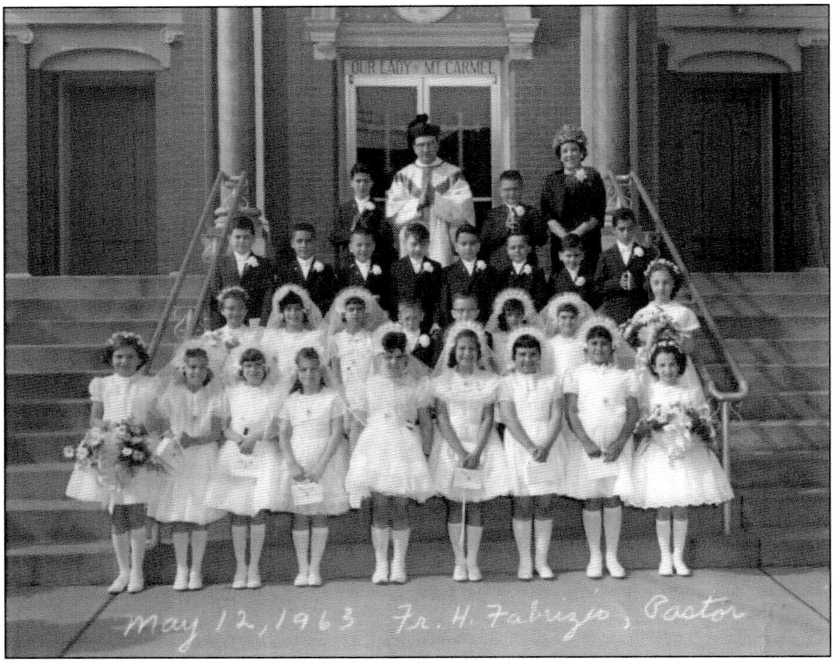

WORSHIP IN YOUNGSTOWN. Most Italians who arrived in the Mahoning Valley in the early 20th century were of the Roman Catholic faith. As soon as their numbers grew large enough, they clamored to have their own ethnic parishes. There were enough Italian Catholics in the city of Youngstown for two parishes, one serving Brier Hill, the other Smoky Hollow. St. Anthony's (below) was founded in Brier Hill in 1898; a large number of Italians settled there to be close to their work in the nearby steel mills. Our Lady of Mount Carmel (above), near Smoky Hollow, was founded in 1908; the current church was built in 1913. The photograph depicts the 1963 First Communion class on the church steps. In 2011, the two parishes merged. Both churches sponsor annual festivals: for St. Anthony's, it is the Brier Hill Festival; for Mount Carmel, it is the Our Lady of Mount Carmel Festival. (Above, courtesy of Our Lady of Mount Carmel Basilica.)

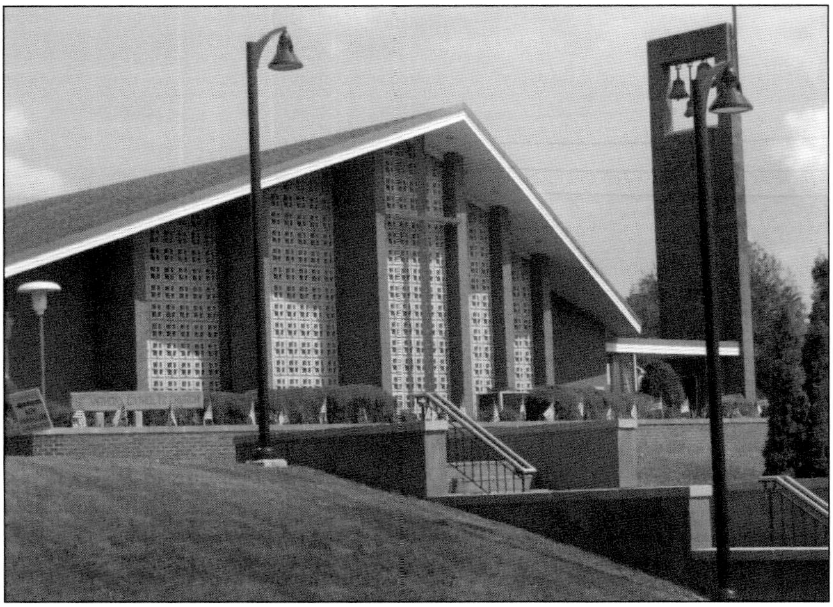

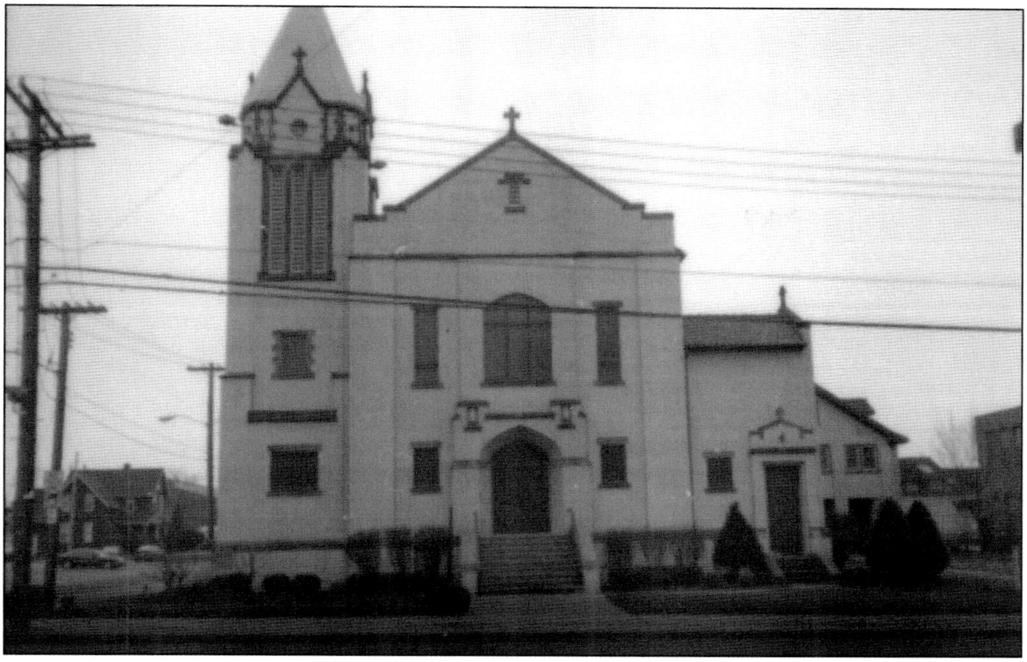

Keeping the Faith. Niles's Italians formed their own parish, Our Lady of Mount Carmel (above), in 1906. The only other Roman Catholic church in Niles was St. Stephen, which started as an ethnically Irish parish. By the early 20th century, Niles's Italian population was large enough for its own congregation. It shares the dates of its annual festival, which began in 1934, during the Feast of Our Lady of Mount Carmel in mid-July, with Our Lady of the Holy Rosary (right), located in Lowellville. Originally, that town's Catholics worshipped in people's homes. The church, established in 1884, acquired its first Italian parishioners in the 1890s. The current building was erected in 1966. The bell tower seen here was constructed in 1980. At its Mount Carmel festival, the Baby Doll Dance is a main attraction.

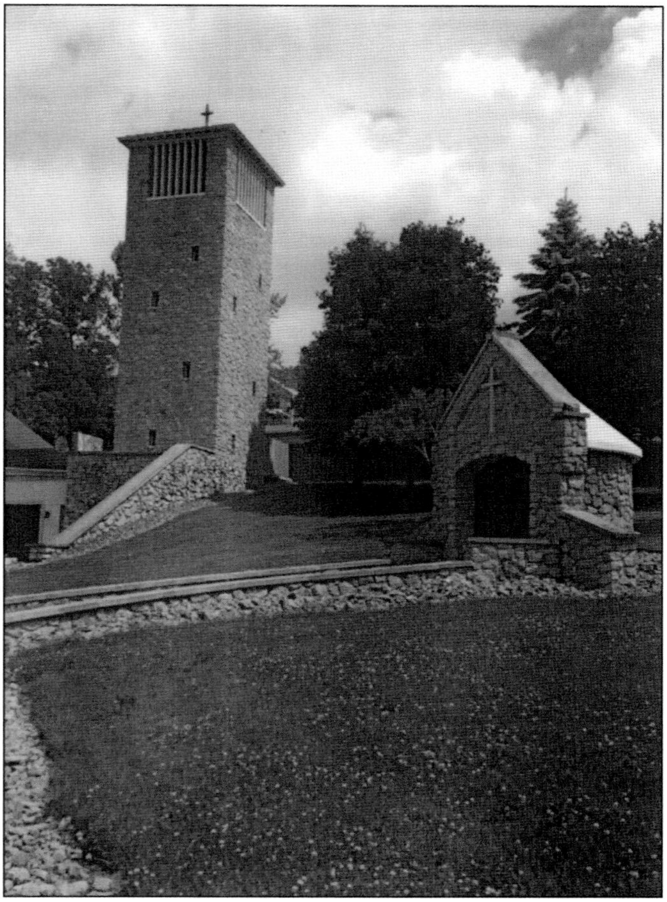

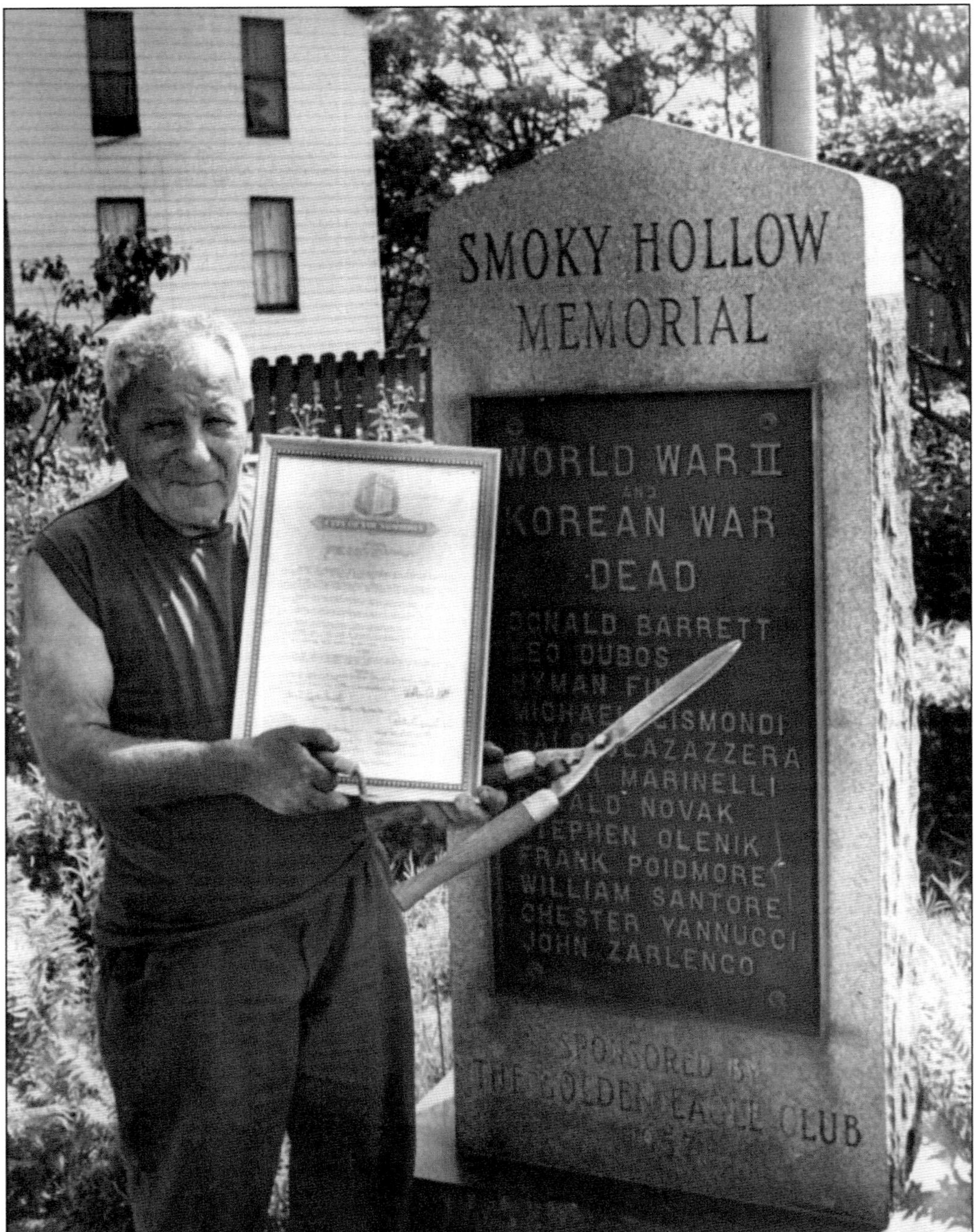

SMOKY HOLLOW MEMORIAL. Dedicated in 1957, the Smoky Hollow Memorial honors those residents of the community who gave their lives for the country in World War II and Korea. In 2015, the Vietnam War was added. Many of the deceased were Italian Americans. It began as a simple monument, but over time, more landscaping made it a shrine worthy of the men it honors. For many years, Atillio DiLallo, a resident of the Hollow, made it his work to care for the memorial. He poses here with the tools of his trade, holding a proclamation from the city of Youngstown honoring him for his hard work and dedication. DiLallo passed away in 1985. (Courtesy of Anthony Worrellia.)

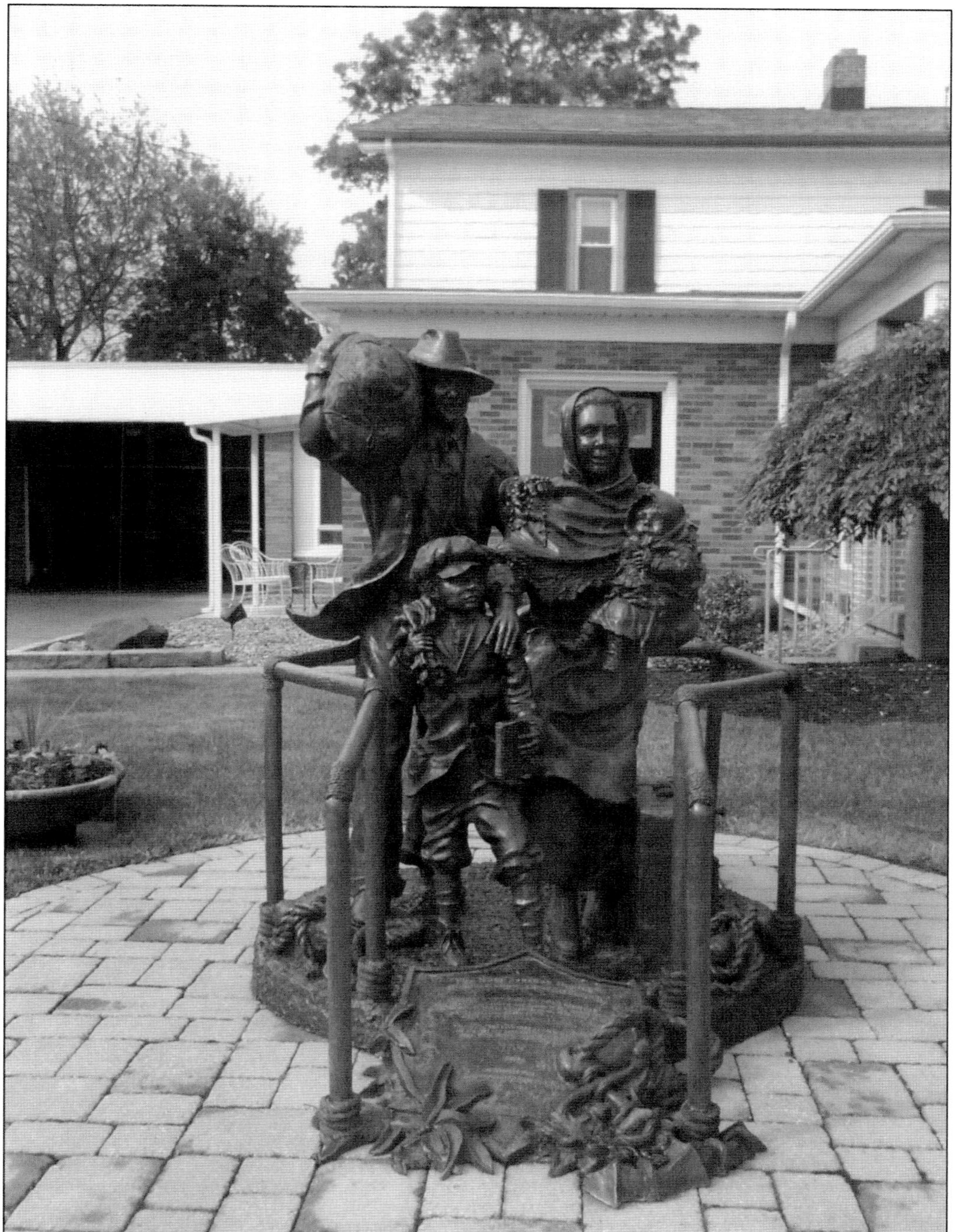

Tribute to Immigration. In 2008, Our Lady of Mount Carmel in Youngstown dedicated this sculpture, *The Next Journey Begins*, as a representation of the spirit and strength of the Italian immigrants to the Mahoning Valley and in recognition of their progeny's continued contributions to the community. Donated by the Tony Lariccia family and sculpted by Tom Antonishak, it commemorates the 100th anniversary of the founding of the church. The work depicts members of an Italian immigrant family as they make the hazardous journey over the Atlantic Ocean to their new homes in the Valley.

Discover Thousands of Local History Books Featuring Millions of Vintage Images

Arcadia Publishing, the leading local history publisher in the United States, is committed to making history accessible and meaningful through publishing books that celebrate and preserve the heritage of America's people and places.

Find more books like this at
www.arcadiapublishing.com

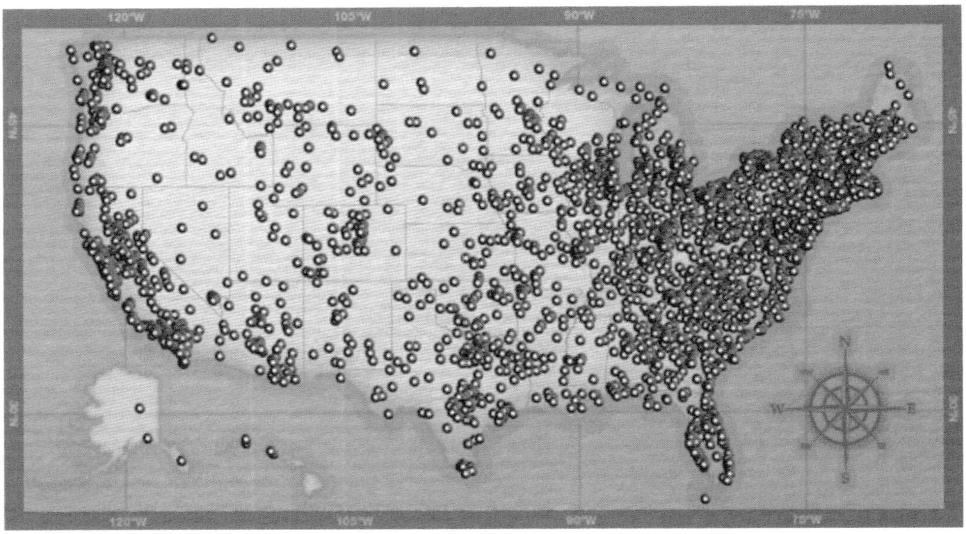

Search for your hometown history, your old stomping grounds, and even your favorite sports team.

Consistent with our mission to preserve history on a local level, this book was printed in South Carolina on American-made paper and manufactured entirely in the United States. Products carrying the accredited Forest Stewardship Council (FSC) label are printed on 100 percent FSC-certified paper.

MADE IN THE USA